Research in Social Care and Social Welfare

of related interest

User Involvement and Participation in Social Care
Research Informing Practice
Edited by Hazel Kemshall and Rosemary Littlechild
ISBN 1 85302 777 4

The Changing Role of Social Care
Edited by Bob Hudson
ISBN 1 85302 732 9
Research Highlights in Social Work 37

Community Care Practice and the Law
Second Edition
Michael Mandelstam
ISBN 1 85302 647 6

Handbook of Theory for Practice Teachers in Social Work
Edited by Joyce Lishman
ISBN 1 85302 098 2

Disability Politics and Community Care
Mark Priestley
ISBN 1 85302 652 2

Effective Ways of Working with Children and their Families
Edited by Malcolm Hill
ISBN 1 85302 619 0
Research Highlights in Social Work 35

Domestic Violence
Guidelines for Research — Informed Practice
Edited by John P. Vincent and Ernest N. Jouriles
ISBN 1 85302 854 1

Ethical Practice and the Abuse of Power in Social Responsibility
Leave No Stone Unturned
Edited by Helen Payne and Brian Littlechild
ISBN 1 85302 743 X

Social Care and Housing
Edited by Ian Shaw, Susan Thomas and David Clapham
ISBN 1 85302 437 6
Research Highlights in Social Work 32

Confidentiality and Mental Health
Edited by Christopher Cordess
ISBN 1 85302 860 6

Research in Social Care and Social Welfare

Issues and Debates for Practice

Edited by Beth Humphries

Jessica Kingsley Publishers
London and Philadelphia

The right of the contributors to be identified as authors of this work has been asserted by them in accordance with the Copyright, Designs and Patents Act 1988.

First published in the United Kingdom in 2000 by
Jessica Kingsley Publishers Ltd,
116 Pentonville Road, London
N1 9JB, England
and
325 Chestnut Street,
Philadelphia, PA 19106, USA.

www.jkp.com

Library of Congress Cataloging in Publication Data
A CIP catalog record for this book is available from the Library of Congress

British Library Cataloguing in Publication Data
A CIP catalogue record for this book is available from the British Library

ISBN 1 85302 900 9

Printed and Bound in Great Britain by
Athenaeum Press, Gateshead, Tyne and Wear

Contents

To the memory of David Boulton
and Steve Morgan

CHAPTER 1

Perspectives on Social Research

Beth Humphries

Introduction

The pattern of research and evaluation in social care and social welfare reflects different and competing discourses. On the one hand there has been a widening of philosophical understandings about the nature of research, the nature of knowledge and the ways in which research is a social product. This is characterised by the growth of 'emancipatory', feminist and other largely qualitative approaches (Broad 1999; Humphries and Truman 1994; Mullender and Ward 1991; Oliver 1990; Stanley 1990; Truman, Mertens and Humphries 2000). On the other hand there is a revival of 'evidence-based' research, which tends to regard positivist-influenced methods as more scientific than subject-orientated perspectives. Increasingly, official statements about a broad range of 'helping professions' assume evidence-based criteria as a building block of practice (see, for example, Audit Commission 1996). As Shaw (1999) points out:

> the very phrase 'evidence-based practice' captures a confident belligerence, a tone of 'prove it or else'. The language of goals, objectives, outcomes and effectiveness challenges reliance on sentimentality, opinion-based practice, intuition or lay knowledge. (p.14)

The chief distinguishing characteristics of this approach are stress on case monitoring and evaluation through single-system designs and, more broadly, the application of scientific perspectives and models in practice; and application of interventions whose effectiveness has been demonstrated through research (see Reid and Zettergren 1999 for a discussion of 'empirical practice'). Moreover, the British Government's view of social research has raised alarm within the research community in its 'illiberal assumption that academic research should be an instrument of governance' (Hammersley 2000, p.10). As a result, research which seeks solutions to problems which are high on the social policy agenda are those most likely to receive funding. This is not only a danger to independent research, but also, in a contemporary climate of management-dominated and bureaucratised practice, this view of research results in a return to the narrow focus on behaviourist and regulatory approaches which gained prominence some years ago (e.g. Jehu 1967; Sheldon 1983) to the virtual exclusion of an examination of social structures and of innovative study in the social sciences. Moreover, the epistemological problems identified in the 'scientific method' in terms of its appropriateness as a model of research for social situations appear to be ignored by its advocates (Everitt 1998). An inherent issue in the approach has been the question of whether particular professional interventions can be isolated or identified as resulting or contributing to changes in problematic behaviour. The 'theoretical neutrality' of empirical-influenced research has been called into question (Stanley 1990), and the direction it points in is the location of social problems in individual behaviours rather than in structural and institutional systems. The normative research which results also tends to exclude particular topics such as 'race' and ethnicity (see, for example, Department of Health 1991, 1995), or to construct such topics in unhelpful and controversial ways (Ahmad and Sheldon 1993), and to stress the need to produce data which will help to control deviant groups (Witkin 2000). Graham (1995) has shown how the production of official statistics in health favours methods which have resulted in the exclusion of minority-group experiences. These techniques, while problematic, also constitute the attractiveness of methods associated with empirical research practice, since they appear to offer definitive tools and answers in the attempt to measure change and productivity. The popularity of such approaches is related directly to a political climate in social care and welfare where management-dominated and performance-based criteria determine the funding environment.

The research orientation of new social movements has sought to make visible those experiences which are misrepresented or ignored by official statistics and by methodological assumptions which result in normative ideas about family life and household structure. Research with women (Stanley and Wise 1993), on disability (Marris 1996), on 'race' (Gordon 1992), on sexuality (Sedgwick 1990), on class (Harvey 1990), on ageing (Arber and Ginn 1991), on youth (Batsleer 1996) and other marginalised identities, has had the effect of exposing the shortcomings of officially sanctioned studies which purport to be objective but in fact are ideologically laden.

This is not to say that some approaches which emphasise 'empowerment' rather than social control, do not have their problems also. For example, those whose theoretical roots are in humanistic psychology may tend to ignore social inequalities and to focus on individual participants, emphasising their need to 'feel good' about involvement in the research process. Critical and feminist social research set out not only to understand the world, but to also change it, linking individual 'conscientization' with the potential for social action – a political model of praxis (Harvey 1990; Humphries 1999; Stanley 1990). (See Humphries, Mertens and Truman 2000 for a fuller discussion of the strengths and limitations of these perspectives.) The association of empowerment research almost exclusively with qualitative methods has worked to its disadvantage in that it is easily caricatured as not objective, neutral or rational, and therefore not legitimate. This is in spite of some outstanding examples of the use of quantitative methods in explicitly political and emancipatory research (e.g. Kelly, Regan and Burton 1995; Truman 2000).

The 'paradigm' debate is fundamentally about the nature of reality. As Truman (2000) points out, a major contribution of feminist epistemology has been to show that 'any knowledge is situated and specific to the way in which it has been produced, and the social location of those who produce it' (p.26). Thus particular and favoured approaches to research and evaluation, feasibility studies and monitoring, will bear the marks of their political authors and audiences. What is needed is the critical scrutiny of these agendas, of assumptions, ideologies and values which underpin policies and practice. Whatever the methods, the aim of a more equal society is a legitimate criterion with which to judge the quality and effectiveness of social care and social welfare.

Background to this Volume

The contributors to this collection, in one way or another, and from different epistemological and political persuasions, are committed broadly to this aim. The majority of them are lecturers and/or researchers within the Department of Applied Community Studies at Manchester Metropolitan University. They are all engaged in social research in a variety of ways, with wide interests and research topics, but all linked to the department's remit of 'applied community studies'. The department is responsible for the professional and post-qualifying training of social workers, youth and community workers, careers guidance advisors, and has a portfolio of courses in these fields, as well as in the area of human communication. Several research groups operate in the department, linked to professional and social policy interests, and a lively research culture has been created through regular seminars and publications. These groups, while overlapping, have distinctive research interests – 'care in the community', 'social divisions', 'human communication'. They each aim to foster and examine studies in these fields.

The book was conceived initially as a resource for colleagues and postgraduate researchers, especially those doing higher degrees, and is one of a number of departmental publications on research produced over the past number of years. The aim was for a collection demonstrating critical reflection, grounded in the experience of doing research, which would be of use both as an example of academic writing and as information about the range of research interests in the department. It became clear that the contents would be useful to a wider audience of policy makers and practitioners in social care and social welfare, and we are pleased that Jessica Kingsley Publishers took up the project.

Permission to reproduce an extract from W. Probyn's *Angel Face: The Making of a Criminal in Chapter 10* was sought from HarperCollins Publishers, who were unable to find contractual evidence for the publication. We are satisfied that every effort was made to secure copyright permission. Appearing in the same chapter is an extract from A.E. Jones's *Juvenile Delinquency and the Law*, published in 1945. We understand that copyright reverted to Mr Jones in 1950, but despite every effort having been made, we have not been able to trace him for permission to reproduce the selection.

Summary of the chapters

The chapter which follows this, by Paul Wilkins, is a contribution to the growing literature on participative models of research. It examines in detail a range of collaborative approaches to research which have emerged out of dissatisfaction with the 'scientific method'. Wilkins discusses their implications in practice, drawing on case studies in both countries of the South and of the North. The chapter examines the claims of collaborative approaches, and reflects on some of their limitations.

Adele Jones draws on her doctoral research to describe how she developed a methodology to construct a framework for understanding the meanings attributed to their experiences by young people affected by immigration controls. She discusses her aim to triangulate theoretical perspectives to support the analysis. This entails an integrated framework of feminist (especially black feminist), participatory and grounded theories which she found particularly relevant. She also raises practical and political questions within the context of her racialised, class-based and gendered identity.

Following this, Mary Searle-Chatterjee opens up and explores assumptions which underpin much research, that of the right of the researcher to speak on behalf of – to represent – 'Others', especially in research carried out by 'the West' on 'the Rest'. She focuses on a number of studies she has carried out as a white woman in India, and examines structures of 'Otherising' implicit in academic and literary traditions. The question is raised as to what extent researchers can do justice to groups of people who are very differently situated from one's self in terms of experience, suffering or culture. She argues that there is still a place for a 'Westerner' to produce texts of her own, if only as a contribution to 'oppositional culture'.

In Chapter 5 Tom Cockburn draws on his experience of researching organisations to examine the contribution of quantitative methods in organisational research, particularly in making sense of records held by organisations. The chapter offers detailed description of the preparation, coding, measurement and summarising of data, and discusses the range of purposes to which findings can be put, supported by a number of examples. Cockburn offers practical examples of coding frames and matrixes of data, and examines the limitations and the politics of quantitative methods.

Beth Humphries and Marion Martin tackle the question of research ethics in Chapter 6. They examine both the purposes and the impact of ethical statements about social research, and bring a feminist critique to bear on concepts such as 'informed consent', 'privacy' and 'deception'. The chapter also considers Western uses of ethics statements in relation to indigenous peoples. Through the use of case studies, the critique foregrounds the ways in which ethics discourses privilege the researcher and represent research subjects as powerless or 'victims'. It offers some feminist-based principles towards a more adequate and inclusive research ethic.

Chapter 7 returns to the problem of meaning in social research, both in interactive methods and in the administration of self-completed questionnaires. David Boulton considers some of the problems raised where researcher and researched do not understand each other, and argues that questions such as 'what do you mean?' (more easily asked by researcher than by researched), can become a tool for exploring special vocabularies. A transcript from an interview is used to explore such topics as abbreviations used by insiders, the importance of 'the ordinary', issues of gender, how 'outsiders' become 'insiders', and 'passing' in research.

Philip Hodgkiss offers a direct challenge to the scientific research model of 'experiment and observe', by asking the question of whether legitimate research may consist of data which the researcher does not directly observe, or is not reported to her/him through a questionnaire or interview. Using a case study of report books in a local authority group home for vulnerable adults, he explores the possibilities of building up a picture from 'elsewhere', working itself out by hearsay, at second-hand, what he describes as 'a world of things going on behind our backs'. Hodgkiss describes a framework for the analysis and asks whether evidence such as this is of any value. He argues such a question is important in the context of Care in the Community, when vulnerable people's well-being might well depend on an informed answer.

Chapter 9, by Carol Packham, makes a link between community development and community auditing. It argues that some research methods are deskilling and exploitative of their subjects, and are therefore inappropriate to use as part of 'community development'. It suggests that 'community auditing' is an empowering process, and describes and evaluates a range of models as to their usefulness to Packham and her colleagues. The chapter includes a discussion of limitations and ethical dilemmas inherent in the approach.

Steve Morgan's chapter introduces readers to the main methodological approaches to documentary and text analysis, and in particular highlights discourse analysis as the focus of a worked example. This consists of a comparison of the text of two extracts from prison autobiographies which construct the causes of delinquency from very different viewpoints. The extracts are deconstructed in detail to demonstrate how autobiographical accounts can challenge the generalising, normalising effects of official discourse.

In Chapter 11, Janet Batsleer draws on the case of 'romantic friendships' as it has been investigated and analysed by feminist historians, to illustrate how new areas for research may emerge in practitioner research. She offers a review of feminist scholarly work in this field, and connects this with her own documentation of the girls work movement in her book, *Working with Girls and Young Women in Community Settings* (1996). She suggests that asking different questions can lead to a very different focus for research.

There are many reasons to believe that storytelling and metaphor are the ordinary language of ordinary people, a universal mode of communication understood in some way by both teller and listener. Because they are a 'natural' form of expression, it makes sense to use them in an investigation of human experience. This is the argument of Chapter 12, which discusses the literature on stories in qualitative research, and draws on Paul Wilkins' own work in art therapy and psychodrama to show that stories told in these contexts have value as investigative tools. Using an extract from his work with a creative therapy group, he demonstrates the possibilities for a different account of group processes than one presented as a number of defined stages and produced by the facilitator alone.

The final chapter, by Ed Mynott, reflects on the experience of completing a PhD, distinguishing between the PhD as a product (i.e. a qualification which potentially allows a person to do things they could not otherwise do), and as a process (the researching and writing of a doctoral thesis). Mynott examines (1) the nature of the academic environment to which the PhD offers access, (2) the conflicting notions of how a PhD should prepare one for the academic environment or status and (3) how different types of student motivation are likely to impact on the experience of studying for a PhD. The chapter highlights the tensions resulting from intellectual aspects on the one hand, and career aspects on the other, and raises the question as to whether studying for a doctorate is always the best way to pursue intellectual work and to achieve what is important to the individual.

References

Ahmad, W. and Sheldon, T. (1993) '"Race" and "statistics".' In M. Hammersley (ed) *Social Research: Philosophy, Politics and Practice.* London: Sage.

Arber, S. and Ginn, J. (1991) *Gender and Later Life: A Sociological Analysis of Resources and Constraints.* London: Sage.

Audit Commission (1996) *Misspent Youth.* London: Audit Commission.

Batsleer, J. (1996) *Working with Girls and Young Women in the Community.* Aldershot: Arena.

Broad, B. (ed) (1999) *The Politics of Social Work Research and Evaluation.* Birmingham: Venture Press.

Department of Health (1991) *Looking after Children: Good Parenting, Good Outcomes.* London: HMSO.

Department of Health (1995) *Child Protection: Messages from Research.* London: HMSO.

Everitt, A. (1998) 'Research and development in social work.' In R. Adams, L. Dominelli and M. Payne (eds) *Social Work: Themes, Issues and Critical Debates.* London: Macmillan.

Gordon, P. (1992) 'The racialization of statistics.' In R. Skellington (ed), *'Race' in Britain Today.* London: Sage.

Graham, H. (1995) 'Diversity, inequality and official data: Some problems of method and measurement in Britain.' *Health and Social Care in the Community 3,* 9–18.

Hammersley, M. *(2000) Times Higher Education Supplement,* 14 April.

Harvey, L. (1990) *Critical Social Research.* London: Unwin Hyman.

Humphries, B. (1999) 'Feminist evaluation.' In I. Shaw and J. Lishman (eds) *Evaluation and Social Work Practice.* London: Sage.

Humphries, B., Mertens, D.M. and Truman, C. (2000) 'Arguments for an emancipatory research paradigm.' In C. Truman, D.M. Mertens and B. Humphries (eds) *Research and Inequality.* London: UCL Press.

Humphries, B. and Truman, C. (eds) (1994) *Rethinking Social Research.* Aldershot: Avebury.

Jehu, D. (1967) *Learning Theory and Social Work.* London: Routledge Kegan Paul.

Kelly, L., Regan, L. and Burton, S. (1995) 'Defending the indefensible? Quantitative methods and feminist research.' In J. Holland and M. Blair, with S. Sheldon (eds) *Debates and Issues in Feminist Research and Pedagogy.* Buckingham: Open University Press.

Marris, V. (1996) *Lives Worth Living.* London: Pandora.

Mullender, A. and Ward, D. (1991) *Self-Directed Groupwork: Users Take Action for Empowerment.* London: Whiting & Birch.

Oliver, M. (1990) *The Politics of Disablement.* London: Macmillan.

Reid, W.J. and Zettergren, P. (1999) 'A perspective on empirical practice.' In I. Shaw and J. Lishman (eds) *Evaluation and Social Work Practice.* London: Sage.

Sedgwick, E.K. (1990) *Epistemology of the Closet.* Berkeley, CA: University of California Press.

Shaw, I. (1999) 'Evidence for practice.' In I. Shaw and J. Lishman (eds) *Evaluation and Social Work Practice.* London: Sage.

Sheldon, B. (1983) 'The use of single-case experimental designs in the evaluation of social work.' *British Journal of Social Work 13,* 477–500.

Stanley, L. (ed) (1990) *Feminist Praxis.* London and New York: Routledge.

Stanley, L. and Wise, S. (1993) *Breaking Out Again.* London: Routledge.

Truman, C. (2000) 'New social movements and social research.' In C. Truman, D.M. Mertens and B. Humphries (eds) *Research and Inequality.* London: UCL Press.

Truman, C., Mertens, D.M. and Humphries, B. (eds) (2000) *Research and Inequality.* London: UCL Press.

Witkin, S. (2000) 'An integrative human rights approach to social research.' In C. Truman, D.M. Mertens and B. Humphries (eds) *Research and Inequality.* London: UCL Press.

CHAPTER 2

Collaborative Approaches to Research

Paul Wilkins

Introduction

Collaborative approaches to research emerged from dissatisfaction with the 'scientific' method as an appropriate way of investigating human experience and the quest for a 'new paradigm' for human inquiry (Reason and Rowan 1981). They offer an approach in which all participants are involved in determining the objectives of research, planning and conducting it, deciding its conclusions and (ideally) sharing in the dissemination of those conclusions. It is research *by* and *with* people; not research *on* people. An essential principle is that people are self-determining, there is value in subjective experience and that power in the research community is shared.

Like many advances in the understanding of human experience, collaborative research has many antecedents. For example, Mearns and McLeod (1984, p.373) write about the importance of the 'researcher' meeting participants in the research as equals. They point out that this is a radical departure from the classical view of the 'subject' as servant of the researcher. Traditionally, the importance of the subject lies not in the person she is, but the extent to which she fits the pre-set criteria of her selection and may be regarded as representative of her population. The fact that she is a multifaceted individual is important only in terms of the nuisance value this individuality creates for the researcher intent on focusing on particular facets while controlling the rest. In this social context, when one person defines the relevance of another, an authority relationship is present from the outset.

Another strand appears in the work of Marshall (1986). Drawing on her study of women managers, she states:

> To learn and develop through research I need to tolerate my not knowing and to seek open encounter with the participants in my research. I seek a measure of equality and wish to be non-alienating in relationships. This involves telling participants what the project is about; discussing its aims and uncertainties; at times revealing where I stand and what I find puzzling and contradictory about the issues raised; and allowing participants to shape the research direction. Whilst, as the researcher, I have a different stake in the project from others, I expect to meet other people's needs as well as my own. (p.196)

Similarly, in his book on heuristic research, Moustakas (1990) makes repeated reference to the importance of *co-researchers*, by which he means all involved in the inquiry process. In the field of transpersonal research methods, too, participation is emphasised. Braud and Anderson (1998) state: 'In an expanded view of research (disciplined inquiry), the researcher's status or importance is not privileged over that of the other research participants. There is democratisation of the research enterprise, with all personnel contributing inputs and able to comment on a study's interpretations and conclusions' (pp.17–18). They go on to say that the terms 'co-researcher' and 'participant' are used, rather than the term 'subject', to emphasise an egalitarian stance towards all contributors to the research project. Those who are most familiar with the experiences being studied – as a result of having had these experiences – are the true experts in any investigation of those experiences.

Reason (1994a, pp.324–339) discusses three approaches to effective participation in human inquiry which he considers to be 'well-articulated in both theory and practice'. These are action inquiry, participatory action research and co-operative inquiry.

Action inquiry

Action inquiry is a form of inquiry into practice. In it there is a 'political' or social dimension in that it is research directed towards the facilitation of social change. Reason (1994b) writes 'action inquiry is concerned with the transformation of organisations and communities towards greater effectiveness and greater justice' (p.49). This requires the researcher, in the role of facilitator and monitor, to become actively and fully involved in a programme which can have such consequences. A philosophical precept of such an approach is that action and research are inseparable.

Action inquiry draws on *action science* (see Argyris, Putnam and Smith 1985; Schon 1983) but whereas the latter focuses on the understanding practitioners have of their behaviour, their thinking and the way they actually behave, the former (as well as with social change) is also concerned with empirical measurement of outcome and the quality of one's own attention (monitored by meditative exercises as one acts). Further, action inquiry addresses the question of how to transform organisations and communities into collaborative, self-reflective communities of inquiry (Reason 1994b, p.49).

Torbert (1991) sees action inquiry as 'a kind of scientific inquiry that is conducted in everyday life' and as 'consciousness in the midst of action' (p.221). Summarising some of Torbert's ideas, Reason (1994b) emphasises the importance of a valid knowledge of four 'territories of human experience to any individual, group or organisation engaging in action inquiry' (pp.49–50). First, knowledge about the system's own *purposes* – an intuitive or spiritual knowledge of what goals are worthy of pursuit and what demands attention at any point in time (and thus knowledge of when another purpose becomes more urgent and pressing). Second, knowledge about its *strategy*, an intellectual or cognitive knowledge of the theories underlying its choices. Third, a knowledge of the *behavioural* choices open to it – essentially a practical knowledge, resting in an awareness of oneself and on behavioural skill. Finally, knowledge of the *outside world*, in particular an empirical knowledge of the consequence of its behaviour.

Krim (1988, pp.145–6), in his account of an action inquiry programme in US city government in which he 'tried to create an organisational culture with a learning strategy (based in action inquiry)', offers a practical translation of this approach as:

1. an understanding and *continual re-evaluation* of the question 'What are we trying to accomplish (in the unit, department, or government as a whole)?

2. the setting up of regular systems to test whether the organisation's strategies and operations in fact match its vision, and to test its effect on the environment

3. the promotion of members' development towards their capacity for exercising 'action inquiry' (continuous learning from experience) – a true school for adults.

Briefly, action inquiry is:

- practical – it is based in real actions taken in real world situations
- political – it is intended to promote positive (and sometimes radical) social change
- participative – it is inclusive of the thoughts, impressions and intuitions of all who are involved
- collaborative – its processes and results are co-owned by the whole research community
- egalitarian – the perspectives of all participants (including the researcher) are seen as of equal value
- critical – the programme of activity and research is carefully evaluated.

Participatory action research

Reason (1994b) describes participatory action research (PAR) as probably the most widely practised collaborative research approach. Like action inquiry, it is fundamentally of a political nature and has been used most widely with oppressed groups – it is an approach which 'starts from the concerns of the people' (Swantz and Vainio-Mattila 1988, p.130). In PAR, the researchers seek to establish a dialogue with the population with which they are working so that they can discover and address their practical, social and political needs. This approach draws on the work of Freire (1970) and shares something with the ideas and practices of Boal (1979) who uses the form of theatre to enable oppressed people to explore their circumstances and seek avenues of change.

Reason (1994b, p.48) sees PAR as having a double objective. One aim is to produce knowledge and action directly useful to a community – through research, through adult education, and through socio-political action. The second aim is consciousness raising, to empower people through the process of constructing and using their own knowledge, so that they can learn to 'see through' the ways in which established interests monopolise the production and use of knowledge for their own benefit.

In many ways, PAR represents an ideology rather than one distinct methodology. Because it is based in a particular community and draws upon the culture of that community, each PAR project will be idiosyncratic. Many methods may be used in any one project – these might derive from the vernacular and are as likely to include group meetings, song, dance and drama as more conventional 'investigatory' techniques. In this sense, PAR demands much more than the technical skills of the traditional researcher. Whitmore (1994, p.97) suggests that, in PAR, there is a need for first of all, a commitment to the empowerment of others and a clarity of class, 'race' and gender analysis (and age, ability/disability as well). It also involves communication skills, an understanding of individual and group dynamics, and an ability and willingness to self-disclose and share personal feelings and experiences.

In some ways, PAR is more resource-intensive than traditional research. To enter so deeply into intra- and inter-personal processes takes time and, as Whitmore (1994) points out in the context of her study:

> [It] includes a willingness to go beyond the immediate task in helping people to cope with poverty. This means helping to provide such basics as transportation, child care and sometimes money. It means mediating with the welfare department on occasion. It often calls for hours spent listening to personal concerns and responding as best one can. In a nutshell, it means recognising all participants as human beings, with all our attendant needs, concerns and joys. It also means working at a broader level, taking action to try to change the larger political, social and economic structures which oppress us. (p.97)

An example of a PAR project is Swantz and Vainio-Mattila (1988) where the study is of people affected by a World Bank financed irrigation scheme in Eastern Kenya. Of their account, the authors argue that it demonstrates 'people do not have to passively accept what is thrust upon them: participatory inquiry may become an important channel for people's action and reaction' (p.127). A variety of techniques was used (including those of traditional ethnography) but *networking* was regarded as the most important. Networking is 'dialogue that has been born within and between groups that have formed temporarily or permanently around a common problem' (p.133).

Whitmore (1994) in which a pre-natal programme for single expectant mothers is evaluated, is another example of a PAR project. In this study, four participants in the pre-natal programme were hired to work with Whitmore as an evaluation team. Whitmore reports that the team decided on a 'mixed method' approach to data collection 'gathering both qualitative and quantitative information from a variety of sources' (p.86). In this account, Whitmore details the interpersonal processes within the group and her own difficulties as an educated woman working with women who were less privileged. She writes:

> One thing is clear to me: as a middle class, university educated researcher, I could never entirely share the meanings of those from less privileged groups, especially those in the most marginalised sectors of society. The verbal barriers are difficult enough. Beyond the verbal – affective, sense-making, one's experience of the world – understanding is class-based, as it is also gender and race based. (p.96)

She considers that although these and other barriers can never be completely overcome, the participatory process can considerably mitigate their effects.

Co-operative inquiry

Co-operative inquiry is a systematic approach to collecting qualitative data of which McLeod (1994) writes:

> this method represents a synthesis of all other qualitative methods, in the context of a distinctive philosophical stance concerning the aims and purposes of research, which must be carried out in a way that respects the *whole* potential for being human, including feelings and spiritual dimensions of experience as well as cognition and behaviour. (p.87)

The product of co-operative inquiry as reports or research papers 'needs to be rooted in and derived from the experiential and practical knowledge of the subjects in the inquiry' (Reason and Heron 1986, p.458). Co-operative inquiry can have the aim of more traditional approaches to research – that is to add to the sum of 'knowledge' about a given topic or area, to provide description and information. Equally, it can be aimed at transformation, exploring practice and effecting change. Heron (1996, pp.48–49) describes 'informative' and 'transformative' aims of co-operative inquiry and explains their interdependence. Co-operative inquiry can also be developmental – that is to do with the personal growth of the inquirers. For example, a collaborative inquiry group of final year undergraduates (all in their early twenties) and I, at their instigation, explored 'life stages'. On one level, this was a straightforward 'informative' exploration – we were seeking to discover and understand patterns in the lives of people in the communities to which we belonged, drawing on our own experience, the experience of others to whom we had access, the literature (fiction, biography and academic) and so on. But there was a deeper meaning to this research. Why should a group of people with relatively little experience of life and its stages be so interested in these patterns? It was clearly linked to what they saw as an imminent (and perhaps radical) change in their own lives. The investigation had a subsidiary (and at first unexpressed) aim of helping group members through a forthcoming change. By understanding life stages in general, they would be better equipped to understand and deal with the changes which were happening to them. This I characerise as developmental co-operative inquiry. Heron (1998) takes co-operative inquiry into the realms of spiritual transformation.

Heron (1996, pp.7–9) considers the areas of overlap between co-operative inquiry and other forms of participatory research (including action inquiry and PAR). In his view, while 'democratisation of content' (that is participants mutually decide upon the objectives of the research) is widely shared, 'democratisation of method' (that is participants deciding upon the operational methods to be used) is only a prominent feature of co-operative inquiry.

Reason and Heron (1986) consider two ideas to be fundamental in the development of co-operative inquiry. First, that people are self-determining, that is 'authors of their own actions – to some degree actually, and to a greater degree potentially' (p.458). Second, that there are at least three kinds of knowledge. These are:

1. *experiential knowledge* which is 'gained through direct encounter with persons, places or things'

2. *practical knowledge* which concerns 'how to do something – it is knowledge demonstrated in a skill or competence'

3. *propositional knowledge* which is 'knowledge about something, and is expressed in statements and theories'.

Heron (1992) added the concept of *presentational knowledge* which Reason (1994b, p.42) describes as the form of knowledge by which we first order our tacit experiential knowledge of the world into spatio-temporal patterns of imagery, and then symbolise our sense of their meaning in movement, sound, colour, shape, line poetry, drama and story. Presentational knowledge forms a bridge between experiential knowledge and propositional knowledge. Heron (1996) states that for each of these forms of knowledge there is an equivalent belief:

> Propositional belief is belief that something is the case. Presentational belief is belief in one's intuitive feel for a meaningful pattern. Practical belief is belief in one's developing skill. Experiential belief is belief in one's dawning sense of a presence. These beliefs form necessary precursors to the relevant forms of knowledge. (pp.53–54)

From these precepts, Reason and Heron (1986) developed a form of participative, person-centred inquiry with a distinctive methodology involving four phases of action and reflection which they examine and explain in the context of a co-operative inquiry into the theory and practice of holistic medicine. These phases are (after Reason and Heron 1986, pp.459–461; Reason 1994b, pp.42–44; Heron 1996, pp.54–55):

1. An initial phase in which a group of co-researchers decide upon an area of inquiry and formulate some basic propositions. They also decide how to conduct the research by agreeing a set of procedures by which they will observe and record their own and each other's

experience. This phase is concerned primarily with propositional knowing but it can also contain forms of presentation (for example, group members may use art or story to articulate their interests and to explore ways of progressing the project). This stage includes both propositional belief and presentational belief regarding what may be useful areas of inquiry and how to start the process.

2.   A second phase in which the group applies these ideas and procedures and which involves a range of special inquiry skills. In informative inquiries, these skills include being fully present with an openness to imagination and intuition. It also means being able to leave aside ingrained conceptual frameworks ('bracketing off') and being prepared to generate new and alternative ways of seeing and interacting with the world. In transformative inquiries, to do with practice, skills include critically appraising all elements of practice both separately and together, interrupting compulsive or conventional behaviours and being prepared to depart from the habitual form of action and to incorporate alternative action frameworks. This all then involves practical belief.

3.   The third phase involves the group in a total immersion in the activity and experience. This is fundamental to the whole process and may involve excitement, boredom, alienation and even forgetting that they are involved in an inquiry process. It is here that the openness of the co-researchers to what is going on for them and their environment allows them to bracket off their prior beliefs and preconceptions and to see their experience in a new way. This is the phase of experiential knowing (and, particularly in the first cycle, of experiential belief).

4.   The fourth phase is a second phase of reflection and occurs after an appropriate period of engagement with the second and third stages and in it the group return to their original propositions and hypotheses and consider them in the light of experience. These ideas are then subject to modification, reformulation, rejection and so on. There is an interplay between propositional and presentational processes; these are now grounded in practice and experience. New hypotheses may be advanced and new strategies adopted. This constitutes a critical return to propositional knowing.

These four stages constitute one complete cycle of the co-operative inquiry process. Reason and Heron (1986) state:

> This cycle of movement from reflection to action and back to reflection needs to be repeated several times so that ideas and discoveries tentatively reached in early cycles may be clarified, refined, deepened and corrected. This 'research cycling' clearly has an important bearing on the empirical validity of the whole inquiry process. (p.461)

These stages can only follow when there is an agreed focus for an investigation but there must be something which precedes the first statement of propositional knowledge. This may be the ideas and enthusiasm of one person or small group of people who then go on to recruit others to their research group. However, it may be more in keeping with the philosophy of co-operative inquiry for the topic of research to somehow emerge from the 'being together' of a group. For example, a collaborative inquiry group based in the Centre for Human Communication, Manchester Metropolitan University meeting in the academic year 1999/2000 proposed an initial stage in the co-operative inquiry process which we have tentatively called 'pre-propositional knowing'. This group met with the intention to work collaboratively, drawing on themselves to investigate some aspect of human experience but with no clear idea of just what the topic of this exploration should be. The early stages of this group were characterised by structured, semi-structured and unstructured efforts at team building. We spent time with each other, hearing each others' stories, sharing enterprises and endeavours (even building a 'hut' in the woods together, sharing lunch on top of a local crag). From this process of simply being together, an issue of interest and concern to us all 'bubbled up' and we decided to concentrate our efforts on understanding life stages. With hindsight, we recognised the events leading up to our first statement of propositional knowledge as essential to the research process and to our evolution as a research community. It was at our second return to propositional knowing that we attached to it the label 'pre-propositional knowing'.

West (1996, pp.347–55) describes a human inquiry project with counsellors who use healing in their practice. He shows how one part of the co-researchers work can be understood in terms of research cycling thus:

Stage 1: The research question agreed on was: how does the use of 'labels' impact on our work? The group decided to explore definitions of labels used for therapists whose work includes healing.

Stage 2: The action taken was that chairs were given labels representing the main positions held by the research participants in relation to therapy and healing. Group members were invited to sit on a chair whose label they identified with and then to describe that position.

Stage 3: Participants used the technique of 'bracketing-off' to focus more fully on the experience of what it felt like to assume that position.

Stage 4: Reflection took the form of group members sharing their feelings about the experience and discussing these. Propositional knowledge was refined in that the group identified the inappropriate use of such labels by supervisors as one of the reasons for supervision difficulties. It was decided to repeat the exercise as described above.

Reason and Heron (1986, pp.466) acknowledge that 'the method is open to all the ways in which human beings fool themselves and each other' and that this poses a threat to the validity of co-operative inquiry and therefore propose a set of procedures to counteract this. These are:

1. *Development of discriminating awareness.* That is the deliberate cultivation of a watchful and mindful state. This is of particular importance in experiential inquiry.

2. *Research cycling, convergence and divergence.* Research cycling provides a series of corrective feedback loops. Convergent cycling allows for checking and rechecking with more and more attention to detail, divergent cycling is a way of affirming the values of heterogeneity and the creativity that comes from taking many different viewpoints.

3. *Authentic collaboration.* Because collaboration is an essential aspect of this form of inquiry, it must in some sense be real. The inquiry group must not be dominated by an individual or clique but must be supportive and (where appropriate) challenging of all participants. All voices must be equally heard. This involves attention to group dynamics and group processes. This 'takes time, willingness and skill'.

4. *Falsification.* In any group, there is a danger of consensus collusion. The deliberate cultivation of a Devil's Advocate role is a counterweight to this. The Devil's Advocate is a group member who temporarily takes on the role of radical critic and who challenges all the assumptions the group seems to make.

5. *Management of unaware projections.* Unacknowledged distress and psychological defences may seriously distort inquiry. This must be dealt with systematically either by bringing it into awareness or allowing it creative expression. Any of a number of approaches to personal growth may be helpful in this context.

6. *Balance of action and reflection.* Collaborative inquiry is a combination of action and reflection. These must be appropriately balanced. It is not possible to prescribe an ideal proportionality because the right sort of balance will depend upon the nature of the inquiry and of the co-researchers.

7. *Chaos.* A descent into chaos will often facilitate the emergence of a new creative order. There is no guarantee that chaos will occur but the key issue is to be prepared for it, be able to tolerate it and be welcoming of it.

Co-operative inquiry in practice

Co-operative inquiry may be part of a larger study, as in West (1997) where it followed a more conventional interview phase, it may emerge because conventional approaches seem inadequate to the task, as in Trayner's (1994) study with health visitors, or be the whole of the study from the outset, as in Heron (1988) where the inquiry was into altered states of consciousness. Whatever the initiating factors of co-operative inquiry, the practicalities are much the same. These include means of recruitment (and retention) of co-researchers, the collection and processing of 'data' and the presentation and ownership of any results and conclusions from the study.

Recruitment to a co-operative inquiry is usually initiated by one or more people. For them, there is the prospect of a reward of some kind, perhaps satisfying an intellectual itch, perhaps the hope of a higher degree or publication. However, co-operative inquiry depends upon the sustained commitment of the co-researchers. One of the issues for recruitment and retention is how the project might be rewarding for all those involved in it.

Most initiators of a co-operative inquiry start by identifying possible co-researchers (perhaps by occupation, perhaps by belief, perhaps by workplace, etc.) and then in some way inviting them to join an inquiry group. For example, Heron (1988) recruited participants by 'advertising a workshop, facilitated by myself, as a co-operative inquiry into altered states of consciousness' (p.183) and Trayner (1994, pp.62–63) invited health visitors she had already met to a seminar in which she outlined her research interests, explained the nature of co-operative inquiry and explained what would be expected of her co-researchers. It is possible that co-researchers recruited in this way will share the initiator's enthusiasm and commitment but real effort must be made to ensure that the group as a whole perceives some benefit from the research. For many co-researchers this may require more than the satisfaction of intellectual curiosity. As no two co-operative inquiry groups are the same, each group must find its own solutions to this issue (it may quite legitimately become part of the group process). Solutions have been found. Whitmore (1994, p.85) in effect employed the participants in her research and for Wilkins *et al.* (1999) the additional reward lay in the contribution the research made to an undergraduate programme of study and thus an academic award. For this and subsequent similar co-operative inquiries, my recruitment strategy was in essence to say: 'Here is an opportunity to work together to investigate a topic or area of mutual interest – we will collectively decide what this is and how to explore it. Contact me if you are interested.' There was always a good response.

Co-operative inquiry data may take many forms – each of the four types of knowledge produces different (but interdependent and related) 'results' and Heron (1996, pp.105–107) describes 'four kinds of outcome'. West (1996) has pointed out that the knowledge of a co-operative inquiry group could as well be 'represented in terms of metaphors, paintings, dance and poetry'(p.353) as a traditional research report. However, methods of analysis and the academic community privilege propositional knowledge above other kinds. For those engaged in this kind of research, this poses a dilemma. Should there be an attempt to condense the expressive and creative findings of collaborative inquiry into a more cognitive framework or can (for example) artistic expression legitimately stand as research output? And who has a responsibility for processing and publishing the output of a co-operative inquiry?

This dilemma is largely unresolved although individual co-operative inquirers have their own solutions. West (1996, pp.353–354) makes an argument for using a grounded theory approach to co-operative inquiry data and asks: Where does the understanding of the phenomena lie? With the research participants as represented in their data analysed by grounded theory? Within the researcher and hence accessible through a heuristic process of exploration? Or co-created as in a human Inquiry group?

West (1996) takes the view that no one form of data analysis is likely to produce a satisfactory report of a co-operative inquiry. He favours a *bricolage*; that is, a mixture of techniques comprising 'a creative composite reflecting the interests and knowledge of the members of the research group at different phases of the inquiry cycle' (p.354).

Heron (1996, pp.101–103) argues of collaborative inquiry that 'anything written down is secondary and subsidiary' to the experience of the people involved in the inquiry but does offer some thoughts on how a report of collaborative inquiry might be compiled and what it should contain. In his view, this is one way of producing a written report:

1. The outline and main content headings of the report, together with any key issues to be included under any heading, are brainstormed, discussed and refined in the whole group.

2. Agreements are made about who will write up which parts, and who will be the co-ordinating editors (who may also be authors of one or more parts).

3. Drafts of the parts are sent to the co-ordinating editors, who produce a complete first draft of the whole report.

4. This is sent to the part-authors and every other member of the inquiry for their comments and suggested amendments, which the editors incorporate as appropriate in a second draft, which is sent round for a final set of comments.

5. The editors take account of the final comments and produce a third and final version of the report, which is then available for publication. (p.101)

The report of Wilkins *et al.* (1999) broadly follows these suggestions and demonstrates a method for moving the personal knowledge of co-researchers to a co-owned knowledge thus:

Our final report was produced by 'story-building'. This occurred in stages:

- the 'telling' of an individual, highly personal story
- the mediation of that story through writing a journal
- the more public re-telling of that story where it was modified by the input and influence of others
- the re-casting of the personal stories in the light of the previous stages and pre-existing stories (the literature) and the production of (an individual) written account
- the synthesis of a group story (by the principal author) from the personal stories in such a way that we all feel and believe 'that is our story – I see myself and my colleagues…'. (Wilkins *et al.* 1999, p.9)

The authors emphasise that these stages are not entirely discrete and that there was a continual cycling through the first three stages (echoing the cycles of co-operative inquiry). The report produced by this process is co-authored by all members of the group.

Alongside this dilemma runs another. In what form should the output of a co-operative inquiry be presented and who is the audience? All the published reports of co-operative inquiry of which I am aware concentrate on the presentation of propositional knowledge. This may be legitimate (although I think that it undervalues other forms of knowing). What I think is more questionable is that these reports are essentially academic in nature. Academic language can at times be relatively impenetrable even to academics and students, arguably, its use exclusive. In a research method which seeks to be egalitarian and to address issues of power this is unsatisfactory. A defence might be that, whatever the form of the published report, the co-researchers benefited from the study and increased their understanding, were empowered, etc., and this would probably be true. But what about a wider audience?

One way out of this dilemma might be to produce reports in a language meaningful to the co-researchers so that others in similar positions will be able to benefit from any new knowledge. As well as being about the words used and the structure of the report, this may be about the use of metaphor and creative expression. Outside the narrow confines of academic and professional journals, people tend to communicate by telling stories. However apparently factual these stories may be, they tend to be enriched by liberal use of metaphor. Many authors (for example, 1976; von Franz 1982) write of how metaphor speaks widely and generally. Jones (1996) writes of the dramatherapy paradox that 'what is fictional is also real' (p.10). Goddard (1996, p.4) has pointed out the 'metaphorical nature of everyday talk'. All this implies that metaphor and stories are the way that human beings communicate their experiences and through which they understand the experiences of others. This has implications for the validity, reliability, accessibility and applicability of the results of research, especially co-operative inquiry and related forms of collaborative research. It may even be that the findings of collaborative inquiry are best presented in a 'fictionalised' form.

Limitations of collaborative approaches to research

The limitations of collaborative approaches include those shared by other 'new paradigm' methods in that, by definition, the researcher is intimately involved with the research and there can be no pretence of objectivity. This opens such research to the charge of bias but there can be rigour in these approaches (see Reason 1994a, pp.331–332). There are, however, practical difficulties.

Any research method aimed at facilitating change may involve the confrontation of established bureaucracy and, even when there is an expressed willingness to co-operate, this can lead to frustration and confusion for all. With all participatory research methods, the commitment of the participants is also an issue. For example, Krim (1988, p.146) reports his difficulty in involving his colleagues fully in his action inquiry process and Casson (1998) working with people who hear voices, reports on the reluctance of participants to attend meetings about the research process even though this was part of their contract. Any collaborative inquiry can be personally demanding of its participants and perhaps especially of the initiator of the research. In this context, Krim (1988, pp.149–150) also writes about the importance of effective supervision from outside the project and the painful necessity to confront aspects of his own behaviour. Reason (1994b) summarises these difficulties:

> Those who wish to take the path of collaborative research be warned: there is no easy way forward. You and your co-researchers may be attracted to the rhetoric of partici-pation; you may think you are deeply committed to the values of participative rela-tionships. Yet for those of us encultured to unconscious participation the leap to a future reflexive participation is immense: there will be doubt and mistrust, there will be disagreement and conflict, there will be failures as well as success. For the birth of a new more integrated consciousness means the death of the old. Future participa-tion means the loss of the myth of certainty, the loss of control, the tempering of the rational mind. It means learning to trust the wisdom of the unknown other. (pp.55–56)

Acknowledgement

I would like to thank Meabh McClean, Wendy Nevin, Zinnia Mitchell-Williams, Karyn Wastell and Rebecca Wheat for permission to draw on their experience and ideas in the development of this argument.

References

Argyris, C., Putnam, R. and Smith, M.C. (1985) *Action Science: Concepts, Methods, and Skills for Research and Interventions.* San Francisco: Jossey-Bass.

Bettleheim, B. (1976) *The Uses of Enchantment.* London: Thames & Hudson.

Boal, A. (1979) *Theatre of the Oppressed.* London: Pluto.

Braud, W. and Anderson, R. (1998) 'Conventional and expanded views of research.' In W. Braud and R. Anderson (eds) *Transpersonal Research Methods for the Social Sciences: Honoring Human Experience.* Thousand Oaks, CA: Sage.

Casson, J. (1998) Personal communication.

Freire, P. (1970) *Pedagogy of the Oppressed.* New York: Herder and Herder.

Goddard, A. (1996) 'Tall stories: The metaphorical nature of everyday talk.' *English in Education 30,* 2, 4–12.

Heron, J. (1988) 'Impressions of the other reality: A co-operative inquiry into altered states of consciousness.' In P. Reason (ed) *Human Inquiry in Action: Developments in New Paradigm Research.* London: Sage.

Heron, J. (1992) *Feeling and Personhood: Psychology in Another Key.* London: Sage.

Heron, J. (1996) *Co-operative Inquiry: Research into the Human Condition.* London: Sage.

Heron, J. (1998) *Sacred Science: Person-centred Inquiry into the Spiritual and the Subtle.* Ross-on-Wye: PCCS Books.

Jones, P. (1996) *Drama as Therapy: Theatre as Living.* London: Routledge.

Krim, R. (1988) 'Managing to learn: Action inquiry in City Hall.' In P. Reason (ed) *Human Inquiry in Action: Developments in New Paradigm Research.* London: Sage.

Marshall J. (1986) 'Exploring the experiences of women managers: Towards rigour in qualitative methods.' In S. Wilkinson (ed) *Feminist Social Psychology: Developing Theory and Practice.* Milton Keynes: Open University Press.

McLeod, J. (1994) *Doing Counselling Research.* London: Sage.

Mearns, D. and McLeod, J. (1984) 'A person-centered approach to research.' In R.F. Levant and J.M. Shlien (eds) *Client-centered Therapy and the Person-centered Approach: New Directions in Theory, Research and Practice.* New York: Praeger.

Moustakas, C. (1990) *Heuristic Research: Design, Methodology and Applications.* Newbury Park, CA: Sage.

Reason, P. (1994a) 'Three approaches to participative inquiry.' In N.K. Denzin and Y.S. Lincoln (eds) *Handbook of Qualitative Research.* Thousand Oaks, CA: Sage.

Reason, P. (1994b) 'Human inquiry as discipline and practice.' In P. Reason (ed) *Participation in Human Inquiry.* London: Sage.

Reason, P. and Heron, J. (1986) 'Research with people: The paradigm of co-operative experiential inquiry.' *Person-Centered Review 1,* 4, 456–476.

Reason, P. and Rowan, J. (eds) (1981) *Human Inquiry: A Sourcebook of New Paradigm Research.* Chichester: Wiley.

Schon, D.A. (1983) *The Reflective Practitioner: How Professionals Think in Action.* New York: Basic Books.

Swantz, M.-J. and Vainio-Mattila, A. (1988) 'Participatory inquiry as an instrument of grass-roots development.' In P. Reason (ed) *Human Inquiry in Action: Developments in New Paradigm Research.* London: Sage.

Torbert, W.R. (1991) *The Power of Balance: Transforming Self, Society, and Scientific Inquiry.* Newbury Park, CA: Sage.

Trayner, H. (1994) 'Confronting hidden agendas: Co-operative inquiry with health visitors.' In P. Reason (ed) *Participation in Human Inquiry.* London: Sage.

von Franz, M.L. (1982) *An Introduction to the Interpretation of Fairy Tales.* Irving, TEXAS: Spring Publications.

West, W. (1996) 'Using human inquiry groups in counselling research.' *British Journal of Guidance and Counselling 24*, 3, 347–355.

West, W. (1997) 'Integrating counselling, psychotherapy and healing: An inquiry into counsellors and psychotherapists whose work includes healing.' *British Journal of Guidance and Counselling, 25*, 3, 291–311.

Whitmore, E. (1994) 'To tell the truth: Working with oppressed groups in participatory approaches to inquiry.' In P. Reason (ed) *Participation in Human Inquiry*. London: Sage.

Wilkins, P., Ambrose, S., Bishop, A., Hall, R., Maugham, P., Pitcher, C., Richards, E., Shortland, J., Turnbull, A., Wilding, S. and Wright, N. (1999) 'Collaborative inquiry as a teaching and learning strategy in a university setting: processes within an experiential group – the group's story.' *Psychology Teaching Review 8*, 1, 4–18.

CHAPTER 3

Exploring Young People's Experience of Immigration Controls
The Search for an Appropriate Methodology
Adele Jones

Introduction

This chapter is concerned with epistemological and methodological questions in research with young people. It is based on a study undertaken as PhD research which involved interviews with 30 young people affected by immigration controls (see Jones 1998). The chapter describes the theoretical perspectives underpinning the study, raises questions about the status of 'empowerment' and argues that claims for representing children and young people are legitimised only inasmuch as they dislodge adult certainties and address inequality.

In developing a methodology I was concerned not to perpetuate a rigid division between theory and method but to ensure that the conceptual framework chosen reflected my substantive concerns (Butt and Jones 1995). I determined not to disclaim bias but to acknowledge it and to make visible standpoints arising from it that were implicit within the approach taken. I did not claim privileged status on the basis of my experience, neither did I make appeals to the respectability and 'infallibility' of science. Instead I suggest that these two positions represent different ways of seeing the world and what is important is not to distance the problem from the methodology but to elucidate the ways in which they connect.

Three major theoretical sources were drawn upon: feminist, participatory and grounded theory; and feminist epistemology provides a connecting thread in the interpretative approach adopted.

Feminist perspectives

Although feminist theory developed in relation to women's oppression, its insights are more widely applicable. Particularly useful to my understandings of young people's experiences were feminist critiques of essentialism, universalism, representation and difference. These take place on two interconnected levels: 'an ideological, discursive level which addresses questions of representation and a material, experiential, daily-life level which focuses on the micro-politics of work, home, family, sexuality, etc. (Mohanty 1991, p.21).

Feminist scholarship is complex, dynamic and contested ground which reflects diverse and often conflicting interests. The field not only provides oppositional agency to dominant discourses but also produces its own hegemonies, insurgents and counter-insurgents. Of particular importance has been the contribution of black feminist scholarship which has led to new understandings on the relational nature of oppression and has challenged universalist assumptions and representations of black women and 'Third World' women by white Western women:

> historicizing and locating political agency is a necessary alternative to formulations of the 'universality' of gendered oppression and struggles... universality of gender oppression is problematic, based as it is on the assumption that the categories of race and class have to be invisible for gender to be visible. In the 1990's, the challenges posed by black and Third World feminists can point the way towards a more precise, transformative feminist politics. Thus the juncture of feminist and anti-racist/Third World/post-colonial studies is of great significance, materially as well as methodologically. (Mohanty 1992, p.75)

Alongside this, and emerging out of the poststructuralist project (i.e. an interrogation of universalisms; opposition to naturalistic theories of difference; celebration of heterogeneity and diversity, and identity constituted through discourse), is a rejection of essentialism and an interrogation of essentialist claims. Essentialist interpretations of the term 'black' for instance, have led to intense debate particularly in the UK and America and have raised concerns about the validity of assertions and their effect on research processes. Amina Mama, in her research on identity formation, argues that essentialist discourse can be a source of oppression, though she recognises that black women have found it necessary to identify with one another's experiences:

> In emphasising the need for unity in the face of multiplicity of oppressive forces, black people risk creating a new discursive regime, namely a set of prescriptions for how to be black and a set of sanctions and epithets for those daring to differ. (Mama 1995, p.156)

Nevertheless, there are also problems with anti-essentialist positions. Anti-essentialism is defined by sociologist Ali Rattansi as:

> [A] maneuver cutting the ground from conceptions of subjects and social forms as reducible to timeless, unchanging, defining and determining elements or ensemble

of elements – 'human nature', for example, or in the case of the social, the logic of the market or mode of production. (Rattansi 1994, cited in Malik 1996 p.5).

Anti-essentialism is in opposition to fixed, determinant, naturalistic theories of social phenomena, challenging the positivist position that social relations are 'merely the surface appearance of a natural essence' (Malik 1996, p.6). Malik suggests this 'renders all determinate relations contingent, bereft of any inner necessity' (Malik 1996, p.6), and to develop the anti-essentialist position would be to assert that all essentialist positions are invalid, even those that recognise relations between the individual and society as a determinant in the formation of identity, since any other stance would contradict the view that social phenomena cannot be reduced to defining properties. Malik's work, and increasingly that of (particularly) black feminists (see Mohanty 1991), while utilising and developing liberatory approaches within some poststructuralisms, questions whether anti-essentialism may erode the very foundations of political struggles of marginalised and oppressed groups since discourse which makes them 'visible', that is, highlights the significance of their difference, can only be of use if there is an *essentialising of difference* constituted out of the experience of oppression. This is both complex and problematic, as it requires, for instance, a view of experience which reduces it to named, understood and accessible properties. It betrays its own universalisms which are an inevitable product of essentialist ideas and it privileges a generalised identity based on an assumed com-monality of interests of oppressed peoples. It underplays issues of power *within* oppressed groups and fails to provide a definition of experience compatible with the notion of a constituted collective. It also does not address the tensions that emerge in the spaces created through discourse and representation. Mohanty (1991) addresses some of these contradictions and argues for a concept of political unity that does not necessitate appropriation, which while accommodating the notion of the personal as political, does not reduce the political to the personal and which regards difference as historically specific. In doing so, Mohanty herself promotes an essentialising of difference in order to develop not only the notion that inequalities are not equal, but that inequality can only be understood within an historical context of social relations.

This issue of the treatment of different inequalities as of equal order of signifi-cance requires some consideration. In an analysis of colonialism as part of the historical context of racist oppression, Sivanandan (1982) writes:

> the economic aspects of colonial exploitation may find analogy in white working class history. But the cultural and psychological dimensions of black oppression are quite unparalleled ... the conquistadors of Europe set up such a mighty edifice of racial and cultural superiority, replete with its own theology of goodness, that the natives were utterly disorientated and dehumanised ... If the white workers' lot at the hands of capitalism was alienation, the blacks underwent complete deracination. And it is this factor which makes black oppression qualitatively different from the

oppression of the white working class. (Sivanandan 1982, cited in Small 1996, p.198)

Sivanandan highlights the fact that white working-class oppression is not the same as black working-class oppression since the latter is given effect through the relations of both race and economics. There is therefore a case to be argued that being black (however this may further be deconstructed) is an essentialising property of racist oppression. While its use brings to the surface the contradictions discussed above, this may help to explain why the term 'black' retains considerable currency as an expression of politicised activity, referring to 'communities' of people who experience, analyse and challenge racist oppression (Mohanty 1991).

Although the study of young people which this chapter describes was not concerned only with black young people, all except one identified themselves as 'black' within the context of their immigration experiences. The current government position is to seek to distance immigration controls from race relations both in order to avoid post-Lawrence charges of racism and also to ease the passage of the Race Relations (Amendment) Bill which seeks to exempt immigration and nationality functions from its provisions to make unlawful any discrimination on grounds of nationality or ethnic or national origins by the police and other public authorities (Race Relations (Amendment) Bill 2000).[1] However, evidence from other studies, and indeed Home Office research, point irrefutably to the structuring and implementation of immigration legislation and policy through the relations of race (the 1961 Commonwealth Immigration Act contained the specific intent of curbing immigration from the Caribbean and the Indian subcontinent). An examination of government archives highlights the prevailing view: 'We are in little doubt that some form of control over coloured immigration will eventually be inescapable' (Cabinet Committee 1956, p.57, quoted in Dean 1993). Research suggests that in the construction and implementation of immigration legislation, race has been an enduring feature with black people consistently affected disproportionately to white people (see, for example, Carter, Harris and Joshi 1987). There is also evidence that women and men are treated differently from each other (Bhabha 1985 Bryan 1985; Women, Immigration and Nationality Group 1985, Dadzie and Scafe). These dimensions were therefore significant within the study and the insights discussed above were important for the research in that they point up:

- On the discursive level, the recognition of how people are constructed within immigration discourse – as 'economic migrants', 'taking advantage of the welfare state', 'bogus refugees', and also as 'pathetic', 'passive', 'needy' and 'victims of war'. The study sought to explore the impact of these images on the young people and the ways they represented themselves, their experiences and their families.

- Related to this, the need to find ways to interrogate universal assumptions about young people affected by immigration control. For example, they are not all refugees, they do not all intend to stay in this country. Their skills and aspirations differ, their experiences vary with geographical, historical, political, gender and cultural differences which should be documented to counter prevailing essentialisms. Such essentialisms are rooted in historical processes which include immigration controls.

- The question of whether an analysis of young people's experiences of immigration controls can accommodate an anti-essentialist position theoretically, whilst embracing an essentialist position for political purposes. That is, being aware of the dangers of reducing characteristics and experiences to naturalistic theories of difference, but recognizing the need for solidarity in opposing policies which affect particular racialised groups differently from others.

- The issue of the construction and implementation of immigration control through relations of race, gender and class and the material realities arising out of this which shape the lived experiences of children and young people.

Participatory research

The study was set within a body of work referred to as 'participatory', 'emancipatory' or 'action' research. Fonow and Cook (1991) have identified several ways in which 'action orientation' may be manifest within the research process:

> [action research] is reflected in the statement of purpose, topic selection, theoretical orientation, choice of method, view of human nature, and definitions of the researcher's roles. This emphasis on action is something feminists share with other traditions of social thought such as Black studies, Marxism, and Gay and Lesbian Studies. (Fonow and Cook 1991, p.5)

'Participatory (or participative) research' suggests a unified body of research, but the field it refers to is one of different, often contradictory approaches to research which draws on several theoretical perspectives (Madden and Humphries 1998). This aside, participatory research remains a useful term for politically motivated research which has had a major impact within the research community through sustained challenge to dominant traditions and the development of methodologies for the inclusion of informants as 'actors' in the research, explicitly addressing inequality. The legitimization of political aims within research has led to intense debate over epistemological claims and the development and articulation of different standpoints. Out of these developments, it is possible to elucidate some common principles and philosophical positions which underpin participatory research.

Madden and Humphries (1998) identify four main influences in the development of participatory research: humanistic psychology; critical theory; feminist research and poststructuralism. Out of these, opposing ideas have developed. For instance, poststructuralists reject humanist ideas, critiquing claims to knowledge based on the positioning of the human subject as central. Rather the human subject 'is not a unitary, given entity acting rationally upon the world, but a site of conflict and difference which is constituted through discourse' (Malik 1996, p.8). However, others, such as Heron (1996), draw on humanist values to argue that a key feature of participatory research is that the researched (and the researcher) are self-determining within the research process and are available to each other in terms of intentionality, reciprocal communication and interpretations of meanings. Critical theorists have contributed to participatory research by questioning the production of knowledge and in making transparent the nature of exploitative processes. Marxist theory has been adapted by feminists to address issues of power and inequality, building on the work of, for example, Freire (1972) whose concern for social justice is predicated on the view that inequality is created and sustained through politically and economically determining social structures and relations. His notion of 'conscientization' as the precursor to action for transformation has had an influence on participatory research (Madden and Humphries 1998).

Postructuralist critiques, rejecting epistemological absolutes and acknowledging multiple, contradictory positions have provided fertile ground for the development of participatory research (see Weedon 1987). These epistemological developments have taken place alongside methodological advances. Participatory research has been promoted and developed by those committed to non-oppressive research methodologies both in order to contribute to an improved 'democratization' of the research process and also in acknowledgement of the realization that informant participation can produce richer data (Mies 1979).

On empowerment

A participative approach in research studies involving young people must embrace principles of empowerment or it risks being no less exploitative than an approach which excludes, marginalises or distorts their views. This requires an acknowledgement of the nature of power relations and an understanding of power as a situational, relational and dynamic concept, referred to as a fluid, multidirectional process (Bhavnani 1991). Approaches which address issues of empowerment do not vest the authority and ability to empower within the researcher and neither can assumptions be made that research participants are in need of being empowered (this is not to underplay issues of power and powerlessness that may exist within the problem being researched) or, indeed, that the process in itself will result in empowerment (although this may be an explicit aim of some studies).

These ideas were attractive to the development of the study. However, the notion of 'empowerment' is complex. Feedback received from some young people who participated was that they experienced the opportunity to tell their stories as 'empowering'. Seductive though this idea might be, the likely explanation is that young people found the experience of being listened to and taken seriously as positive, and maybe even helpful. But beyond the moment – the affirming possibilities created by researcher interest and concern as interviews unfolded – I suggest that meaningful empowerment lies not so much in the interaction with the researcher but in the potential to utilise findings to effect change. Empowerment sought *within*, rather than *beyond* the research interview can be achieved where the methodology employed uses 'therapeutic theoretical orientations and models to guide the interviews' (Hutchinson and Wilson 1994, p.304). However, there is a danger of exaggerated claims for empowerment as specific outcome rather than as social phenomenon. It may be more helpful to understand empowerment as a precursor to action and this as the precursor to change. Also, descriptions of empowerment within research projects rarely discuss reciprocity, as if the act of listening, interpreting and feeding back data is the only way in which empowerment is achieved. In studies involving the sharing of personal and painful information, the emotional investment of the storyteller may result in empowering the researcher more than the researched.

Oakley frames empowerment as 'therapeutic effects':

> Nearly three-quarters of the women said that being interviewed had affected them and the three most common forms this influence took were in leading them to reflect on their experiences more than they would otherwise have done; in reducing the level of their anxiety and/or in reassuring them of their normality ... There were many references to the 'therapeutic effect' of talking: 'getting it out of your system'. (Oakley 1981, p.50)

Claims made about the achievement of empowerment within participatory research are difficult to substantiate and my view is that integrity lies elsewhere – in locating responsibility with the researcher to ensure that the process is neither experienced as disempowering nor has disempowering outcomes, and in seeking informant validation on the interpretation of data. The focus of participative research should be as much about *disempowerment* therefore as empowerment, meaning that there must be a personal and political understanding and commitment to identifying and dismantling disempowering processes both at the level of personal dynamics and also in achieving change within a wider social context. It requires of the researcher a political consciousness and declaration of perspectives which provide the baseline for the researcher's own participation in the process.

Participative approaches to research and a commitment to empowerment are not concepts existing within a research vacuum. The intervention seeks to advance both the researcher and the subjects of the research in line with declared political positioning. Neither should such approaches be confused with achieving an egalitarian basis within a professional research relationship, although this is often implied. The researcher designs and leads the research project and inevitably 'calls the shots'. While at the level of personal interaction there may be shifts in the nature, location and exercise of power, the interpretation, presentation, ownership and use of data (even where there are attempts to share power) prevent equality within the relationship. As is clear, participative research is not unproblematic. It implies a consensus in determining the research design and the method adopted that in reality may be difficult to achieve. And, where agreement is not reached, questions remain such as whose agenda is progressed and whose motives are frustrated.

Insufficient attention in the work of those promoting empowerment as a legitimate aim of action research, is given to issues of power *within*, and although Bhavnani (1991) talks about shifting power, this does not adequately address power within the process. The declared position of the researcher may be that she is motivated at the level of personal interaction and research aims in a politicised way by feminism and/or anti-racist struggles (or any other political agenda) and these may be advanced by the research. There is gain here, therefore, not only for those whose rights might be progressed, but also for the researcher who advances a personal (political) agenda, utilising the power of the researcher within a rationale of challenging social injustice.

Sharing power within the research process has led to researchers, particularly some feminist researchers, sharing personal information with research subjects (Oakley 1981). This was a position that I initially adopted, since I had personal experience of immigration proceedings. Early reflection on the process, however, led to scepticism of the benefits of this to young people as informants, since they required no validation of the researcher's interest in or knowledge of the topic, and the sharing of personal information did little to equalise power and seemed a diversion from the purpose of the interviews. I became acutely aware that rather than serving to establish rapport and a common basis of understanding (important in the approach adopted), this seemed at times merely to further burden young people, much as a researcher investigating the effects of sexual abuse might should she reveal to informants that she, too, had experienced abuse.

The significance of my immersion as researcher in the interview process was not lessened by this realization, it simply meant that, aided by greater clarity about the sharing of personal information, subsequent interviews were unencumbered by unwelcome disclosures. This reveals distinctive characteristics of research with children and young people: the protective role adopted by the researcher; issues of power that are played out in assumptions about when and why young people need 'protection'; and the influence of constructions of childhood and youth which frame young people as vulnerable.

In participative research, the researcher is both participant and researcher. The first of these roles legitimises fulfilment of personal and professional goals (own political agenda; a desire for the work to be well received both by the participants and those who commissioned the work; academic credibility; etc.). However, the researcher is in a position to advance her own goals even where these are in conflict with those of other participants. This is particularly true in studies in which informants are children and young people.

The approach adopted was one where the primary source of data emanated from the experiences of young people. However they were not involved in initiating the project or in decisions about the areas of study since these had grown out of professional interests. There were difficulties in identifying research informants, and the involvement of young people from the outset in developing methods for achieving this might have led to a different outcome. This suggests that the participatory principles adopted were subject to fairly arbitrary rules as to when a participatory approach was applied and when it was not. These limits to the sharing of power also extend to other aspects of research such as research design, data analysis, allocation of research funds, publication and dissemination.

In summary, claims made of participative research must be scrutinised to unravel contradictions and dilemmas. This is necessary not to undermine participative research but to reaffirm it on the basis of improved understanding, clarity and integrity.

Researching the experiences of young people

While I sought to make a contribution to a growing body of social research seeking to confront oppression and exploitation in the production of knowledge (Fonow and Cook 1991), I was aware that to view the experiences of immigration simply as experiences of oppression would underplay the strengths of young people and effectively reduce them to victims of circumstance, rather than active players or survivors, and my primary concern therefore was to ensure that the processes of oppression were not replicated through the project. This created a dilemma – the discriminatory nature of immigration proceedings was established early in the study and preliminary data analysis indicated that most of the young people did feel that they were victims of oppression. To seek an interpretation of data which included acknowledging strengths and strategies for coping (an important aspect of emancipatory research) seemed, given the severe anxiety and distress that some of the young people expressed about their circumstances, at times insensitive and irrelevant. It also raised questions about the dangers of interpretations being used to minimise hardship created by conditions that obtain in the lives of those being researched.

In planning interviews, I was mindful of several concerns which emerged during the preliminary stage of the work and which I addressed through establishing interview principles as follows:

- Young people should experience the process as positive and affirming
- In the sharing of painful information, the opportunity for the interview to provide the means of a young person obtaining support should be registered as an explicitly-stated possibility
- To avoid replicating investigative situations the interviewees may have experienced in their dealings with immigration authorities, factual information be sought at a late stage, once trust had been established
- Young people be given the opportunity to determine their own interview conditions (e.g. venue, location, time, accompanied if required, the right to refuse permission for interviews to be taped)
- The right to withdraw information from inclusion in the findings

- The right to stop the interview at any point.

There are a number of implications of adopting these principles which I have discussed in detail elsewhere (Jones 1998). For example, young people may have questioned the wisdom of their involvement in a project that might be critical of institutions from which they were seeking support. Further, in allowing the young people to set the venue for interviews, I may have placed myself at risk on occasions (such as finding myself in a run-down area of London late at night). I justified these decisions on the grounds that they were empowering for the young people involved.

Grounded theory – feminist reframing of grounded theory method

The third strand informing the methodology was grounded theory. I was not concerned in any purist sense with protecting the 'culture' of the school of grounded theory (Stern 1994, p.217) either by remaining true to the principle of 'letting theory emerge' (Glaser 1992, in Morse 1994) or in the more positivist explication promoted by Strauss and Corbin (1991) which uses highly structured codification of data to exhaust all possible explanations and contingencies. These differences that have evolved in the approaches of Glaser and Strauss (1967), who articulated grounded theory as a 'systematic, phenomenologically based method for social research, an alternative to the dominant natural science paradigm of knowledge' (Reissman 1994, p.2), reflect developments of the method although they are also indicative of the 'looseness' and difficulties of verification that have been the source of criticism of the original description. Grounded theorists differ in orientation, in adaptations and in applications of the method, but the principle of theory emanating from data as opposed to the logical testing of hypotheses has led to the generation of important knowledge.

Feminist reframing of the method challenges the notion of 'discovery' and offers a socially constructed, interpretative view of reality (Gregg 1994). This approach is based on the view that theory is not simply waiting to be discovered, or uncovered as if by magic, but is created through social construction of meaning. In line with a grounded theory approach, the study was derived from a problem identified by young people themselves through preliminary work which was the first stage of the research. In a process of continuous refinement and reflection the themes that emerged from initial engagement with young people were reimmersed in further interviews and the developing theory made explicit and tested back with them. The young people were thus 'main actors' not only in the sense that they were fully involved in immigration proceedings in their own right and spoke from the authority of their own experience, but they were also 'main actors' in directing the research and in ensuring that the interpretations given to the data were relevant to them as informants and to others.

The method rests on a consciousness of interaction and a reflective and critical awareness of the dynamics of engagement with the informant in which the investigation, rather than testing preformed ideas, checks out hypotheses generated by the study. The purpose of the interviews with young people was to enable the articulation and description of their experiences, to get them to describe, assess, illuminate and develop their own perceptions. This required my involvement *within* the process, being attuned to the information shared and providing feedback and revision on interpretations. Preliminary data analysis was carried out at the end of each first contact. As transcriptions of interviews were examined for possible themes and concepts, ideas that emerged were developed through subsequent interviews and the data refined and revised in the light of informant validation or modification.

Prolonged engagement with informants is a major cornerstone of grounded theory both in order to test out interpretations and also to achieve saturation (satisfaction that nothing new is emerging from the data). This was an important means by which informants were able to contribute to the direction and development of the study. The themes were scrutinised for their significance to welfare work, and semi-structured interviews with practitioners provided the data through which I was able to identify implications for practice of the ideas that were developing. A theoretical examination of material was used to investigate the relationship between immigration and child care legislation.

Although immersed within the interview process, I was at the same time outside of it, observing reflexively my role as researcher, the dynamics of the situation and my own interpretations of the emerging data. Fundamental to obtaining rich material was the quality of my relationship as researcher to those whose experiences I sought to understand. Data collection was a process rather than an event and drew from a range of human activity.

Re-presentations of children and young people

Several writers have problematised the notion of children's representation and I have borrowed the term 're-presentation' (Alldred 1998; Hall 1992; James and Prout 1997) to highlight here that it is *my* reading of the data that is presented rather than representation (as portrayal) of children and young people's views. Within the study, I draw attention to the ways in which identity constructions of young people subject to immigration controls were *part* of those controls and I analyse young people's narratives to demonstrate a reclamation of self-representation as an oppositional and political act. The theoretical positions I am concerned with here, however, are those that underpin the conceptual tools used in making sense of children and young people's experiences and the ways in which claims for speaking on behalf of children might be authorised. For instance, how do theories of social constructionism inform representations of childhood and youth? If the process of interpretation is one of a socially constructed reality, is it possible to identify principles which justify one particular 'reading' of data rather than any other?

The concept of social constructionism is based on a rejection of naturalistic, totalizing theories of social relations and places emphasis on the importance of language and discourses not just in describing social reality but in constructing it.

Subjectivities are constituted through discursive representations whose meanings are not fixed or inherent but are dynamic, contested, contextualised and conflictual (Madden and Humphries 1998). An important aspect of the theoretical framework within which the study was set was attention to the discursive fields in which the material realities, identities and concerns of the young people whose experiences were central to the problem were constituted.

Hegemonic discourses on childhood and youth are important sites through which the identities of young people are contested and reveal underlying ideological tensions. Within Western societies the acquisition of rights, responsibilities and freedoms for children and young people are linked to defining biological stages such as 'puberty' which position childhood and adolescence as natural states underlined by physiological differences between them and adults (Griffin 1993). Here children are presented as 'innocent', 'vulnerable' and in need of protection and special treatment (unless, that is, they display a lack of innocence). This idea is incompatible with notions of children as sexual, political or self-determining subjects, and partly explains unease with other conceptualisations of rights, such as those which privilege the views of children with authority and status unmediated by others. Adolescents have been largely constructed as problematic, not authoritative. Authority, such as exists, seems to be confined to the 'authority' of being cast as consumers – young people's experience collapsed into the category 'youth culture', commodified and sold back to them. Beyond this, constructs of 'youth' largely constitute young people as a uniform social category and promote a homogenised view of young people which 'flattens out' difference and diversity. Youth research rarely privileges young people since 'exaggerated' attention on particular groups of young people often stems from policy concerns about controlling their behaviour. Even where the focus is on social problems, discourses of youth are permeated with ideas of biological determinism so that young people are seen as challenging authority, testing out, experimenting and so on, as a precursor to adulthood – a 'natural' process of transition – the emphasis on 'being' merely a means of determining 'becoming'. Pervasive ideas on the immutability of the child or adolescent state, theories which seek to underscore the dependency of children and underscrutinised claims to representation, however, leave uncontested the systems of domination and adult authority that such ideas serve. My concern was that many studies which claim to provide a voice for the views and experiences of children and young people leave unquestioned the power differentials between researcher and researched. I suggest that what is required is a theoretical approach to the reading of children's experience.

Theorising children's experience

How does the sharing of the detail of aspects of one's life constitute knowledge? What authority does experience of oppression claim? How does one both address the specificities of marginalised groups (such as young people in immigration cases) and at the same time respond to counter-claims for equal recognition of experience which may threaten to level out privileging status for previously silenced voices? How is common sense different to experience that speaks as knowledge?

These important epistemological questions have been at the centre of recent feminist scholarship. Chandra Talpade Mohanty (1992) and Gail Lewis (1996) have argued that it is only by theorizing experience that these questions can be addressed. Lewis (1996) points to the endurance of the category of experience as evidence of its importance both in terms of political action and in questioning dominant epistemologies:

> in creating a legitimacy to speak from experience, feminists (black and white) had made it possible to begin to undo established ideas about what it means to 'know'. This, together with the adoption of some post-structuralist insights such as the category of 'the subject', cast new light on and raised new problems about the ways in which social categories and the social/psychic selves which inhabit them are constituted. Those who had erstwhile understood themselves as 'individuals' could now cast new meaning on their lives and think of themselves as historically constituted 'subjects'. (p.25)

In her text *Situated Voices* (1996) Lewis is concerned primarily with gendered, class-based and racialised notions of self, and interrogates the category 'experience' through an examination of the ways in which it surfaces and is utilised by black women. She draws on theoretical perspectives articulated by Joan Scott who comes from 'a profound sense of opposition to the status of 'experience'…constituted as 'uncontestable evidence and as an originary point of explanation – as a foundation upon which analysis is based' (Lewis 1996, p.25) and who promotes an alternative view in which experience speaks with authority only in so far as it is contextualised in terms of historical relations (Scott 1992). Mohanty's (1992) work, on the other hand, questions epistemological formulations which position experience as a unitary notion. She unpacks universalising claims about experience and raises questions about the implications of underscrutinised anti-essentialist positions. She develops Scott's ideas by contextualising experience within 'a politics of location' in which representations of identities, difference and oppression are subject to intense interrogation and attention is focused on the socially constructed meanings (racialised, gendered, class-based, etc.) ascribed to subjectivities at 'historical moments' rather than on social categories themselves. For Mohanty, being female does not of itself privilege women with incontestable claims to knowledge based on the experience of sexist oppression. While she acknowledges that all women are affected by experiences of oppression, not all women experience oppression in the same way. It is not sameness or the shared aspects of experience which give it its epistemological value, but its social, political and historical location and the interrelationship between different axes of power.

I suggest that the work of feminists such as Scott, Mohanty and Lewis provides an important theoretical framework through which claims for the re-presentation of children's voices can be authorised. The voices of young people emerged as authoritative precisely because the 'situational reading' of experience *validated* the specificities of their daily lives, *grounded* localised descriptions within the configurations of historical, social and political relations and *centred* the young people as subjects, or active agents in which they 'claim the space from which to speak' (Lewis's terminology).

Children and young people's experience does not have ontological status simply because they have been excluded from the processes through which knowledge is validated. While feminists have challenged dominant ideas about what it means 'to know' and in the process have opened up the potential of liberatory epistemologies, there is a gap in relation to theory on the status of children's experience. The application of theory produced by feminists such as Lewis and Mohanty lead us to an acknowledgement of two important positions which may take us forward: the experience of being oppressed and disempowered by virtue of being a child legitimates the 'claim to space from which children speak' but is not necessarily a 'claim to know'; and what is required is for individual subjectivities produced out of children and young people's experiences and conceptualisations of 'child' discursively constructed to be analysed in relation to race, gender, disability, sexuality, class, and so on, and located within a wider social and political context. In centring children and young people's experiences and perceptions of immigration proceedings, the aim was to shift the pivotal position assumed by adults, professionals and the like. The term 'shift' operates here as a linguistic device which suggests movement, but might be better visualised as an 'opening up' of discursive monopolies, shaking adult certainties and creating possibilities – even the smallest of possibilities, for the briefest of moments, for seeing things differently. This requires making visible the position of the adult in discourses of children and young people. Adults own the processes of representation; we allege that we speak for children but our speech is normative and limits children's agency. In our discourses we name as distinct the category 'child' but we are not named, *our* position is assumed, authoritative, central. We represent all people but children only represent children, and are often denied even this. While adults, too, are affected by the structures of inequality and processes of oppression which determine who speaks for whom and in whose interests, it is nevertheless adults who speak for children and young people – not the other way round. Children and young people do not claim to speak for the whole of humanity. This simple observation is very important. In studies and activities which seek to obtain the views of children and young people, we (adults) are usually concerned to know what children think and what they do – the child is the observed, the 'gazed upon'. While my approach also makes focal the experiences of children and young people, the intention was to dislodge or at least influence dominant discourses, to chisel through the authority from which adults/professionals speak and to create the space in which the meaning children and young people ascribe to their experiences challenge hegemonic approaches to, for example, the notion of children's rights. To 'gaze upon' the child, but also to scrutinise the assertions and assumptions of those who claim to speak for the child.

The questions arise, how do children construct themselves as subjects in identity formations and locations that are defined for them, how *do* they invent themselves and how do they counter hegemonic discourses in which they are objectified? The current hegemony of children's rights, for instance, seems to deny children agency, both in that the construct 'child' is largely constituted outside of the child subject and also in collapsing children's potential for utilising personal power through notions such as 'best interests' where meaning is determined by authoritative others – adults. However, in applying the theoretical approach I have described, it is possible for oppositional agency and 'transformative' critique to emerge from the spaces created not only by young people's voices but also their silences, and to provide the opportunity for a more liberatory approach to rights.

Conclusion

In this chapter I examined issues presented by the approach adopted which used grounded theory (Glaser and Strauss 1967) and which provides an exploration of feminist re-framing of grounded theory concerned with the social interpretation of meaning. The method seeks to demonstrate compatibility with principles of participative and empowering research methodologies developed by feminists which advocate commitment to change as a legitimate aim of research activity (Humphries 1994; Mama 1989; Mohanty 1991). I located personal and political positions underpinning the project, described the research paradigm and discussed contradictions that arose in the development of an appropriate methodology. Finally, I provided a reflexive account of the process and discussed the theoretical positions that underpinned my claims to re-presenting children and young people's voices. The methodology extends feminist research by applying perspectives highlighted through feminist discourse to an area of study which is not solely concerned with women.

Note

1   *The Stephen Lawrence Inquiry: Report of an Inquiry by Sir William Macpherson of Cluny* presented to Parliament, February 1999 stated in its conclusion: 'The conclusions to be drawn from all the evidence in connection with the investigation of Stephen Lawrence's racist murder are clear. There is no doubt that there were fundamental errors. The investigation was marred by a combination of professional incompetence, instituional racism and a failure of leadership by senior officers.' (Chapter 46.1)

References

Alldred, P. (1998) 'Ethnography and discourse analysis: Dilemmas in representing the voices of children.' In J. Ribbens and R. Edwards (eds) *Feminist Dilemmas in Qualitative Research*. London: Sage.

Bhabha, J. (ed) (1985) *Worlds Apart: Women under Immigration and Nationality Law*. London and Sydney: Pluto Press.

Bhavnani, K.-K. (1991) *Talking Politics: a Psychological Framing for Views from Youth in Britain.* Cambridge: Cambridge University Press.

Bryan, B., Dadzie, S. and Scafe, S. (eds) (1985) *The Heart of the Race.* London: Virago.

Butt, J. and Jones, A.D. (1995) *Taking the Initiative: A Study of Child Protection Services to Black Children and Families.* London: NISW, REU and NSPCC.

Cabinet committee on Possible Legislation to Control Immigration from the Commonwealth, (1956) PRO CAB 129/81 CP125.

Carter, B., Harris, C. and Joshi, S. (1987) *The 1951–55 Conservative Government and the Racialisation of Black Immigration.* Warwick: Warwick University.

Fonow, M.M. and Cook, J.A. (1991) *Beyond Methodology: Feminist Scholarship as Lived Research.* Indianapolis: Indiana University Press.

Freire, P. (1972) *Pedagogy of the Oppressed.* London: Penguin.

Glaser, B. and Strauss, A. (1967) *The Discovery of Grounded Theory.* Chicago: Aldine.

Glaser, B.G. (1992) *Basics of Grounded Theory Analysis.* Mill Valley, CA: Sociology Press.

Gregg, R. (1994) 'Explorations of pregnancy and choice in a high-tech age.' In C.K. Reissman (ed) *Qualitative Studies in Social Work Research.* London: Sage.

Hall, S. (1992) 'New ethnicities.' In J. Donald and A. Rattansi (eds) *'Race', Culture and Difference.* London: Sage, in association with the Open University.

Heron, J. (1996) *Co-operative Inquiry: Research into the Human Condition.* London: Sage.

Humphries, B. (1994) 'Empowerment and social research: Elements for an analytic framework.' In B. Humphries and C. Truman (eds) *Rethinking Social Research.* Aldershot: Avebury and Ashgate.

Hutchinson, S. and Wilson, H. (1994) 'Research and therapeutic interviews: A poststructuralist perspective.' In J.M. Morse (ed) *Critical Issues in Qualitative Research Methods.* Thousand Oaks, CA: Sage.

James, A. and Prout, A. (eds) (1997) *Constructing and Reconstructing Childhood: Contemporary Issues in the Sociological Study of Childhood.* 2nd edn. London: Falmer Press.

Jones, A.D. (1998) *The Child Welfare Implications of UK Immigration and Asylum Policy.* Manchester: Manchester Metropolitan University, Applied Community Studies.

Macpherson, W. (1999) *The Stephen Lawrence Inquiry: Report of an Inquiry by Sir William Macpherson of Cluny.* London: The Stationery Office.

Madden, M. and Humphries, B. (1998) *The Construction of Social Research Knowledge.* Vol. 2. Manchester: Manchester Metropolitan University.

Malik, K. (1996) 'Universalism and difference: Race and the postmodernists.' *Race and Class* 37, 3, 1–17.

Mama, A. (1989) *The Hidden Struggle.* London: Race and Housing Research Unit.

Mama, A. (1995) *Beyond the Masks: Race, Gender and Subjectivity.* London: Routledge.

Mies, M. (1979) *Towards a methodology of women's studies.* Working Paper 77, The Hague, Netherlands Institute of Social Studies

Mohanty, C. (1991) 'Cartographies of struggle: Third World women and the politics of feminism.' In C.T. Mohanty, A. Russo and L. Torres (eds) *Third World Women and the Politics of Feminism.* Indianapolis: Indiana University Press.

Morse, J.M. (ed) (1994) *Critical Issues in Qualitative Research Methods.* Thousand Oaks, CA: Sage.

Oakley, A. (1981) 'Interviewing women: A contradiction in terms?' In H. Roberts (ed) *Doing Feminist Research.* London: Routledge & Kegan Paul, 30–61.

Race Relations (Amendments) Bill (2000) HCB 60, London: The Stationery Office. http://www.homeoffice.gov.uk/leg.htm

Rattansi, A. (1994) '"Western" Rasims, Ethnicities and Identities' in Rattan, A. amd Westwood, S. (eds) *Racism, Modernity and Identity: on the western front.* Cambridge: Polity Press.

Reissman, C.K. (1994) *Qualitative Studies in Social Work Research., London: Sage.*

Sivanandan, A. (1982) *A Different Hunger: Writings on Black Resistance.* London: Pluto Press.

Small, S. (1996) *Racialised Barriers: The Black Experience in the United States and England in the 1980s.* London: Routledge.

Stern, P.N. (1994) 'Eroding Grounded Theory.' In J.M. Morse (ed), *Critical Issues in Qualitative Research Methods* CA: Sage.

Strauss, A. and Corbin, J. (1991) *Basics of Qualitative Research.* Thousand Oaks, CA: Sage.

Weedon, C. (1987) *Feminist Practice and Poststructuralist Theory.* Oxford: Basil Blackwell.

Women, Immigration and Nationality Group in Bhabha, J. (ed) (1985) *Worlds Apart: Women under Immigration and Nationality Law.* London and Sydney: Pluto Press.

CHAPTER 4

Studying 'Others'

Research and Representation

Mary Searle-Chatterjee

Introduction

There is a vast literature debating the functions and characteristics of writing by researchers from the 'West' on the 'Rest'. It has been argued that in practice much research has served not so much to shed light on any reality or to achieve emancipatory purposes but to construct images of an imagined 'Other'. People from colonised regions have been presented as fundamentally different or, worse still, as inferior and less evolved. Such images have provided support for the view that non-white people are less fit for self-government or, today, for political and economic equality or dominance. They are said to constitute a set of literary practices whose effect is to produce 'selfhood' as well as 'otherness'. A key example is 'orientalising', that is to say, the process by which a vast array of diverse individuals, societies and traditions, particularly among Muslims, but also among South Asians, are lumped together as if they have had a single, unchanging 'essence' throughout history (Said 1978, pp.1–48; Sayyid 1997). The argument then does not relate simply to bias, blindness or arrogance on the part of the researcher's attitudes (Shohat and Stam 1994), but to 'otherising' structures of thinking implicit in academic and literary traditions. It should be noted, however, that some scholars who are, in general terms, sympathetic to Said's approach have pointed to contradictory complexities in some of the historical texts (Dirks 1996; Gunew 1990, pp.99–120). Similar points have been made about white researchers studying racial minorities within the metropolis. Indeed, the same critiques can be made of much research on less powerful groups in general, whether defined in terms of religion, class, age, gender or sexuality.

A second area of debate relates to the issue of how far a researcher is affected and restricted by her/his own standpoint: is it possible to do justice to groups of people who are very differently situated from one's self in terms of experience, suffering or culture? 'Strong' forms of this argument have led in practice to the relativist position that knowledge of others is not possible.

Contrary to these critiques is the view often expressed by anthropologists and comparative sociologists that it is better for a researcher to be an 'outsider'. Anthropologists who study 'at home' still have a struggle to prove themselves. The argument has been that fieldwork abroad aids the 'distanciation process that is necessary if we are to see ourselves as others see us' (Jackson 1987, p.14), indeed, that a person who has rarely encountered social and cultural difference at close quarters is unlikely to be able to see social processes for what they are. That this is not on the face of it an absurd position can be seen by the major contributions which have been made to sociology and anthropology by people who are not complete insiders, that is to say, by Jewish academics and people of 'mixed' background, 'cultural hybrids' to use the now fashionable term (see Bauman 1991; Kuklick 1991).

In practice, most of the debate has revolved around 'Western' researchers. Anthropologists from other societies have tended to study people in their own country and I know of no evidence that their supervisors have tried to persuade them to do otherwise, to study dominant groups in the 'West'. That is to everyone's loss, in my view. The fact that it has not been seen as a Western priority to fund researchers from ex-colonised countries to do research on metropolitan populations speaks for itself. However, it is worth considering M. Strathern's view (1987, pp.30–31), that it may be a form of eurocentrism to think that a non-European studying 'at home' is doing the same thing as a Westerner studying 'at home'. The issue is not just one of authorial perspective but of the relation between the cultural and social practice implicit in the discipline and the cultural and social practice of the people being studied. The focus here, then, is on constitutive aspects of culture more fundamental than racist and colonial attitudes. From this point of view the 'non-Western' anthropologist who studies the 'West' would not simply produce a reversal of perspectives because she is herself by definition moulded by Western assumptions. This, of course, raises the issue of where is home and who is an insider. One can only be labelled as such in relation to a particular moment and context. Nita Kumar (1992) in her study of artisans of Benares claims that their life was as alien to her upper-class home life in Lucknow as it would have been to any 'foreign' researcher. We all have multi-hyphenated identities (Shohat and Stam 1994). It is these which can provide both a reasoned and felt grounding for the humanist position that communication among groups, however flawed, is not only a possibility but perhaps even an inevitability.

The issue of 'insider' and 'outsider' social scientists studying Indian society has been lengthily debated by Indian academics in the journal *Contributions to Indian Sociology* published in Delhi, as has the issue raised by Strathern. Most of the contributors have come down strongly in support of the view that we can all participate in a universal project to find general knowledge. Indeed, it is the Indian contributors to the journal who have insisted on this most strongly and who have rejected the 'otherising' endeavours of persons such as M. Marriott who claim to recognise 'difference' and avoid eurocentrism by charting an 'Indian sociology' based on distinctively 'Indian' foundations. The Enlightenment, with its universalist project, is, they argue, no longer a Western possession but belongs to 'the world' (Marriott 1991; Singh in Marriott 1991; Sharma in Marriott 1991. For an alternative view, rejecting current sociological approaches to India in favour of literary expression, see Tharu and Lalita 1993). The debate in *Contributions to Indian Sociology* has focused not on the process of doing research but on the possibility of acquiring knowledge, as well as, to a lesser degree, on the construction of sociological texts about a society 'other' than one's 'own'. Here, for reasons of space, I shall focus only on the third aspect of this question, that of the writing of texts for particular audiences. I shall focus on the production of texts by mainly white 'Westerners'.

I wish to argue that despite the validity of the critiques of 'Western' writing about people in other societies, there is still a place for the 'Westerner', like anyone else, not only to produce texts critiquing existing texts, but also to produce texts of her own, if only as a contribution to 'oppositional culture' within the metropolis (Said 1993, p.316). I do not argue that this is the only justification for such writing but this is the one on which I will focus here. Other justifications include developing reflexive self-awareness, personal, cultural and social enrichment, and correcting the distortions in so-called 'general' theory produced in the West. Whether it is justifiable to 'use' people for such purposes is an issue for all social research, and depends, to a considerable degree, on the way in which the research is conducted. Here I shall focus only on the presentation of research, rather than on the process of doing it.

I recognise that most of my readers will not be as fortunate as myself in having had the opportunity to study and do research both in Britain and India. I spent four years studying at an Indian university of which two involved field research. However, I think that aspects of the issue I discuss are to some extent present in all research and particularly need to be borne in mind when studying racialised minorities who originated from previously colonised states. One of the tasks for overseas research conceived within an oppositional tradition is to address itself to the 'West', to undermine common 'orientalised' stereotypes, and homogenising tendencies, which may be as common among so-called 'radicals' as among traditionalists. The task is to uncover the social patterns underlying surface differences by showing how cultural practices, trends and movements are the product of historical processes and liable to change as do circumstances, and to try to show how agency and structure interweave. Within this framework there is a continuum of views as to how best to work. One approach favours being free with ones 'translation' of difference in an attempt to facilitate empathy and understanding. Those at the other end of the continuum argue for being more 'literal', in an attempt to avoid the ethnocentrism implicit in forcing the logic of other peoples' frameworks to fit one's own mould. It may be difficult to achieve that without falling into either incomprehensibility or relativism. I do not see it as the task of such research 'to give a voice to others': one may re-present or 'reinscribe' them, to use Spivak's distinction (1990, p.57). Indeed one can not do otherwise. The 'translation', if that is what it is, is authored, a result of selection, and should be recognised as such. It may have been useful as a critical programme to point to the unimportance of the role of the author when analysing bodies of texts to find common themes and presumptions (Foucault 1984). As a basis for one's own work this can only lead to a fudging of authorial responsibility. A presentation should be recognised for what it is, an argument which can be scrutinised and discussed.

Case study: narratives on temple demolitions

In the light of the preceding discussion, I shall now look at some of the problems and possibilities which I have encountered in my own writings on Muslims in India. I shall look at three pieces of writing on aspects of self-identification among Muslim men in the city of Benares (Varanasi), a major centre of Hindu tradition, and one on elite Muslim women in the city of Hyderabad, a major centre of Islamic culture. One of the subjects I wanted to explore was how Muslims relate to their Islamic identity, given that negative narratives and images are current both in popular Indian culture and in writings about India. In Benares, Muslims constitute about a quarter of the population; in Hyderabad 43 per cent. The writing is based on research done in 1985 and 1986. I conceived the writing of these papers partly as an attempt to intervene, in a small way, into arenas in which Islamophobia is a dominating cultural mindset. In Europe, Muslims have long served as an image of the 'other' constitutive of self-definition: the same has more recently become true for many Hindu Indians. One of the core themes in both European and Hindu traditions of Islamophobia is of the Muslim as iconoclast, intolerant and prone to violence. The image of the Muslim as past destroyer of temples has erupted with fury into the public arena in India since 1985. Temple destruction narratives have become a legitimating charter for Hindu nationalists' destruction of a mosque at a contested historical site and for subsequent attempts to change the nature of the Indian polity. This has occurred in the context of the breakup of the electoral dominance of the Congress party and the emergence of increasingly fragmented electoral coalitions, in which high-status groups in particular make use of any identities available, including religious ones, to further their electoral ambitions. 'Otherising' narratives about Muslims were promulgated vigorously by the British when in India. Historians differ on the issue of the relative influence of Britons and Indians in the early development of such themes (Bayly 1988; Pandey 1990). One of the implications of such narratives is that those erstwhile rulers of India who were Muslims were ruling by virtue of their religious identity. Their class or ethnic identity as Moghuls, Pathans, Turks, Afghans, etc. is not foregrounded. The cause or motive for their actions is similarly taken as self-evidently religion. The British, then, were to be perceived as a welcome refuge, and as protectors of Hindus from Muslim onslaught. A widespread motif in British texts is of the British male as defender of Hindu females both from violent Muslims and from wife-burning Hindus. For a recent example of this see the widespread popularity of *Far Pavilions* (discussed by Sunder Rajan 1993). The motif of the Muslim as violent iconoclast is found in many, if not most, history and travel books written about India, regardless of the nationality of the author. Not being a historian

I was not able to enter the historical debate: what I did was to collect current oral narratives, by interviewing Muslims (as well as some Hindus), of a variety of social backgrounds, about what they believed had been the cause of the destruction of the central ruin in the city of Benares. I also collected current narratives relating to a Muslim saint and martyr at whose local shrine many people, both Hindu and Muslim, worship. I found parallels in the two types of narrative which in most cases were an inversion of the 'Muslim as destroyer of temples' motif dominant in the larger Indian society. In brief, most of these narratives conceded that some Hindu temples had been destroyed. However, they explained this destruction in a reverse way as being due to the efforts of a Muslim hero to protect Hindu women (and their sons) from the violence of Hindu kings or priests. Regardless, then, of what was the historical 'reality', i.e. who destroyed what for what purpose in what context, this suggested that present-day Muslims in this city not only did not glorify iconoclasm but preferred to believe that such a thing was never done by members of a group with which they identify.

In presenting this material (Searle-Chatterjee 1990), I felt it necessary to include some brief reference to the fact that historians differ in their accounts of the periods to which these narratives claim to relate, and I made a point of including reference to the work of Indian historians who do not underwrite the Muslim as iconoclast theme. I also included some comparative material about border raids in medieval England in which Christian Scots destroyed the churches of Christian English, in order to show that attributed religious identity is not necessarily the most salient marker in such a context. I presented my informants' narratives alongside published narratives originating from various 'Hindu' and nineteenth-century British (Christian?) sources to show structural reversals and parallels. I also included reference to a contemporary Afghani version. My writing was an attempt to undermine demonising images of Muslims and to show how perceptions of history are shaped by group of identification. I also made some attempt to consider class dimensions, not only religious and 'ethnic' ones. I showed for example that the 'lowest' Hindu groups had no interest in or knowledge of such narratives.

My presentation, however, was not without problems. Although I always included qualifiers such as 'generally', 'often', etc., my tabular presentation, linking particular types of narrative to particular ethnic/religious groups, could have been read as implying that 'Hindus' think one way, 'Muslims' another, nineteenth-century Britons in another and contemporary Afghans in yet another. Individual variation and the processes by which people debate narratives did not appear in my papers. This could therefore perhaps be seen as encouraging an 'essentialising' approach despite the oppositional aims of the work. To capture debate in process over time does of course involve extended and highly intensive research with a very high level of linguistic skills. Indeed, it is historical, rather than purely sociological, work which seems most likely to accomplish such a goal. Another key problem, as always, relates to the issue of who will be the reader, or what will be the variety of types of reader for the paper. Is it possible to speak to them all? Some readers might have considered reference to Scottish border raids intrusive. Indeed, for a reader not in any way infected by a tendency to stereotype Muslims, my whole argument might have seemed laboured and unnecessary, even patronising. In writing about dominant groups it is not usually necessary to include much contextual material, as any particular piece of writing is only one among many kinds of information available to the reader. In the case of studies of minority, or less powerful, groups it is necessary to build in material to counter the distorted way in which many readers will encounter the material (however 'accurate' it may be) because of the spectacles through which they already view the world. One cannot place a certificate on one's work restricting its readership to those who share certain assumptions. A study of black single parents in Britain, for example, might be accurate in a narrow sense, but deeply misleading, given the likely nature of the readership, if it does not include a breakdown by socio-economic class, some consideration of the larger socio-economic context for people of Caribbean origin, both in Britain today as well, perhaps, as in the Caribbean in the past, and comparative data from different 'racial' groups or societies in similar structural situations. An account of polygamy in Nigeria, or among American Mormons, might be 'accurate' and written respectfully by an anthropologist who herself even decides to enter such a social arrangement, yet still be received by the reader or listener as a confirmation of prejudices already held, unless, and perhaps even then, a huge amount of contextual material is included.

Who then, was my paper written for and who might have welcomed it? Clearly many Muslim readers would welcome it. Hindu nationalists, on the other hand, could not be expected to. They could argue that a focus on current images, rather than on past 'facts', or laying out all narratives as if they are in some sense equivalent, is seriously distorting. Non-nationalist Hindus might, of course, find the material interesting as might Britons of various types. Note that I have not specified academics. This is because I always hope that my writing will be read beyond the confines of the academic world. This adds to the problem of multiple audiences.

A second paper presenting this material, and including more information relating to local dimensions of the historical debate, appeared in an American book on the city authored by Religious Studies specialists on Hinduism (Searle-Chatterjee 1993). All of the other chapters focused on Hindus, often on high-caste Brahminical perspectives. I felt, therefore, that the inclusion of my paper in this context produced a useful counterweight, particularly as such a volume is likely to be read by people who have been very exposed to 'the Muslim as iconoclast' theme, including visitors to the city.

Case study: social mobility or religious 'fundamentalism'?

A third paper on Benares (Searle-Chatterjee 1994) was written in awareness of the related image of the Muslim as narrow-minded and religiously obsessed 'fundamentalist'. This image has, of course, a long history in Europe and has surfaced very prominently in Britain in the last decade. In this paper I described the historical process by which a group of merchant weavers became members of a sect popularly known as Wahabis by other Muslims though strictly speaking they are Ahli Hadiths. They are becoming more zealous in their observance and are placing more emphasis on scriptural 'purity'. As such, they are often regarded as 'fundamentalist'. I begin by pointing out that the concept of fundamentalism tends to be used without careful definition whenever Islamic religiosity appears in the public domain. The Ahli Hadiths in Benares are certainly reformist. They express a concern to return to the 'fundamentals' of the 'true' religion, to purify it of what they see as harmful or non-essential accretions in the form of 'superstition'. They also seek to banish 'scholastic legalism', another characteristic often taken to indicate a 'fundamentalist' approach (Hiro 1988). They reject the authority of the four law schools. However, they are not 'fundamentalist' in so far as they do not reject the Hadith (the Traditions). Nor do they reject the doctrine of ijtihad, reinterpretation of the Quran and Hadith in the light of the spirit of Islam. Personal experience may count for more than the medieval jurists. In that sense, they are like 'modernists'. Nor do they have a political project, another characteristic often associated with 'fundamentalists'. My main argument, however, was that rather than regarding this group as yet another example of a worldwide process of Islamicisation, it was more appropriate to view the sectarianism as an expression of upward mobility by a group of newly rich merchants of the 'lowly' community of Weavers. Adopting a form of Islam stressing the simple egalitarianism of faith, rather than the intellectual subtleties of the 'experts', serves to stake out a claim to moral superiority and equality with former elite groups. The Ahli Hadiths were stressing religious values where these can be seen to imply that inherited birth rank is less important than virtue. They were not attempting to emulate the old Shia elite which is more versed in feudal and courtly styles, nor the Westernised elite, for they do not have pre-existing skills or dispositions of that kind (though they have remarkable artistic and trading skills). By increasing their religious observance, they set in train a competitive process among other Sunni Muslims in the city. Although I presented these developments in the terms of a 'detached' sociologist, I tried not to diminish my informants by presenting their activities as manipulative attempts to secure status. I spoke of them 'expressing their new sense of worth' (Searle-Chatterjee 1994, p.87). One can think of similarities in the history of non-conformist sectarianism in Britain, or, indeed, today, with competition for moral superiority among white anti-racists.

This paper was, in my view, 'successful' in so far as it contributed to the work of those who attempt to undermine the obsession with religious motivation in accounts of Muslims. It also attempted to undermine the category of 'fundamentalism'. However, it too was not without problems from the point of view of an oppositional project. First, it is clear that the Ahli Hadiths would not themselves describe their religious activities in terms of social mobility but in terms of seeing the truth. There was clearly a disparity between my perspective and theirs. It was also not impossible that my work could have been used to assist local politicians and others in surveillance of local groups though I am pretty sure that the shrewder operators would not have needed any help from me, nor would they have been likely to see my paper which was published by a journal in Oxford in which Muslim academics, particularly political scientists, have a major editorial presence. Might my work, however, at some future time be useful to CIA operators seeking information about potentially destabilising divisions? In what contexts is it helpful to point to variation and divisions among minority groups? It is often important to undermine generalised and essentialised images and to show how identities are fluid and emerge in changing circumstances, but at other times this may be perceived to contradict the interests of members of that minority group, or of sections within it, who may consider a claim to unity (Searle-Chatterjee 1987), what Spivak (1990) calls a 'strategic essentialism' (p.51), to be in their political interest. The issue has to be decided partly in terms of the nature of the publication and the presumed readership. One cannot, however, predict with full certainty who will be the reader. In the case of the paper in question I felt that this was probably not a problem. All of us as readers, of course, have fragmented and fluctuating thinking processes. At some level, all 'Westerners', as well as all people in Benares, know that every Muslim is a unique individual. At another level of consciousness, or in different contexts, people speak and act as though Muslims are all the same. The productions of cultural workers such as writers and researchers may have little effect as they will be used selectively.

Case study: gender, religion and national identity

The final piece of writing which I wish to discuss relates to elite Muslim women in Hyderabad (Searle-Chatterjee, in press). It is based on extended interviews with five women, supplemented by material from a couple of others. This research was particularly satisfying to me as not only did I find it very enjoyable but so too, I believe, did the women concerned as evidenced in their wish to meet me again and to maintain contact. In these interviews we discussed issues of religion and nationhood, the meaning for them of being a Muslim woman in the context of being a citizen of the Indian Union, given that images of women often become emblematic of group identity, both for 'insiders' and 'outsiders'. In an international context this has become particularly true for Muslims, both in relation to Europeans and 'Christians' (Ahmed 1992; Kabbani 1986; Kandiyoti 1991), as well as in relation to Hindus (Sarkar and Butalia 1995). At the time I felt that the material was of limited value because my informants were few in number and only of a particular and limited class range. I now feel that this was one of the merits of the work. Most of the sociological literature about Muslim women in India simply generalises about them as if they form a single category. My informants were all of elite groups despite the variation in their income levels and endogamous groups. They shared very many socio-economic characteristics. They had all been born before, or around, the time of Independence and Partition. They were all married, well educated in English and also in one or more other languages, usually including Urdu, and had major activities beyond the domestic sphere. They were all highly articulate and could, and did, express their views in public. Three of them at least were writers in several languages. What I did not know in advance was that they were all also religiously observant. The high degree of convergence in their social characteristics meant that the divergence in their views could be taken to indicate something about the range of individual variation possible from within a shared social matrix. The individual had at last not disappeared from my analysis. I showed that though each woman had her own individual approach to every issue we discussed, they all participated in the same ongoing conversation with themselves and others about what it means to be a Muslim, and a woman, in India today. Indeed, it could be said that an essential part of the experience of being a Muslim woman in India is taking part in debates about what that situation is and could be. The meaning of a Muslim identity is not something given and uncontested.

What were the problems in the presentation of this research? Clearly my presentation, like any other, involved a selection and arrangement in terms of what I considered to be important. I mostly used the womens' own words. However, I grouped these according to a series of themes, and sometimes summarised in order to avoid excessive repetition. Direct speech was often converted into indirect forms. I highlighted similarities and differences. Occasionally I introduced a comment in order to suggest a larger context in which a woman's words could be placed. I do not think that this fragmenting and recombining of voices meant that the individuality of each woman was lost. Did it mean that I was distorting their voices? Again, I hope not. I was certainly not 'speaking for' them. They did not need me to do that. They were all confident and already do speak in the public domain. One potential problem was that the very fact that their individuality was not lost meant that problems of confidentiality could arise, particularly as these women are prominent and could fairly easily be identified despite the changing of their names. I scrutinised my material carefully, trying to weigh up whether any comment or quotation might possibly cause offence. On reflection, as I write this, I realise that I ought to have sent a copy of my proposed paper to each of the women for comments. However, 12 years have elapsed between the interviews and the writing of the paper.

The writing up of research is a process fraught with difficulty and dilemma. Inevitably it will be affected to some degree by the social location of the writer. It may be shaped by the guiding light of an experientially, doctrinally or politically grounded standpoint related to the particular topic of research, or by the assumptions implicit in the conventions of the discipline or genre within which the writer works. That is not, however, to argue that only people with particular identities may study particular subjects, but rather that what we have to attempt to do is to make transparent the assumptions which shape our work. Nor is it to argue that we should never move beyond the narcissistic world of self-analysis. It is the movement of stepping out beyond that, to face the risk of being challenged by 'facts', perspectives, remote from one's own experience that can make research such a life-enhancing activity.

References

Ahmed, L. (1992) *Women and Gender in Islam*. New Haven, CT: Yale University Press.

Bauman, Z. (1991) *Modernity and Ambivalence*. Cambridge: Polity Press.

Bayly, C.A. (1988) *Indian Society and the Making of the British Empire*. New Cambridge History of India. Cambridge: Cambridge University Press.

Dirks, B. (1996) 'Recasting Tamil society: The politics of caste and race.' In C. Fuller (ed) *Caste Today*. Delhi: Oxford University Press.

Foucault, M. (1984) 'What is an author?' in P. Rabinow (ed) *The Foucault Reader*. Harmondsworth: Penguin.

Gunew, S. (1990) 'Denaturalising cultural nationalisms.' In H. Bhabha (ed) *Nation and Narration*. London: Routledge.

Hiro, D. (1988) *Islamic Fundamentalism*. London: Paladin.

Jackson, A. (1987) *Anthropology at Home*. London: Tavistock.

Kabbani, R. (1986) *Europe's Myths of Orient*. London: Pandora.

Kandiyoti, D. (1991) *Women, Islam and the State*. Basingstoke: Macmillan.

Kuklick, H. (1991) *The Savage Within: The Social History of British Anthropology*. Cambridge: Cambridge University Press.

Kumar, N. (1992) *Friends, Brothers and Informants: Fieldwork Memoirs of Benares*. Berkeley, CA: University of California Press.

Marriott, M. (1991) 'On constructing an Indian ethnosociology.' In *Contributions to Indian Sociology*, 25, 2, 295–308.

Pandey, G. (1990) *The Construction of Communalism in Colonial India*. Delhi: Oxford University Press.

Said, E. (1978) *Orientalism*. Harmondsworth: Penguin.

Said, E. (1993) *Culture and Imperialism*. London: Chatto & Windus.

Sarkar, T. and Butalia, U. (1995) *Women and Right-wing Movements*. London: Zed Press.

Sayyid, B. (1997) *A Fundamental Fear: Eurocentrism and the Emergence of Islamism*. London: Zed Press.

Searle-Chatterjee, M. (1987) 'The anthropologist exposed.' *Anthropology Today*, August, 3,3, 16–18.

Searle-Chatterjee, M. (1990) 'The Muslim hero as defender of Hindus: Mythic reversals and ethnicity among Benares Muslims.' In P. Werbner (ed) *Person, Myth and Society in South Asian Islam*, Special Issue of *Social Analysis 28*, Adelaide: University of Adelaide.

Searle-Chatterjee, M. (1993) 'Religious division and the mythology of the past.' In B. Hertel and C. Humes (eds) *Living Banares*. New York: State University of New York Press.

Searle-Chatterjee, M. (1994) "Wahabi" sectarianism among Muslims of Benares.' *Contemporary South Asia 3*, 2, 83–93.

Searle-Chatterjee, M. (in press) 'Women, Islam and nationhood in Hyderabad.' In M. Unnithan and V. Damodaran (eds) *Identities, Nation-State and Global Culture* Delhi, India: Manohar.

Shohat, E. and Stam, R. (1994) *Unthinking Eurocentrism*. London: Routledge.

Spivak, G.C. (1990) *The Post-Colonial Critic.* Edited by S. Harasym. New York: Routledge.

Strathern, M. (1987) 'The limits of auto-anthropology.' In A. Jackson (ed) *Anthropology at Home.* London: Tavistock.

Sunder Rajan, R. (1993) *Real and Imagined Women: Gender, Culture and Post-colonialism.* London: Routledge.

Tharu, S. and Lalita, K. (1993) *Women Writing in India.* Delhi: Oxford University Press.

CHAPTER 5

Case Studying Organisations: The Use of Quantitative Approaches

Tom Cockburn

Introduction

Many of the case studies in this book emphasise the methodological benefits of looking qualitatively at individuals, groups or organisations, in order to develop a more detailed understanding of particular cases. The collection, collation and analysis of statistics and quantitative information in looking at cases provides necessary and important information on the background or context of cases. In relation to case studies of community organisations the contexts include information and profiles of the communities in which the organisation is located. For instance, in case studying a community centre, it is important to not only look at the 'internal' aspects of the organisation (the work roles of staff, means of communication, hierarchy models, etc.), but also at the social context of the community, such as the age, income levels, and numbers and type of ethnic communities in the vicinity. Clearly, the context is reliant on quantitative information such as census returns or local government figures. Indeed, some organisations gather their own information on their communities (private companies may spend huge amounts of money on 'market research'). Yet organisations may hold substantial amounts of quantitative information that, if analysed appropriately, may have enormous benefits for the aims of organisations and the delivery of their services. Furthermore, in the spirit of this collection an analysis of internally produced quantitative data will help with case studying organisations.

This has completely a different aim than any 'qualitative' work that may be applied to case studies. Qualitative researchers will seek to analyse the meanings and practices of the workers in the agency (Silverman 1993; Zimmerman 1973) that are often different to the more statistical analysis that I am seeking to promote. A quantitative approach, on the other hand, first, provides the researcher a generalised view of their case study, whereby researchers will enable an agency to make generalisations about the type of organisation they are, who works for them and what are their 'typical' clients. Second, a quantitative approach may enable an easier and more comprehensive survey and identification of gaps in provision. Third, a quantitative approach offers measurements of the nature of the organisation rather than unquantified 'feelings' or 'perspectives'. Fourth, quantitative approaches allows an exact quantification of things such as staff, clients, successes, workload allocation, service provisions, etc. Fifth, quantitative approaches facilitate a formalised, quantifiable and publicly transparent evaluation of services offered. Finally, quantitative approaches make it possible to aid the case study of the organisation by providing a measurable base in which valid and reliable comparisons can be made with other similar organisations.

This chapter will enable a case study of an agency or organisation to be undertaken using a quantitative approach. Due to space constraints, readers are asked to see Kane (1987) for a basic introduction to research design and data production, or Gilbert (1993) and Ritchie, Taket and Bryent (1994) for a slightly more detailed discussion of research design and data production, although these texts do not focus on a quantitative analysis of case studies. It is hoped that this chapter will bring those people unfamiliar with quantitative approaches to consider using and applying statistical analytic techniques to their particular cases. This contribution does not examine doing questionnaires or interviews, as these have been adequately discussed by other authors (see Fink 1995; Fowler 1995; Hakim 1987; May 1997; Moser and Kalton 1971; Oppenheim 1992; Rose and Sullivan 1996; Sarantakos 1993). Later I will suggest to readers where they can find out about the wealth of statistical techniques available for analysis. I begin here by introducing someone unfamiliar with quantitative and statistical approaches to making sense out of records held by organisations. The main aim is for the reader to become acquainted with the preparation, coding and summarising of data.

Making sense of case files

An analysis of organisational records is very useful to agencies in helping them become reflexive about their operations and to have an overall and accurate picture of their practices over a period of time (Hall and Hall 1996). The information gained by researchers could help point out any gaps in services. The information may illustrate biases that may have built up in terms of their client base. The analysis may provide the agency with information concerning their 'success rates' that in turn may be included in annual reports or to help them bid for extra resources.

So what kind of data do organisations have that may be quantified and analysed? There are many records held by organisations (see Hakim 1993 for overview).[1] There are a variety of record books, visitors books and registers where there may be names and addresses of visitors, the organisations they represent, the length of visit or the purpose of business. Clearly a quantification of this material would be useful to the organisation, in terms of building up a profile of their clients. There are also a number of diaries held by agency workers that could merit quantification and analysis. Hospital admissions statistics, committee reports or court reports are also documents worthy of analytic attention. Finally, agencies usually hold case files (or case notes) of clients and it is to this source that the article focuses attention. Case files are documents not usually assumed to be data resources and are relatively unwieldy in being quantified and aggregated. Yet the benefits of going back through case files are worth the effort in terms of the detailed information contained in them that could be retrieved and quantified.

A number of professionals use case files including social workers, probation officers, educational welfare officers, housing officers, GPs, district nurses, counsellors, psychiatrists, mentors, solicitors, court officials, among others. Numerous institutions keep case files including schools, prisons, residential care homes and hospitals. Organisations may also keep case files on agency workers. The contents of case files vary as much as the type and quality of case worker, that is they may be brief or they may be thick with detail and description. The content of case files also depends on how long the client has been involved with the organisation. It is usually the rule that the longer the involvement in the agency the larger the file. Using case files has added advantages in that they often provide a rich seam of detailed information and researchers can learn a great deal about the client's case history and how staff have dealt with each particular case (Scott 1990; Stake 1995). In my own quantitative work with case files I have found that they keep reiterating that what I am quantifying are real people, often with important and moving problems, not merely numbers, percentages, ratios, averages and proportions (Cockburn 1995).

Case files often contain information that quantitative researchers are constantly searching for which can be fairly easily turned into quantifiable 'variables'. They usually have crucial background information on their clients such as their age, gender and ethnicity, details about their religion, where they live and details about their families. They may contain information that allows researchers to understand how practitioners work as they might contain details about which staff are allocated to the case and what programmes the client has undertaken, and include notes on what methods of work are applied to the client. From case files a profile of the agency's inter-agency work can be constructed as there is often information on what organisations have made the referrals and what happened to clients that have passed through the system. Analysing case files can often measure the effectiveness of organisations by quantifying successes and failures (if there is an established criterion for measuring success or failure).

It needs stating that alongside these many advantages there are a number of problems that may arise for researchers. Not least, access to case files might be restricted due to an organisation's policies on confidentiality, although agencies may permit access to case files with the understanding that anonymity and confidentiality are absolutely assured. There is another obstacle to working with case files and this is the physical problem that the files are sometimes thick and detailed documents containing a huge amount of information that may make it difficult to extract quantifiable information. Case files are often written up in a hurry and consequently handwriting may be difficult to read, or they may be written in the vernacular of the profession to which the researcher may not be acquainted. It is also possible that the case files contain contradictory information that may be hard to clarify. As Gordon (1988) says: 'case records are rich in detail about daily life and personal relations. They are not, however, universally reliable, understandable, or easy to use' (p.12).

Despite these serious obstacles, on the whole I have found the rewards greatly counterbalance any disadvantages. The best way to minimise problems is to prepare adequately prior to working with them and to establish a clear set of aims and objectives.

Preparing numerical data

The second step in the research after negotiating access to the case files is to commence with the coding of information in the files into a format that will provide the means for quantitative analysis. The coding stage is one where the data is tidied up for categorisation and analysis. The process of coding is sometimes referred to as 'handling' the data (Swift 1996), which means the shaping of the raw data so that they are transformed into variables to allow us to inspect or analyse them more readily. Before this is finalised it is necessary for the researcher to spend time familiarising themselves with the files; researchers need to 'tune in' to the meanings and messages of the data. This is accomplished by exploring the characteristics and structure of the case file. How are the covering forms laid out? How were they written? Do they include correspondence with other agencies? What other documents were referred to? And so on.

It is important to record as much as possible numerically. Even with data referring to 'categories' or 'types' (technically referred to as *Nominal* or *Categorical* data), it is better to translate these categories into coded numbers. Here numbers are just labels for discrete items (where no ordering is implied); examples include gender, religion, organisations, ethnicity and so on. This will probably be the most commonly used scale (in contrast to numerical and ranked data). By applying each label with a discrete number rather than a word, it is surprising just what can be quantified and thus is susceptible to statistical tests at a later stage. For example, with gender assign each gender with a number (for instance, female $= 0$; male $= 1$) or with each religion assign a number (for instance, Roman Catholic $= 1$; Church of England $= 2$; Presbyterian $= 3$; Jewish $= 4$, etc.). With numerical and ranked data it is usually best at this stage to record the raw figures.[2,3]

'Closing' data

As I alluded to in the previous section, the data is best transformed from its raw form into numbers. After familiarising oneself with the case files the next step should be an examination of a representative sample of the case files (say 40 cases). Record on to the top of sheets of paper the information which is of interest and below that copy the corresponding information contained in the other files. Eventually one is able to look at the information and to categorise and code it into numbers.

How many categories is it necessary to have? If there were no constraints, and we wished to avoid any distortion of the data, we may like to have as many categories as there are case files, grouping under one heading only those that are identical. This clearly is not a practical prospect. In my experience, a category that will, in the final analysis, hold fewer than 20 cases must be regarded as a luxury. It should also be mentioned that for a great many of categories there are some already designed coding frames available ready made. For instance, classifications for occupation or ethnicity (Irvine, Miles and Evans 1979; Marsh 1988) are already available and widely used. Although, as Dorling and Simpson (1999) point out, they are far from being unproblematic and may not suit one's own study's particular needs.

It is worth noting that in imposing a set of classificatory categories, perhaps eight or ten in number, on a very much larger and probably very varied set of details, some important details of the data will be 'lost' in recording the details of case files into numbers. However, quantifying the contents of case files enables researchers to have an overview of the work performed by agencies, allows the running of comparisons and enables statistical tests and measurements.

After the researcher has identified a type and number of categories, it is then possible to go on to code the rest of the case files. It is worth working on the smaller sample as it will later speed up the process by having a list of previously determined codes for those aspects of the files that one is interested in. Instead of writing down the words of the files, the researcher rings a predetermined numerical code to indicate what information is being measured. For instance, if a researcher is working on the case files of a residential children's home she may be interested in where the referrals were made and could attach numerical codes to different types of agency. In this way, social services becomes 1, parents/carers become 2, voluntary agencies become 3, other residential care homes become 4, and so on.

Getting the data ready for analysis

The next stage is to shape the raw data into variables so that they may be inspected or analysed. It is necessary for the data to be presented in such a way that the data becomes elements of a data matrix. This may seem to be an off-putting term but is in fact quite simple. People use matrixes throughout their daily lives, for example bus or train timetables or home-shopping catalogue summaries. It seems that most public-sector utilities are presenting the outcomes of their services in league tables that are themselves raw figures and values placed in a matrix. Data matrices are best suited to computer or machine-based analysis but it is also possible to 'hand count' matrices or 'tally frequencies' held on paper (Sarantakos 1993).

Table 5.1. An example of a coding frame

Column	Variables or codes
1	Gender 1 = Girl 2 = Boy
2–3	Age (2 digits)
4	Ethnicity 1 = White 2 = Black Afro-Caribbean 3 = Black Asian 4 = Black other
5	Religion 1 = Roman Catholic 2 = Protestant 3 = Jewish 4 = Muslim 5 = Other
6–7	Length of stay in months (2 digits)
8	Referring agency 1 = Social services 2 = Parents/carers 3 = Voluntary organisations 4 = Other
9	Programmes 1 = Counselling 2 = Outdoor activities 3 = Family therapy 4 = Work experience
10	Outcomes 1 = Family of origin 2 = Fostering 3 = Adoption 4 = Other voluntary organisation 5 = Other residential care home

Data is constructed by the researcher and does not appear magically. It is the coding frame that constructs the data. The codes are derived from the data as a result of decisions taken by the researcher. In order to adopt one's own data matrix for the case files being used, it may be helpful for me to invent a fictitious coding frame of a residential care home for children, as outlined in Table 5.1. On the left-hand side are the column numbers that will appear on the top of the data matrix. For each digit in the matrix there needs to be a column. There are ten columns representing eight variables. Note that two variables require two columns, as they are each likely to need two digits. The ages of children will say range from 9 to 13, therefore any young person aged ten and above will need space for two digits (see Table 5.2: columns 2 to 3 are reserved for the category 'age'). Similarly, a young person may stay in the home for a number of years, and if cases stay for ten or more months they will need space for two digits (columns 6 to 7 in Table 5.2 are for the category 'length of stay' represented in months). It is necessary to point out that technically a person could stay in the institution for more than 99 months and if this was the case then space will be needed for three digits. However, in our fictitious example the longest stay for a resident is 34 months.

Table 5.2. Research data matrix									
1	**2**	**3**	**4**	**5**	**6**	**7**	**8**	**9**	**10**
1	1	2	1	2	2	3	1	4	1
2	1	0	1	2	2	2	2	1	5
2	0	9	1	5	0	4	1	4	5
1	1	1	2	2	1	8	1	2	5
1	1	3	1	1	2	2	1	3	1
1	1	0	1	2	0	3	1	1	1
1	1	1	1	2	0	7	3	1	5
2	1	2	3	4	2	5	1	4	2
1	1	0	1	2	3	4	1	4	3
2	1	1	1	2	0	2	1	2	1

I have provided an example matrix in Table 5.2 that corresponds to the example coding frame outlined in Table 5.1. The size of the sample is only restricted to ten cases but already we can observe at a close glance a number of facts that may be important to the agency. In the first column we can see that girls outnumber boys. In the second and third columns we can see that the ages range from 9 to 13. In the fourth column eight out of the sample of ten are white, and by looking at the fifth column we can see that most of the children are Protestant. From column 8 we learn that eight out of ten clients are referred to by social services. Columns 9 and 10 also tell us concisely what programmes the children participated in and what happened to them after they left the home. This information may not mean too much to the general reader with only ten cases, but if presented with a population of 500 it will not be readily visible and could have important meanings to the workers. For instance, they may wish to reassess how they deal with minority communities given the high proportion of white clients. They may wish to step up efforts to return the young people to their families of origin. These are important issues that the agency needs information to act upon. Furthermore, although I have restricted the sample to only ten in order to introduce the reader to matrixes, if the case files are backdated trends may also be determined over time. Very often organisations wish to have information about how their practices today compare with those in the past. Summarising information from case files into a matrix will identify patterns and trends, patterns that would otherwise be locked in filing cabinets.

Analysis of larger data and introducing statistical analysis

It is quite easy to read and interpret figures from a matrix with just ten cases. The problem arises when the cases number over 100 and it becomes difficult for the eye to catch patterns and trends unless the data is treated in some way. Here it becomes important to use some simple statistics. It is well beyond the possibilities of this chapter to present more than a very brief pointer to simple statistics. The reader is strongly recommended to read specialised introductory statistical texts (such as de Vaus 1991; Erickson and Nosenchuck 1983; Healey 1990; Howells 1985; Huff 1981; Marsh 1988). However, as a minimum, percentages can be displayed for each category. These percentages can be easily presented graphically, in a bar chart or pie chart, using the 'graphs' function of most modern word processors.

Once percentages have been gained it is useful to read the specialist books listed above and to look at descriptive and frequency statistics, including measures of central tendency and measures of spread (using diagrammatic forms of analysis, such as stem and leaf diagrams). Then comparisons between variables can be made where differences and correlations can be made. For those who wish to go into their statistical analysis in greater depth, good introductions to advanced statistical techniques are available (including Agresti 1996; Cohen 1969; Hair 1998; Kendale 1952; Stuart and Ord 1987).

With large sets of data it is still possible to use pen and paper to work out frequencies and distributions. However, it is far easier to use a computer. Modern statistical packages such as SPSS or MINITAB are able to provide statistics at a press of a button, once the raw figures are entered. Moreover, when we want to present our collected data to an audience, whether for the agency concerned or for academic reports or dissertations, the advantages of computers in providing diagrams, pie charts, bar charts and histograms become irresistible. Good introductions to using statistical packages include Bryman and Cramer 1997; Foster 1993; Healey and Earle 1997; Kinnear 1999; Rose and Sullivan 1996.

Presenting data in a clear and understandable way is important (see Chapman and Mahon 1988). This can be aided not just by specialist statistical packages, but also by databases, and even some spreadsheet computer packages are able to transfer data into a presentable format. Similarly to statistical packages, there are good introductory texts to using databases and spreadsheets (for example, Erickson 1999; Neibauer 1997; Pelosi 1998; Weisskopf 1999). However, they have limitations in terms of developing statistical analyses.

Notes

1   Catherine Hakim's (1993) article is extremely rewarding in giving an overview of 'official and business records', though it does not discuss the records of voluntary organisations. Neither does it mention the use of case files, a source of data this chapter aims to highlight.

2   Numerical data is usually referred to as 'Interval data', that is, data that refers to points or measurements which are at equal distance from each other; for example, defined intervals of time such as years or weeks (this information may prove useful for working out the amount of time a client has been on the books, attendance on programmes or for differences in age). Also, money is scaled in intervals of pounds.

3   Ranked data such as preference scales or measures of responsibility are referred to as 'Ordinal' data. Ordinal data is ordered, but the intervals are not necessarily constant (like interval data) and can be rank ordered. Objects can be ordered in criterion from highest to lowest. Examples of this could be educational qualifications such as GCSE, 'A' level, diploma and degree. Also, certain skills can be arranged according to rank and importance.

References

Agresti, A. (1996) *An Introduction to Categorical Data Analysis*. New York: John Wiley.

Bryman, A. and Cramer, D. (1997) *Quantitative Data Analysis with SPSS for Windows*. London: Routledge.

Chapman, M. and Mahon, B. (1988) *Plain Figures*. London: HMSO.

Cockburn, T. (1995) 'Child abuse and protection: The Manchester Boys' and Girls' Refuges and the NSPCC, 1884–1894.' Sociology Department Occasional Paper Number 42. Manchester: University of Manchester.

Cohen, J. (1969) *Statistical Power Analysis in the Behavioural Sciences*. New York: Academic.

de Vaus, D.A. (1991) *Surveys in Social Research*. London: UCL Press.

Erickson, B. and Nosenchuck, T. (1983) *Understanding Data*. Milton Keynes: Open University Press.

Erickson, L. (1999) *Quick, Simple Microsoft Access 2000*. New Jersey: Prentice-Hall.

Fink, A. (1995) *The Survey Kit*. London: Sage.

Foster, J. (1993) *Starting SPSS/PC+ and SPPP for Windows: A Beginners Guide*. Wilmslow: Sigma.

Fowler, F.J. (1995) *Improving Survey Questions: Design and Evaluation*. London: Sage.

Gilbert, N. (ed) (1993) *Researching Social Life* London: Sage.

Gordon, L. (1988) *Heroes of their Own Lives: The Politics and History of Family Violence, Boston 1880–1960.* New York: Penguin.

Hair, J. *(1998) Multivariate Data Analysis.* New Jersey: Prentice-Hall.

Hakim, C. (1987) *Research Design: Strategies and Choices in the Design of Social Research.* London: Unwin Hyman.

Hakim, C. (1993) 'Research analysis of administrative records.' In M. Hammersley (ed) *Social Research: Philosophy, Politics and Practice.* London: Sage.

Hall, D. and Hall, I. (1996) *Practical Social Research: Project Work in the Community.* London: Macmillan.

Healey, J. (1990) *Statistics: A Tool for Social Research.* London: Chapman & Hall.

Healey, J. and Earle, R. (1997) *Exploring Social Issues using SPSS for Windows.* London: Sage.

Howells, D. (1985) *Fundamental Statistics for the Behavioural Sciences.* Boston: PWS Publishers.

Huff, D. (1981) *How to Lie with Statistics.* Harmondsworth: Penguin.

Irvine, J., Miles, I. and Evans, J. (1979) *Demystifying Social Statistics.* London: Pluto.

Kane, E. (1987) *Doing Your Own Research: How to Do Basic Descriptive Research in the Social Sciences and Humanities.* London: Marion Boyars.

Kendall, M. (1952) *The Advanced Theory of Statistics.* London: Griffin.

Kinnear, P. (1999) *SPSS for Windows Made Simple.* Hove: Psychology.

Marsh, C. (1988) *Exploring Data: An Introduction to Data Analysis for Social Scientists.* Cambridge: Polity Press.

May, T. (1997) *Social Research: Issues, Methods and Process.* Bristol: Open University Press.

Moser, C. and Kalton, G. (1971) *Survey Methods in Social Investigation.* Aldershot: Gower.

Neibauer, A. (1997) *Access for Busy People.* London: Osborne.

Oppenheim, A.N. (1992) *Questionnaire Design and Attitude Measurement.* London: Heinemann.

Pelosi, M. (1998) *Doing Statistics with Excel 97.* New York: Wiley.

Ritchie, C., Taket, A. and Bryant, J. (eds) (1994) *Community Works.* Sheffield: Pavic.

Rose, D. and Sullivan, O. (1996) *Introducing Data Analysis for Social Scientists.* 2nd edn. Buckingham: Open University Press.

Sarantakos, S. (1993) *Social Research.* London: Macmillan.

Scott, J. (1990) *A Matter of Record: Documentary Sources in Social Research.* Cambridge: Polity Press.

Silverman, D. (1993) *Interpreting Qualitative Data: Methods for Analysing Talk, Text and Interaction.* London: Sage.

Stake, R.E. (1995) *The Art of Case Study Research.* London: Sage.

Stuart, I. and Ord, K. (1987) *Kendall's Advanced Theory of Statistics.* London: Arnold.

Swift, B. (1996) 'Preparing numerical data.' In R. Sapsford and V. Jupp (eds) *Data Collection and Analysis.* London: Sage.

Weisskopf, G. (1999) *Excel 2000: No Experience Required.* London: Sibex.

Zimmerman, D. (1973) 'The practicalities of Rule Use,' In J. Douglas (ed) *Understanding Everyday Life.* London: Routledge & Kegan Paul.

CHAPTER 6

Disrupting Ethics in Social Research

Beth Humphries and Marion Martin

Introduction

In research approved by a scientific community a basic demand is that it should be ethical, but ethics is not separate from the planning and the choice of methods in social research, a kind of 'bolt on' which is only considered when one is engaged in doing research, and then only at certain points. Ethics is fundamental to making claims about knowledge, and ethical behaviour is no less important in other aspects of professional or personal life. A classical concept of ethics or moral philosophy involves the theory of 'the good life', the study of value, not just the empirical question of what people actually value, but the normative question of what it is *right* to value. The study of ethics has produced a number of monolithic systems of explanation. Although these operate from a position of supposed detachment, there has been a growing realisation that particular people, notably marginalised others, have been ill-served by the tenets of existing systems. The critique extends to the interests of women, to colonised peoples and other subordinate groups: 'there is nothing remotely resembling pure social data whose meaning and truth are incontestably self-evident' (Goldberg 1993, p.154). Knowledge, especially knowledge of and about the social, is not produced in a vacuum. Knowledge producers are set in social milieus. Smith (1999) speaks of 'research through imperial eyes' (p.56), seeing research as an important part of the colonisation process because it is concerned with defining legitimate knowledge. She describes the ways assumptions of Western male ideals about the most fundamental things are regarded as the only rational ideas which will make sense of the world, of social life and of human beings, leaving a foundation of ideologically laden data about indigenous societies (p.170).

Western feminist approaches have been in danger of inscribing themselves on research in similar ways (see Mohanty's 1991b critique). At the same time Mohanty (1991a) has described how women worldwide have engaged with women's oppression in its different forms, but very much in the context of anti-imperialist movements, in the 'fight against racist colonialist states and for national independence' (p.9). We want here to engage with this wider view of feminism and anti-imperialism in the spirit of bell hooks (1989): 'we must understand that patriarchal domination shares an ideological foundation with racism and other forms of group oppression.' (p.22) We should not try to isolate feminism from these other struggles.

In this chapter we examine orthodox understandings of research ethics, drawing out an approach to ethical research which is informed by the above view of feminist knowledge, and which takes into account not only the interests of women, but of other 'Others'. This involves uncovering the illusion of objectivity and impartiality on which ethics claims are made, and revealing the power relationships which are concealed by ethical statements. The objective is not to suggest an alternative system, because there is no final absolute answer to moral dilemmas, or make pronounce-ments which can apply authoritatively across time and space. Rather it is to unsettle taken-for-granted categories in ways which might begin to work in the interests of all those who fall outside normative paradigms.

Statements of ethics

Bulmer's notion of ethics is widely accepted:

> the scientific community has responsibilities not only to the ideals of the pursuit of objective truth and the search for knowledge, but also to the subjects of their research ... the researcher has always to take account of the effects of his (sic) actions upon ... subjects and act in such a way as to preserve their rights and integrity as human beings. Such behaviour is ethical research. (Bulmer 1982, p.3)

Codes of ethics concern not only the protection of subjects of research, but also the interests of the academic discipline or profession. They regulate the conduct of researchers regarding:

- academic freedom – the right to research, publish and promote academic research

- professional integrity – claims made about expertise, and the reputation of their academic discipline

- reporting findings truthfully – commitment not to falsify or distort data, and to ensure the research is justified for the furtherance of knowledge

- the well-being of research participants – that they are unharmed physically, socially or psychologically.

Ethical theories result from the experience of a particular human community. Aspects of the way of life of influential groups become elevated to represent the view of all, are presented to the world as neutral, objective and universally applicable, and their origins become concealed. The dominant codes of ethics in Western societies are constructed on liberal humanist ideas in the interests of a scientific community, and have been absorbed as reasonable by researchers and others (Shildrick 1997). However, social science is not neutral inquiry into human behaviours and institu-tions, but is deeply implicated in the project of social control, ultimately serving the interests of dominant groups (Foucault 1980). Western codes of ethics have also been applied to the situation of developing countries, with the assumption that the values that underpin them are held by all people everywhere (Smith 1999). The study of non-European languages and cultures, for example, forms a significant thread in Western discourse about 'primitive' culture and racial inferiority, and in victim-blaming educational theories (Cameron *et al.* 1992; Goldberg 1993; Rodney 1972).

Liberal humanist ideas which inform ethical statements are based on a conception of the moral and social order, dominant since the seventeenth-century Enlightenment, in which gender-neutral, individual and autonomous actors conduct their lives and enter into contractual relationships with other individuals on the basis of free will and rationality. As we shall show, these ideas lead to problems and illusions in the proper conduct of social research, because they make assumptions about questions of virtue, rights, justice, equality and freedom.

> historically the knowledge-makers, guardians and teachers … have been male [and] 'knowledge' is by definition rational, scientific and universal…counterposed against those of emotionality, the natural and particular, and these and related characteristics are associated with the known characteristics of the sexes. (Stanley 1997, pp.2–3)

Artefacts such as codes of ethics, therefore, should not be taken at face value, and actually serve *two* main functions: (1) enhancement of a group's or discipline's reputation, and (2) as guarantees to research subjects. We are concerned here primarily with the latter, but there are some brief points to be made about the former.

The enhancement of a discipline's or group's status

In terms of the purpose of ethical guidelines to protect the interests of institutions and professional bodies, Friedson's (1970) well-known study of medicine as a profession concluded that the distinguishing feature of a profession is the fact of autonomy – the legitimate control of an occupation over its work. It must persuade the State that its work is 'reliable and valuable'. Codes of ethics serve as one of a number of means used to convince the State of this. They are 'campaign documents' in the push for autonomy, public confidence and resources.

Codes of ethics assume the moral requirement to rest on the conduct of the researcher. So long as she or he is seen to exercise proper moral agency, the injunction to ethical behaviour is satisfied. The position of the 'subject' is characterised as passive and dependent. It is of limited ethical interest in that no moral agency is attributed to the respondent. The dominant discourse of autonomy of all people to act freely and rationally is called into question by this move, which privileges the researcher, and research subjects are denied full moral agency. They are required to give consent, but this notion too is problematic for reasons we discuss later.

For now, as a means of protection of an institution or a profession, such principles as, for example, 'informed consent', on the face of it designed to protect research subjects, can be used as a defence if research subjects subsequently disagree with the findings (for example, Udry and Billy 1987). Among the purposes of ethical codes, then, are propaganda and self-protection.

Protection of the rights of research subjects

With regard to the protection of the rights of research subjects, most guidelines (see, for example, British Sociological Association (BSA) (1995) and Manchester Metropolitan University undated) identify a number of interlinked areas as of key importance in the research process:

- the social impact of research
- informed consent
- privacy
- deception.

For research to be ethical it should be informed by moral principles which avoid harming others, promote the good and are respectful and fair. However, this is not as straightforward as it appears. First, codes of ethics are voluntary, premised on professional norms, but with no penalties for breach of ethics. Indeed, where discussion of ethics appears in the research literature, it usually consists of the researcher justifying her/his ethical behaviour (for example, Davidson and Layder 1994). We know of few accounts of ethics where the researcher admits to unethical practice. One might conclude that discussions about ethics are ineffectual, because not only are codes voluntary, not only are there no penalties for breach, but in any case there are no measures of poor practice except the scrutiny of a research committee which *may* act as discouragement to bad practice.

Another problem with codes of ethics is that they are framed in binary opposites, as illustrated by Singer's (1991) statement: 'ethics deals… with good and bad, with right and wrong' (p.xxi). This is a definition of ethics which assumes values as absolutes. 'Absolute ethics' are prescriptive and proscriptive moral injunctions about what one ought /ought not to do. But this does not measure up to real life, where in the process of constructing social knowledge, researchers grapple with ethics in grounded situations which are often in between the binary – dilemmas that a menu of dos and don'ts does not help to resolve. This insight leads a number of feminists to argue for 'contextual ethics' (for example, Benhabib 1992; Shildrick 1997), about which we say more later.

Codes of ethics do not take account of the impact of differences of power in relation to the principles of 'consent', deception, and so on. The BSA code acknowledges power differences, but encourages the researcher to develop 'trust' (British Sociological Association 1995, p.1). This discourse assumes power is possessed by the researcher and none by the subjects. It also assumes the issue of power can be overcome, rather than be seen as an inherent condition of the research situation. The consequences for subjects are that, under this construction of ethical behaviour, they are dependent on the goodwill of researchers *whether or not a code of ethics is applied*. The conception of power here is very different from that described by Foucault (1980), who views it as a force and an effect circulating in a web of social interaction:

> power is employed and exercised through a net-like organisation. And not only do individuals circulate between its threads; they are always in the position of simultaneously undergoing and exercising this power ... In other words, individuals are the vehicles of power, not its point of application. (p.98)

Foucault argues that power is not monolithic, but is multifaceted within social relations. While agreeing that power can be understood as a multiple relation, we do not deny that power can also be understood as a property which some people in some contexts have more of than others (nor does Foucault). However, we find Foucault's notion of micro-power a useful one in unpacking the impact of ethical statements. Dominant discourses of ethical codes privilege the researcher as the source of power, a position which we regard as inadequate to capture the complexities of social relations. Some of the difficulties can be demonstrated by a closer look at the expectations ethical codes have of researchers, and at some examples from research practice. Above we identified four areas where researchers are urged to look after their research subjects – social impact; informed consent; privacy; deception. Each of these is considered below to examine their complexity.

Social impact

This refers to a warning not to cause disruption to people's lives during or after the research process is conducted. It is as if the researcher can dig out bits of information while leaving the whole intact and undisturbed. The idea of non-disturbance is related to positivist notions of science and objectivity – the benign, observing, objective researcher working in a controlled, laboratory-like environment. Feminists have been critical of these assumptions, saying it is neither possible nor desirable to conduct research in that way. This 'hit-and-run' model of research ignores the relationships which might be built between researcher and researched in discussing sensitive or shared concerns. Oakley's (1981) work is a case in point. She interviewed women about the experience of becoming a mother. Contrary to all the rules she shared her own experiences with them, answered their questions, had dinner with them, and for some of them was present at the birth of their children. Oakley argued that because women have experiences in common they engage with each other emotionally and empathically, making the interview experience much richer. This approach has been criticised because it ignores differences of class, 'race', ability, age, sexuality, culture and geography (Kothari 1997; Mohanty 1991a, 1991b; Trinh 1989). The problem with discussions about ethics is that because they are framed within sanitised 'professional' ideals, they evade the issue of power and politics which are inherent in the research process. The context in which research is conducted, the social characteristics of researched and researcher, methods, strategies, conclusions, all have implications of power. As we have argued, where power is recognised in conventional discussions of ethics, it is often framed in terms of acknowledging the disparate power of the researcher and researched, and of taking steps to protect the vulnerability of the researched (British Sociological Association 1995; see also Herzog 1996, ch. 14). This implies that all those being researched are powerless and vulnerable. But being a researcher does not cancel out other power relationships. Bhavnani (1991) carried out research with a group of young black and white working-class women and men. She wrote about her experience of the back and forward movement of power which she as a black woman researcher experienced in interviewing young black men and women and young white men and women, and how at times she herself felt vulnerable. The power relations that exist around gender, 'race' and class did not disappear because of her position of power as a researcher. And people being researched are not powerless, as we argued earlier. Power engenders resistance and is always being resisted. There are myriad ways people can withhold co-operation, mislead researchers or otherwise engage with the dynamic of attempting to gain and exercise power. Some writers attempt to excise the issue of power, suggesting the problems of representing other people's experiences and perspectives can be dealt with by declaring their social characteristics ('I am white, heterosexual, middle class...'), or through identity matching of researcher with researched. The first of these rather glibly implies that power is dealt with by such a declaration. The second assumes that the researcher sees what the subject sees and will share insight into the 'true' knowledge which is produced by oppression on the basis of shared identity or similar experience. This suggests all people with similar characteristics share the same experiences and understand those experiences in similar ways; it presents research as a kind of mirror which can reflect reality if held in the right hands, and it ignores the highly complex business of how people's experiences are represented in research reports. Research is seen as the result of 'discovery' rather than as a subjective and social construction. A study of black women social workers shows the complexity of research with people who appear to share similar characteristics but who are differently positioned at different times (Lewis 1996).

Informed consent

Homan (1991) argues that the principle of informed consent is not an ethic, but a procedure widely agreed to safeguard the rights of subjects to know what research is being conducted, and to approve their own participation. It is also a mechanism through which research can be achieved without the loss of reputation of researchers, and works to the benefit of professional organisations and individual researchers. Guidelines agree that informed consent must be obtained before entering into a research relationship. This involves giving information to prospective research subjects about the research, obtaining their permission to be a subject of the study, and assuring them of confidentiality. This is emphasised in research involving relatively powerless groups in order to prevent their exploitation. But questions arise about the amount and level of information people require in order to give fully informed consent, and indeed whether such consent has been obtained. A signature or a nod does not necessarily signify understanding. The circumstances in which information is given and its timing are also important. Research may change radically or subtly as it develops, bringing into question the validity of seeking one-off permission at the beginning. Children in a classroom, mentally ill people in hospital and prison inmates, for example, may feel constrained to take part in a study, even when they have been told they are free not to participate. In these circumstances, taking into account the context and the status of the agent, the ideal of informed consent turns out to give strictly limited protection to subjects. There needs to be freedom from coercion and intimidation, the consentor must be capable of consenting, and in possession of at least minimal information about what is at stake. Sometimes researchers argue they can only get the information they want by withholding informed consent. Milgram's (1963) study of obedience examined the extent to which ordinary people would obey an authority figure. Subjects were told they were taking part in a 'learning study', were asked to sit in a cubicle next door to a student, and to administer increasingly severe electric shocks to the student. When the (fictitious) shocks were administered, subjects heard cries through the partition walls. Many expressed doubt and anxiety about their role but were urged on by the experimenter. Some continued to administer shocks to the maximum level. Milgram concluded that normal individuals were more likely to obey orders from an authority figure than to obey their own moral code.

He defended his research by saying the experiment provided an opportunity to learn more about the conditions of human action. Giving full information could make it impossible to conduct the experiment. However, he violated the principle of informed consent by withholding comprehensive information which would have allowed exercise of choice, informed by full understanding of what was involved. Even in less controversial situations, the moral imperative to secure informed consent often conflicts with the practical imperative to gain co-operation. Milgram and others argue that subjects who know exactly what the researcher is investigating may alter their behaviour, so being less than frank is justified. Some ethical guidelines (for example, Manchester Metropolitan University undated), have an opt-out clause written in on these very grounds. Permission to withhold information may be given by an ethics committee if a convincing argument is submitted. This dilemma is based on positivist notions that social science investigators can achieve the level of control assumed in a laboratory experiment where external influences are controlled. But human subjects are conscious, intelligent actors, and refusing to tell them what the experiment is all about does not gain total control for the researcher. If research subjects are not told what the experiment is investigating, they will draw their own inferences about its purpose. These inferences, whether right or wrong, will then affect their behaviour in the laboratory. The argument that giving full information will distort the research results is based on beliefs arising from positivist philosophical foundations, but there is no doubt that it is also an expedient one to ensure that ambitions for investigation are not thwarted by a refusal of consent. It also illustrates the provisional nature of apparently unambiguous statements in codes of ethics.

Privacy

As a general principle, ethical guidelines suggest that privacy should be respected, and the topic is discussed mainly in relation to covert methods. Protecting the anonymity and privacy of the research is usually represented as protecting the subject but, as we said earlier, it may also protect the researcher from disputes about the research. The discourse that research subjects are powerless and researchers are powerful works very much in the interests of the researcher. Humphreys' (1970) well-known study of men's sexual behaviour in public toilets justified its covert methods by arguing that, in order to help these vulnerable men politically and socially, it was necessary to acquire information about their needs and practices, obtainable only through research which invaded their privacy. Apart from the pater-nalistic tone of this argument, it is questionable whether Humphreys' research did offer support, and whether the men considered themselves in need of it.

Researchers frequently defend an invasion of privacy in the interests of gaining knowledge. Julia Davidson (Davidson and Layder 1994) studied power and control in the interactions of a sex worker with her clients.[1] With the co-operation of the sex worker – Desiree – Davidson took on a number of roles, including that of recep-tionist. She listened in to conversations between the punters and Desiree, and had conversations with Desiree about their sexual preferences. Davidson was untroubled by her intrusion into these men's world. Her reasons were (1) the clients remained completely anonymous to her, and she was not in a position to secure or disclose information which could harm them; and (2) Desiree had willingly offered details of their interaction, and since this knowledge belonged to Desiree, she was entitled to do what she liked with it. Davidson argued that in any case virtually all social research is exploitative and intrusive to some degree, because research is seldom undertaken at the request of its human subjects and it is rarely undertaken without a view to the professional advancement of the researcher. Ethical dilemmas can therefore only be resolved 'through reference to the researcher's own moral and political values' (p.215). This reference to the researcher's own values demonstrates the limits of codes of ethics in actual, grounded situations. With a wide range of possible motives, what values will inform such judgements? Different political and moral allegiances and personal ambitions will result in very different decisions as to what is for the 'common good' and in the interests of the wider community. Codes of ethics become redundant in such a scenario. Davidson made it clear she respected Desiree but had no wish to advance the interests of Desiree's clients, did not particu-larly like them and had no real sympathy for them. She said:

> I have a professional obligation to preserve and protect their anonymity and to ensure they are not harmed by my research, but I feel no qualms about being less

than frank with them, and no obligation to allow them to choose whether or not their actions are recorded. (Davidson and Layder 1994 p.215).

This example also demonstrates that the ownership of information is not always a straightforward matter, and can be reinterpreted to legitimate the behaviour of the researcher. Here it was expedient for Davidson to perceive Desiree as the owner of the knowledge the researcher wanted, but there are numerous situations where such a view may be contested (parents or professionals giving information about children, partners giving information about each other, for instance). Moreover, in nearly all discussions of privacy, the bounds of privacy are defined by subjects and not by researchers (power is momentarily attributed to subjects). This relies on the sensitivities of subjects to protect their own privacy, and exonerates the researcher who might sometimes be more aware of how intrusive an investigation has become. Subjects of research may be oblivious to the intrusion, or feel unable to set boundaries which are comfortable for them. But the researcher is 'off the hook' by passing that responsibility to the subject's judgement, and can then push for as much co-operation as she or he can get.

This discussion relates to the use of covert research methods, but there are issues of privacy which relate to open methods. Unstructured and informal interviewing styles have as their strength the drawing out of information which would otherwise not be available to the researcher. The researcher may have something in common with the subjects which helps put them at ease, encouraging informality and disclosure. Oakley (1981) and Finch (1984) both celebrated this approach in interviewing women, but still felt free to publish their transactions. Of the two, Finch alone expressed concern that she might be exploiting her subjects. More generally, interviewers are trained to begin an interview with non-threatening questions, putting the respondent at ease before asking intimate or sensitive questions (this also applies to self-administered questionnaires). If privacy is defined as the respondents' mechanisms for self-protection, these may vary with the degree of charm and the characteristics of the interviewer, or the amount of choice the respondent perceives her/himself to have.

Obtaining information from third parties is also an ambiguous area. In Davidson's research, Desiree's perspective was important, but a study of power in commercial sexual encounters could legitimately include punters. Consider the likelihood of Desiree's clients consenting to be interviewed. By using Desiree as informant, Davidson by-passed the requirement of obtaining consent of others involved, and entered into their private world without their knowledge.

There is a more complex response to the issue of ethical scruples about methods. Cameron et al. (1992) make the point that this question is not one which can be confined to the practical level of research method. It inheres in the research relationship itself, and has to be seen as part of the problem of representation. However the data is collected and however carefully negotiated the agendas may have been, when the researcher produces representations of the research for an outside audience control of the data and its meanings shift towards her/him: 'research inevitably involves the recontextualisation of utterances, and so even the most deliberate discourses are likely to be reinterpreted' (p.132). We return to representation later (and see also Searle-Chatterjee in this volume).

Deception

Deception is key to many aspects of invasion of privacy and informed consent as discussed above, but it also merits attention separately. Homan (1991) identifies four kinds of research in which deceit is central: (1) concealment – for example, bugging, the use of hidden cameras or tape recorders; (2) misrepresentation – direct lying, giving false names; (3) camouflage – being a real policeman or whatever, before adding the role of researcher, or retrospectively using previous knowledge; (4) acquisition of confidential documents, which are then used to contact respondents, or as the focus of analysis. There are examples of all of these in published research, some of which we have considered here. Most ethical guidelines prohibit covert research and the deceit inherent in it, *unless an exceptional case is made*. There are on record some blatant cases of deceit which have had damaging consequences for the research subjects. The American Tuskagee project used black men with syphilis as a control group in testing treatment, giving them a placebo (Coney 1988). In 1988 in New Zealand, women with pre-cancer symptoms were assigned to one of two groups without their knowledge or consent. One group received treatment and the other did not (Smith 1999). In both these cases an argument was advanced justifying the studies as in the public interest. It is worth reflecting on the fact that the subjects in both cases were from poor, undervalued groups whose rights were presumably not worth the researchers bothering to consider. *Their* interests were excluded from 'the public interest'. The conclusion of this critique of liberal humanist conceptions of research ethics is that dominant discourses about ethics conceal gendered and racialised power relationships, where assumptions based on male, universalist, Western views of human relationships are privileged, and result in fallacious claims to fairness, equality, justice and human rights. The yearning for the certainty of absolutes has resulted historically not in justice or equality, but in the denial of moral personhood to those categories of living beings who cannot be identified in terms of the ideal standard (Shildrick 1997, p.213). Is it possible then to seek new constructions which do not operate on the basis of such an exclusion? What might be the pre-conditions for an adequate response?

Feminist anti-imperialist ethics

Feminists and anti-racists are critical of dominant ethical codes because they claim universal applicability, and because they purport to be impartial and objective but in fact are exposed as in the interests of powerful groups. Our argument here is that there is no final absolute answer to moral dilemmas, no self-complete system which can satisfy all the demands made of it, or which can apply with universal authority.

Our goal is not to depose existing systems of ethics in favour of others, but to disrupt them, to contextualise them and to limit the grounds of their applications. What is intended here, then, is not a replacement of one set of static ethics positions with another. We aim not for a reconstruction of rules of behaviour, but we draw on a range of feminist and anti-imperialist understandings to construct principles which we think reflect a dynamic approach to a moral basis for action. It would be naive or disingenuous to treat these principles as straightforward and without complexity. We confront and explore the complexities, an approach which we argue enhances rather than undermines their usefulness.

The principle of partiality

At the core of a progressive ethic must be an acknowledgement of the situatedness of all research, and its partiality in terms of both bias and its lack of completion. Maria Mies (1993) speaks of feminist 'conscious partiality', a notion which cuts across ideas about neutral and value-free researchers, achieved through partial identification with research subjects. The sharing of the experience of being women, and therefore knowing a common oppression, leads to empathy and connection, and therefore greater validity of research data. There is of course a limit to and dangers in identification where the experiences of researched and researcher are different, and there is a risk of Western feminists in particular falling back on universalistic assumptions about 'common' experience. This is why Mies' notion of *partial* identification is crucial. Identification must take account of difference, which we shall discuss presently. The point here is that ideas of a static, ahistorical view of ethics is unhelpful. All knowledge is provisional, subject to change with changing conditions.

Locating the researcher

Feminist methodology involves putting the researcher into the processes of production, rather than obscuring the relationship of researchers to the people they study. The positivist idea that researchers ideally would produce wholly objective representations of reality, that even though they will always fall short of the ideal, they should distance themselves as far as possible, seems to us to be both unrealistic and self-deceiving. Researchers are inevitably socially located persons:

> all knowledge, necessarily, results from the conditions of its production, is contextu-
> ally located, and irrevocably bears the marks of its origins in the minds and intellec-
> tual practices of those lay and professional theorists and researchers who give voice
> to it. (Stanley and Wise 1990, p.39)

Researchers bring their histories, biographies and subjectivities into every stage of the research process, and this influences the questions they ask, how they ask them and the ways in which they try to find answers. The subjectivity of the researcher should not be seen as a regrettable intrusion, but as a factor in the interactions involved in doing research.

Research subjects are active, reflexive beings

A related point is that research subjects are themselves active, reflexive beings who have insights into their situations and experiences. As Cameron *et al.* (1992) comment, 'they cannot be observed as if they were asteroids, inanimate lumps of matter: they have to be interacted with' (p.5). Moreover, they should not be seen as the passive providers of information, or as the victims of social and other forces. Mohanty (1991b) reviewed nine studies carried out by Western feminists on women of the South, and concluded that few addressed the social agency of women. Women as subjects do have a critical perspective on their situations, and do organise collectively against their oppressors. A dominant discourse of imperialist texts, including some feminist work, entails problematising women and men labelled Other. As a result they are located in terms of underdevelopment, oppressive traditions, high illiteracy, rural and urban poverty, religious fanaticism and overpopulation, and these become the defining characteristics of 'Third World women'. The lives of subordinated groups need to be addressed in their own terms, not as 'problematic' in relation to those of dominant groups. A different voice formulates different truths and values, no less compelling than those of the dominant culture.

The other side of this coin is to define black women and women of the South as 'strong', 'achieving', 'wise', 'coping', 'matriarchal', presenting a romanticised and unrealistic view of them. A disruptive ethic insists on a recognition of the dynamic oppositional agency of individuals and collectives as they engage with the researcher and with their daily lives. Such a recognition might lead to different emphases for research – on strategies for opposition rather than on attributes of victimhood, for example, and towards an avoidance of the objectification which characterises some research.

Cameron *et al.* (1992) suggest a basic precept for empowering research to be that 'persons are not objects and should not be treated as objects' (p.131). In their view this should mean the use of interactive methods, where research subjects become actively involved in the research process, consciously influencing the researcher. This implies that interactive methods are the only legitimate ones, and that quantitative approaches are excluded. Clearly there are times when interactive methods are not appropriate, and Truman's (1999; 2000) descriptions of large-scale research which involved service users in controlling its direction is an example of the possibilities of recognition, whatever the methods.

Representing others

Producing text on behalf of people studied, raises points of conflict. On the one hand empowering intentions might be to 'bring people to voice'; to allow subordinated and invisible voices to be heard and heeded. This is a core aim of feminist research. But the problems are put in this quote from Asad (1986):

> It remains the case that the ethnographer's translation/representation of a particular culture is inevitably a textual construct, that as representation it cannot normally be

contested by the people to whom it is attributed, and that as a 'scientific text' it eventually becomes a privileged element in the potential stores of historical memory. (p.163)

Regardless of how open research methods are, or how extensive the opportunities for people to offer their view or comment on research, or how faithfully their verbatim words are recorded, at the end of the day it is the researcher who makes choices as to which opinions are put forward and what interpretations are placed on them, and who generally mediates the talk of her subjects. The varieties of views expressed, the contradictions, the opportunities for redefinition in interaction, reveal research subjects as many-sided and complex. The moment of textual representation creates fixed, one-dimensional, 'reified' subjects. The same process applies to the researcher, who in the monologue of reported research also loses part of her fluidity. A number of writers advocate feedback to research subjects during the process of analysis and writing up (for example, Martin 1994, 1996; Rampton 1992), as a way of ensuring their continued influence.

There is another dimension to the issue of representation. Mohanty has identified what she calls disconcerting similarities between the typically authorising signature of Western feminist writings on women in the Third World, and the authorising signature of the project of humanism in general: 'humanism as a Western ideological and political project which involves the necessary recuperation of the "East" and "Woman" as Others' (Mohanty 1991b, p.73). In other words, much research from Western feminists and non-feminists alike produces work which repeatedly confirms and legitimates Western man/humanism as central. The idea of the supremacy of countries of the North is reinforced by a projection of images of peoples of the South as inferior, and of Southern women as passive, uneducated, oppressed and powerless in comparison with Western women. Mohanty challenges this move in the research she examined and calls for us to challenge Marx's dictum: 'they cannot represent themselves; they must be represented' (1991b, p.74).

Encompassing difference

The discussion of representation invokes the recognition of difference. A number of black women and women of the South have written about the assumption in much research on women (and other groups, but women particularly) as an already consti-tuted, coherent group with identical interests and desires, regardless of class, ethnic or racial location, implying a notion of gender which can be applied universally and cross-culturally. As a result, women's interests have been homogenised, and difference denied (see Carby 1982; hooks 1989; Lorde 1984; Mohanty 1991a, 1991b). Moreover, the model of women's interests has been taken to be that which applies to those who are white, Western, middle class, heterosexual, able-bodied and young. There is a need to rethink overgeneralised and underresearched categories such as 'woman' and 'gender' (Stanley and Wise 1990, p.21). The question has been raised as to whether indeed the notion 'woman' is any longer a useful one, given the wide differences among women (Riley 1987). The category 'woman' is fractured, as are the categories 'race', 'sexuality', 'disability'. It is important to take account of the different oppressions experienced by different groups of women and other Others. Does this lead to the relativistic conclusion that therefore it is not possible to say anything about a generalised oppression of women worldwide? Or is there after all a place for universal understandings? Some feminists who have taken up this point argue for retaining a general theory of women's oppression while taking account of the particular and the local circumstances in which women find themselves (Humphries 1998; McNay 1992; Soper 1993). Benhabib (1992, p.158) proposes a concept of 'interactive universalism' where every universal other is recognised as a concrete other, with specific needs and desires and experiences. Lister (1997), in her discussion of citizenship, suggests a notion of 'differentiated universalism, which gives equal status to women and men in their diversity. A woman-friendly citizenship is thus rooted in difference' (p.197). In the light of such a position, the practical question for research becomes how the process concerned with 'actual living, breathing, thinking, theorising people should proceed at the level of methodology translated into method' (Stanley and Wise 1990, p.40).

Contextualising research

All of the principles discussed above are implied in a concept of contextualising research. In particular, as Mohanty (1991b, p.56) says, 'the discursively consensual homogeneity' of groups of people such as 'women' is mistaken for historically specific material reality. That is, although there may be an agreement that particular groups are everywhere oppressed, it should not be assumed that such oppression will take the same form across geographical, historical, cultural boundaries: this focus whereby women are seen as a coherent group across contexts, regardless of class or ethnicity, structures the world in ultimately binary, dichotomous terms, where women are always seen in opposition to men, patriarchy is always necessarily male dominance, and the religious, legal, economic and familial systems are implicitly assumed to be constructed by men (Mohanty 1991b, p.70). This is not to say that an entirely relativist position should pertain. It is not necessary to give up on a general theory of oppression and exploitation in order to insist on the need to understand the local and the particular. It is in the imposition of the ethnocentric gaze that the colonising move takes place.

Accountability to communities

Discussions of accountability usually assume a fundamental accountability to a research community, with obligations to research subjects seldom considered beyond ethical behaviour during fieldwork. The possibility of any accountability beyond an individualistic model seems not to be an option. Definitions of ethics are framed in ways which contain the Western sense of the individual and of individualised property. We saw this earlier in the discussion of the right of the individual to give her/his own knowledge, and the right to give informed consent. Community rights or views are generally not recognised or respected. As a Maori woman, Linda Smith asserts that what is important in community research is the community itself making its own definitions (Smith 1999). Respect for cultural tradition, for the range of views, feelings and interests within a community are crucial aspects of research practice within an alternative research ethic.

This is not to adopt a simplistic notion of 'community', or to say that there are not conflicting interests within communities, and these are major issues for relatively powerless and undervalued groups. Nor is it to ignore 'communities of interest' which do not depend on geographical location or boundary, but which have formed around priorities and particularities. But it is the case that for many indigenous women, for example, writing and talking about their own experiences has developed into a major research priority for them: 'there is a burgeoning of a distinctive indigenous women's literature which actively works against Western literary categories' (Smith 1999, p.127). The processes of methodology and method are expected to embody an ethic of respectfulness and healing. They are expected to lead one small step further towards self-determination, mobilisation, decolonisation and transformation. These goals are far from the objectives embodied within the codes of ethics of disciplines and research communities which we considered earlier.

Conclusion

In this chapter we have engaged with a critique of orthodox statements of ethics in order to show their limitations and the ways they support the interests of dominant groups. We have offered some principles which we believe should influence research aims in improving the social position of subordinate groups, and in making their voices heard. We have acknowledged the complexities involved in any declaration of a research ethic, and we are of the view that simplistic dichotomies are misleading. The position taken by Benhabib (1992) summarises the aim of any research which strives to be ethical, 'a reversing of perspectives and a willingness to reason from the other's (Other's) point of view, does not guarantee consent; it demonstrates the will and the readiness to seek understanding with the other and to seek some reasonable agreement in an open-ended moral conversation'.

Note

1   Davidson's research did not claim to be feminist research. It appears to have been a conventional study using methods of participant observation.

References

Asad, T. (1986) 'The concept of cultural translation in British social anthropology.' In J. Clifford and G. Marcus (eds) *Writing Culture*. Berkeley, CA: University of California Press.

Benhabib, S. (1992) *Situating the Self: Gender, Community and Postmodernism in Contemporary Ethics*. Cambridge: Polity Press.

Bhavnani, K.K. (1991) 'What's power got to do with it? Empowerment and social research.' In R. Parker and J. Shotter (eds) *Deconstructing Social Psychology*. London: Routledge.

British Sociological Association (1995) *Statement of Ethical Practice*. London: BSA

Bulmer, M. (ed) (1982) *Social Research Ethics*. New York: Holmes & Meier.

Cameron, D., Frazer, E., Harvey, P., Rampton, M.B.H. and Richardson, K. (1992) *Researching Language: Issues of Power and Method*. London and New York: Routledge.

Carby, H. (1982) 'White women listen! Black feminism and the boundaries of sisterhood.' In Centre for Contemporary Cultural Studies, *The Empire Strikes Back: Race and Racism in 70s Britain*. London: Hutchinson.

Coney, S. (1988) *The Unfortunate Experiment*. Auckland: Penguin.

Davidson, J.O'C. and Layder, D. (1994) *Methods, Sex and Madness*. London: Routledge.

Finch, J. (1984), "It's great to have someone to talk to": The ethics and politics of interviewing women.' In C. Bell and H. Roberts (eds) *Social Researching*. London: Routledge & Kegan Paul.

Foucault, M. (1980) *Power/Knowledge: Selected Interviews and Other Writings 1972–77*. C. Gordon (ed). Brighton: Harvester.

Friedson, E. (1970) *The Profession of Medicine*. New York: Dodd, Mead & Co.

Goldberg, D. T. (1993) *Racist Culture: Philosophy and the Politics of Meaning*. Oxford: Blackwell.

Herzog, T. (1996) *Research Methods in the Social Sciences*. New York: HarperCollins.

Homan, R. (1991) *The Ethics of Social Research*. Harlow: Longman.

hooks, b. (1989) *Talking Back: Thinking Feminist, Thinking Black*. London: Sheba.

Humphreys, L. (1970) *Tearoom Trade: Impersonal Sex in Public Places*. Chicago: Aldine.

Humphries, B. (1998) 'The baby and the bath water: Hammersley, Cealey Harrison, Hood-Williams and the emancipatory research debate.' *Sociological Research Online 3*, 1, http://www.socresonline.org.uk/socresonline/3/1/9.html

Kothari, U. (1997) 'Identity and representation: Experiences of teaching a neo-colonial discipline.' In L. Stanley (ed) *Knowing Feminisms*. London: Sage.

Lewis, G. (1996) 'Situated voices: Black women's experience and social work. *Feminist Review 53*, Summer, 24–56.

Lister, R. (1997) *Citizenship: Feminist Perspectives*. London: Macmillan.

Lorde, A. (1984) *Sister Outsider*. New York: Crossing Press.

Manchester Metropolitan University (undated) *Guidelines for Ethics in Research*. Manchester: Department of Applied Community Studies.

Martin, M. (1994) 'Developing a feminist participative framework: Evaluating the process.' In B. Humphries and C. Truman (eds) *Rethinking Social Research*. Aldershot: Avebury.

Martin, M. (1996) 'Issues of power in the participatory research process.' In K. de Koning and M. Martin (eds) *Participatory Research in Health: Issues and Experiences*. London and New Jersey: Zed Books.

McNay, L. (1992) *Foucault and Feminism*. Cambridge: Polity Press.

Mies, M. (1993) 'Feminist research: Science, violence and responsibility.' in M. Mies and V. Shiva (eds) *Ecofeminism*. London: Zed Books.

Milgram, S. (1963) 'Behavioral study of obedience.' *Journal of Abnormal and Social Psychology* 67, 371–378.

Mohanty, C.T. (1991a) 'Cartographies of struggle: Third World women and the politics of feminism.' In C.T. Mohanty, A. Russo and L. Torres (eds) *Third World Women and the Politics of Feminism.* Bloomington Indiana: Indiana University Press.

Mohanty, C.T. (1991b) 'Under Western eyes: Feminist scholarship and colonial discourses.' In C.T. Mohanty, A. Russo and L. Torres (eds) *Third World Women and the Politics of Feminism.* Bloomington Indiana: Indiana University Press.

Oakley, A. (1981) 'Interviewing women: A contradiction in terms?' In H. Roberts (ed) *Doing Feminist Research.* London: Routledge & Kegan Paul.

Rampton, M.B.H. (1992) 'Scope for empowerment in sociolinguistics?' In D. Cameron, E. Frazer, P. Harvey, M.B.H. Rampton and K. Richardson, *Researching Language: Issues of Power and Method.* London and New York: Routledge.

Riley, D. (1987) *Am I That Name? Feminism and the Category of 'Women' in History.* London: Macmillan.

Rodney, W. (1972) *How Europe Underdeveloped Africa.* London: Bogle-L'Ouverture Publishers.

Shildrick, M. (1997) *Leaky Bodies and Boundaries: Feminism, Postmodernism and (Bio)Ethics.* London: Routledge.

Singer, P. (1991) *A Companion to Ethics.* Oxford: Basil Blackwell

Smith, L.T. (1999) *Decolonizing Methodologies: Research and Indigenous Peoples.* London and New York: Zed Books.

Soper, K. (1993) 'Postmodernism, subjectivity and the question of value.' In J. Squires (ed) *Principled Positions: Postmodernism and the Rediscovery of Value.* London: Lawrence & Wishart.

Stanley, L. (1997) 'Introduction: On academic borders, territories, tribes and knowledges.' In L. Stanley (ed) *Knowing Feminisms.* London: Sage.

Stanley, L. and Wise, S. (1990) 'Method, methodology and epistemology in feminist research processes.' In L. Stanley (ed) *Feminist Praxis.* London: Routledge.

Trinh T Minh-ha (1989) *Woman, Native, Other.* Bloomington Indiana: Indiana University Press.

Truman, C. (1999) 'User involvement in large scale research: Bridging the gap between service users and service providers?' In B Broad (ed) *The Politics of Social Work Research and Evaluation.* Birmingham: Venture Press.

Truman, C. (2000) 'New social movements and social research.' In C. Truman, D.M. Mertens and B. Humphries (eds) *Research and Inequality.* London: UCL Press.

Udry, J.R. and Billy, J.O.G. (1987) 'Initiation of coitus in early adolescence.' *American Sociological Review 52*, 84–155.

CHAPTER 7

Unusual Terms

What Do You Mean By...?

David Boulton

Introduction

The use of language is such that we get by mostly without a full, or exact, under-standing of what others are thinking. In extreme situations the lack of exact under-standing can be fatal. Imagine two young men, up to no good, discovered on a roof by a policeman who asks them to give him a gun that the younger of them is carrying. The older says: 'Give it to 'im', the younger shoots the policeman and the older of the two, having been found guilty of murder, is hung.

As a medium for research a 'more-or-less' understanding can lead to problems which threaten the validity of the claims a researcher may make. On the other hand such problems of meaning can provide the researcher with keys for unlocking doors to otherwise undiscoverable worlds.

The exploration which follows uses an oversimplified model of the research act in which those who are hoping to discover something about the everyday world are referred to as 'researchers' and those who provide information which might be used as the basis for discovery are referred to as 'informants'. The roles of 'infor-mant-as-researcher' and 'researcher-as-informant' are left on one side because by definition they are unlikely to encounter terms which are considered unusual.

The depth of knowledge which a researcher has of the world under study is a variable – in some cases researchers will have considerable knowledge but often the researcher is a complete stranger to that world. A questionnaire sent to people who were invited for screening for bowel cancer offered informants a five-point response scale to record their agreement/disagreement with the statement 'Most people with polyps do not have symptoms'. 'Polyp', as with other medical terms, has a meaning taken for granted by health care practitioners and is also likely to be meaningful to frequent 'visitors' to medical worlds such as 'people with polyps', or 'people suspected of having polyps'. There will be many, however, who will ask: 'What's a polyp?' At this point the researcher has lost contact with the informant. This is of special importance where the researcher, or interviewer, is not present to answer the question. Thus all self-completed questionnaires will suffer from this problem to a greater or lesser extent and all questioning where digression from the interview script is forbidden will suffer too. What suffers finally is the validity of the findings. What is at fault is the researcher's assumption that his/her conceptualisation of the social world is understood by informants.

So far the accusation is that often informants do not understand researchers as a result of a mismatch between their different vocabularies. Where the mismatch is the other way round, that is, the researcher does not understand the informant, opportunities open up for discovering something which is so special to the informant that he/she has a word, or phrase, which is opaque to the researcher and perhaps also to others who do not inhabit the informant's world. Insider terms, that is, words and abbreviations which are special to the world the informant occupies and which will appear strange to us if we are outsiders, can provide a useful gateway to the informant's world. For example Becker, Geer and Strauss (1961) observed that medical students in a state medical school in the USA used the word 'crock' to describe some patients. For the students a 'crock' was a patient who did not have an identifiable illness. The pursuit of this observation led to a more general examination of the ways in which one group of people (students) in the medical school classified another (patients) in terms of the problems raised by the one for the other.

A case in point

Questions such as 'what do you mean by...?' can become a tool for exploring special vocabularies of the world under study, potentially enabling the researcher to enter rather than merely observe from the other side of the fence. Consider the following extract from a response by an informant to the question, 'Tell me about your work':

> For instance when we encouraged the staff to set up a women's group which was a
> 2 traditional crafts-type group in order to get the women to start coming into the DC – to
> start to get used to the DC surroundings and not to be scared of the noise that was
> 4 going on or of the men wandering in and out with their hands in their pockets – that
> sort of thing – and that to me – although it's just a traditional type of woman's group
> 6 actually had a marvellous spin–off effect – I've got someone who is now wanting to do
> photography – one of the women was doing art and went from there in doing
> 8 woodwork because she wanted to make her own frame for a picture and I think that is
> a big benefit – these women used the DC as a drop in centre – coming in voluntary –
> 10 we now have facilities for female Schedule 11 orders – we didn't until the beginning
> of this year because the place was just too male orientated and as a female PO
> 12 coming into the DC it is one of the things that I am naturally very interested in – and
> yes we do now because now we have the facilities either to incorporate women in a
> 14 group through the DC or to run a completely individual programme – if you can't cope
> with groups you can use the DC and learn from the DC without having to go into a
> 16 group and where women are concerned if they can't cope with the number of blokes
> we have there then certainly we can find an individual programme for them – we
> 18 haven't yet had any Schedule 11 orders for women although I can see them on the
> horizon coming up but we haven't had any so far and that's got a lot to do with the

20 way the justice system treats women – but we don't actually have that many female
   clients in this office – the percentage is very low and therefore the percentage of
22 women that come and do Schedule 11 will be very low too – but at the moment out of
   a total caseload of about 250 in this office 30 are doing Schedule 11 – I don't know
24 what percentage of female clients we have – we have women offenders doing
   Schedule 11 4A one of whom did Money Management and also the crafts group as
26 part of a specific attendance and we have also had women who have done Schedule
   11 4A with alcohol education groups.

Two acronyms are evident in the text: PO (line 11) and DC (lines 2, 3, 9, 12, 14 and 15). When a phrase is signified by its initial letters, or some other form of abbreviation, it is certain that this results from its frequent use by insiders. An abbreviation which initially serves as shorthand becomes a marker which signifies membership or non-membership of the world in which it was generated. To a qualitative researcher PO would be likely to refer to 'participant observation', to a map-reader 'post office' or to those who inhabit a world of women offenders (line 24) 'probation officer'. Similarly DC could variously mean 'direct current' (not likely here), 'detective constable' (very unlikely here since DC seems to be a place), 'detention centre' (a possibility) or its intended meaning in this context 'day centre'. In order to choose the right construct, where there is no possibility of questioning the informant, the researcher needs access to a complete dictionary of alternative meanings and enough clues to select the right context. The problem on the roof was that knowing the context did not indicate one meaning rather than another.

In entering the world of a day centre where men and women offenders complete aspects of their sentence under the supervision of a probation officer we also find that people 'have Schedule 11 orders', 'do Schedule 11' (lines 22–23, 25 and 27) and that in the first two cases it is 'Schedule 11' but in the last two it is 'Schedule 11 4A' that is done. Clearly 'Schedule 11' is important and since its first use is combined with 'orders' we could guess that it has something to do with the type of sentence imposed on the offender by the court. If we ask the question, 'What do you mean by Schedule 11?' the reply will help us to develop our insight into sentences as alternatives to custody at the time in history when the interview was carried out. 'Schedule 11' refers to Schedule 11 of the Criminal Justice Act 1982 which is labelled 'Probation and After-Care'. '4A' (and '4B', not mentioned in the interview) were insertions, specified in the 1982 Act, into Section 4 (day training centres) of the Powers of Criminal Courts Act 1973.

In section 2(3) of that Act (Powers of Criminal Courts Act 1973) for the words 'and 4' there shall be substituted the words '4A and 4B'

The 1982 Act then goes on to describe 4A as a requirement for an offender to (a) 'present himself to a person or persons specified in the order at a place or places so specified' and (b) 'to participate or refrain from participating in activities specified in the order'. 4B is described as a requirement 'to attend at a day centre specified in the order'.

So to 'do Schedule 11 4A' is to attend at a place and to participate in activities – in this example to attend at the day centre and to attend a group looking at money management (line 25) or one involved in education on the use of alcohol (line 27). To 'do Schedule 11', without the specification of 4A or 4B, would presumably require attendance at the day centre, with or without a requirement to participate in activities. The basic question has already led to a consideration of the history of one aspect of the criminal justice system in the 1970s and 1980s. It is also worth noting the way in which the sections of the two Acts are used to create a concept/description of what was done in day centres, that is 'Schedule 11' was done, 'Schedule 11 4A' was done too. No longer! The Criminal Justice Act 1991 changed the pattern of community sentences.

Discussion

Although this technique has clear advantages, the most obvious danger of searching for 'special languages', or focusing on the unusual, is that we miss the 'ordinary'. It may just be that the ordinary, the everyday, the taken-for-granted tells us much, or more, about the social world of those we are studying than does the unusual. For example, the outsider to the world of the day centre would be likely to discover that the ratio of female to male offenders is low and an examination of court statistics might reinforce a view that crime is essentially a male preoccupation.

At face value, then, it points to different numbers of men and women attending the day centre – nothing surprising, it is a numbers issue: 'We don't actually have that many female clients in this office – the percentage is very low and therefore the percentage of women that come and do Schedule 11 will be very low too.' However, the phrase: 'That's got a lot to do with the way the justice system treats women' (lines 19–20), used in the context of a reported lack of Schedule 11 orders for women, led to the most important finding of this piece of research. In response to the question: 'What do you mean – the way the justice system treats women?' a series of steps were taken which led to the discovery that magistrates, male and female, stereotyped women offenders in such a way that sentences which used alternatives to custody, such as community service and Schedule 11 orders, were seen as inappropriate to their stereotyped view of how women spend time. Thus the extent to which researchers are themselves insiders may lead them to miss important issues.

In collecting data for social research there is clearly a variety of stances available for adoption and these are independent of the form the data will take. The dimension which is considered here, for modelling this variety, ranges from polar positions of 'outsider' to 'insider'.

Wherever a researcher meets an 'unusual' word or phrase he or she is marked as an outsider, to some degree. Such terms can be seen to signify belonging for users and exclusion for non-users. This suggests that there will be difficulty for the researcher in taking the role of Other and therefore in 'understanding' the insider/respondent, and that there will be additional difficulty in capturing the insider/respondent's reality as a result of being cast as an outsider. The mutual recognition of the researcher's outsider status by both researcher and respondent can be seen to mark a boundary between their worlds. The extent to which such boundaries become barriers to understanding must be considered.

It should be stated, initially, that the effects of boundaries are not only a problem for researchers; they are an integral part of the process of living our everyday lives. The way we share language enables us to signify our membership of multiple realities and, where we do not understand, our non-membership is similarly signified. Part of the process of moving from non-membership to membership involves learning the words, phrases, accents, gestures, ways of dressing and so on, which signify membership, allow entry and enable the granting, by others, of insider status. For a British-born, English-speaking person, learning a new language so as to pass, for example, as Greek, may take many years with no guarantee of success. For a person beginning a university course it is unlikely to be many weeks before he or she will pass successfully as a student – indeed she/he *is* a student.

In the first case the language boundary stands as a barrier to the researcher whose likely strategy would be to engage the services of an insider as interpreter in order to break through. Whyte (1943), in his classic 'participant observation' study of a street corner gang in Boston, after either being rejected or getting nowhere with his intended research idea following direct attempts to talk to people in Cornerville, was introduced by a social worker to Doc, who became his mentor, guide, sponsor and interpreter.

Whyte also came to realise that he could never pass as a Cornerville person – he was Bill from the university – and when he tried to talk like Cornerville people Doc admonished him, pointing out that he was different and that was how people wanted him to be. Here the researcher was able to notice the unusual because, even though he was an outsider, his sponsor safeguarded and legitimised his presence on the inside.

Wiseman (1970) faced similar difficulties in her study of 'Skid Row alcoholics'. As a woman in a predominantly male world she passed as a woman friend of an alcoholic, and as a woman looking for friends who might be living on Skid Row. She indicated that she dressed down in order to meet the expectations of those she met. She also noted that there were many places where she would have been denied access either as a woman or as a researcher. For these settings Wiseman hired researchers who were more easily able to maintain their presence as observers. In this case the researcher was able to notice the unusual because, although she was an outsider, she was able to maintain her presence in a legitimised 'stranger' role. The interviewer role is just such a legitimised stranger role.

At the opposite end of the continuum is research carried out by a researcher who is already an insider. In this situation there is no barrier for the researcher to break through – there is no boundary to cross. Sanders (1973) reports spending three months researching a pool hall on the west coast of the USA and indicates that in addition to observing as a player and a 'game watcher' he talked to people about what was going on. 'Interviewing was done in such a manner as it was not seen to be "interviewing" by the subjects, in other words, questions concerning features and practices were asked in normal conversations' (p.50). The danger here was that those ordinary, routine, everyday things which are essential to an understanding of the world being researched would remain unnoticed.

There may well be philosophical or value-based reasons which drive the researcher to select a particular point on this insider–outsider continuum but there may well be a case for incorporating the opposite perspective as a routine part of the data-combing process so as to ensure that (1) 'what is taken for granted and unnoticed' by insiders is not lost; or (2) 'what is meaningful' to insiders is brought to the notice of outsiders.

Conclusion

To summarise, one can make a number of statements about the attempt to understand different 'languages':

- Informants know things which researchers want to know.
- Insiders – people who share membership of a partnership, a group, a network or an organisation – also share special vocabularies which enable and enhance communication between insiders.
- Enquiries about the use of such special vocabularies can provide researchers with insights into the 'world-being-researched'.
- Researchers know things which are irrelevant to informants.
- Researchers are also members of groups which share special vocabularies.
- Where researchers use their special vocabularies with informants, communication can be hindered.
- Outsiders as well as insiders can provide valuable insights into the meaning of data.

References

Becker, H.S., Geer, B. and Stauss, A. (1961) *Boys in White*. London: University of Chicago Press.

Sanders, W.B. (1973) 'Pinball Occasions.' In A. Birenbaum and E. Sagarin (eds) *People in Places: The Sociology of the Familiar*. London: Nelson.

Whyte, W.F. (1943) *Street Corner Society*. Chicago: University of Chicago Press.

Wiseman, J.P. (1970) *Stations of the Lost: The Treatment of Skid Row Alcoholics*. Chicago: University of Chicago Press.

CHAPTER 8

Casing the Joint

An Illegitimate Take on a Community of Care

Philip Hodgkiss

Introduction

Have you ever wondered what goes on when you're not around? For my part, and to anticipate your answer, so have I! Such an oblique quandary, however, has not exercised empirical social science overlong. After all, you can't quantify, interview or participant observe an absence or negation. This, by the way, is not the 'not being there' of subsequently discovering what people did or say they did in answer to a questionnaire. Instead, this is the equivalent of participant observation but observation of something you are not with at the time. This might appear to be far-fetched, but we have been placing former patients and inmates at the furthest reaches of our care, from which point we should have been able to take a 'reading'. We appear, however, to have lacked the wherewithal to get our bearings. People (clients) being cared for in the community have been pushed out there into ongoing existential encounters while we have had precious few means of monitoring the situation and little idea of how to 'control' for it theoretically or methodologically.

Monitoring vulnerable people and what they get up to when carers are not, or cannot be, around has begun to exercise the minds of health care professionals (for example, the keeping of a peripatetic diary) but not so, so far, more systematic research 'engines'. As researchers we need to shake off the shibboleth of science: experiment and observe. With regards to observation, in particular, we have to imagine an existence to which we are not party and not a confidante; a world of things going on behind our backs to which we are not witness. From this region we dimly feel the impact of 'elsewhere' working itself out by hearsay, second hand; we may have our suspicions of what is going on or, conversely, not the slightest clue. This is our absence of presence with a world where something untoward comes to pass; a parallel universe where we are turned over *in absentia* by distant intervention. There is a quality of experience and relation unfolding there; *not* suspended animation, though it is hard to distil movement out of such a fleeting world. This is the 'place' it is almost as difficult to describe as time and space without recourse to metaphor. Almost, but not quite! This is the moment your house is burgled or your car stolen, which is best accessed when captured on security cameras. (Of those who saw it, who will ever forget the scenes of the Bulger child being 'abducted' from the shopping precinct.) These 'grainy' pictures are the best shot we have of being with ongoing events when, as we would say, 'we weren't there'. Out of such footage fine-grained analysis of social movement might emerge of that something in the offing – a fait accompli in the making. Certainly, we need to rely on closed-circuit technology, when and where available, but we need to have the nous to think our way into this world 'apart' by every means at our disposal.

The case study

With this in mind, this chapter is based on a reading of the report books of a local authority group home in a metropolitan area taken over an 18-month period (July 1993 to December 1994) during the initial phase of the Care in the Community initiative. The group home is generally acknowledged as a model for other accommodation for users and clients in the city and it is important to take stock of this stage or type of halfway-house provision because the emphasis is increasingly on individual rehabilitation into the community. The report books were chosen as one of the few available records (police reports might have proved comparable) of events and occurrences involving a small group of people in a social setting in a given locality. Technically speaking it involves the use of a documentary source and a hermeneutic approach to the data contained therein (see May 1993; Plummer 1983). The approach to the report books, similar to that with diaries and journals, involves examination of contemporaneous day-by-day entries by two health care professionals whose main aim, unlike the often self-conscious diarist with an eventual audience in mind, is to report what has happened (in so far as it has been witnessed or can be reconstructed) to inform their co-worker of the 'state of play' when they take over. The group home is not permanently staffed, but visited daily by peripatetic social services staff. The report books are, therefore, an indispensable means of information exchange. The group home provides higher dependency accommodation for seven adults with severe and enduring mental illness (men *and* women, ages 16–65). It is located two miles from the city centre in an area of multiethnic composition, situated between old terraced house properties and a large local authority housing estate. Unemployment, poverty and deprivation in the area are high. According to the report books the characteristic features of the group home appear to be: an 'informal' economy of residents taking from each other food and money without consent and a great deal of borrowing (bartering) (there is also the buying of things for others, running up of debts at local shops and losing of money outside); an interpersonal melange of occasional violent exchanges and sexual encounters (often exhibitionism); and the context for indulging in alcohol, cigarettes and occasionally drugs. But most of all it is the only home environment of seven extremely vulnerable people.

There is no mention in the report books of residents (as they are referred to) being part of any structured social activity outside the group home. Apart from visits to day centres and to residents in other group homes (and very occasionally to families of origin), there is no reporting of someone setting out to a gathering or an event or returning from one (visits to public houses are excluded in this definition). It cannot be assumed that this is a nil return, but the actual instances of residents being party to and part of structured social activity during the period under scrutiny must be very few and far between indeed. It might be speculated at this juncture that lack of structured social activity (for example, playing or watching sport, going to the cinema, attending places of worship) among residents is as likely to be highly correlated with institutionalisation, lack of knowledge, skills and role models from families of origin and general disorientation and dislocation in the area itself as it is to individual pathology or a wider social malaise. Once 'placed' in that community the residents live out an ambiguous status: are they to be viewed particularistically (as 'different') or universalistically (as 'the same')? The answer to this in the ongoing context of the community will be much more rough and ready than it will be on case conference agendas. Of course, what is deconstructed here is not uniform by age, gender and ethnicity – there is just one person (elderly male) of Indian subcontinent, Islamic origin. In particular, it is males, young males and young women, who figure in the incidents reported here. Drugs, alcohol and sex play a crucial part of exposure to situations which may result in a reported incident, in addition to any recognised individual pathology or condition. There are differences, then, on the basis of gender and stage in the life-course. However, to characterise the situation as one of predation on the weak and vulnerable would be only partially accurate as several of the incidents resulted from networking with consociates (see below). In addition, there are recorded in the report books what will be described as 'invasive' encounters where the clients' personal social space or their dwelling place is invaded without their knowledge or consent but not always without their duplicity and complicity.

The invasive incidents that occurred in this particular group home, according to the report books, fall into four main types: (1) youth generated; (2) networking; (3) sneak-thieving; and (4) interaction with the local economy. Of course, this data can be cross-cut and sliced in any number of different ways.

1. Youth generated (where youths have been implicated in the account):

    (a) A coping stone thrown through a resident's window. '[a resident]'s windows were smashed by stones that would have killed him had he been in bed [another resident] saw young men running away'. (Police called)

    (b) Youths at the door demanding from the residents something they say belongs to them. (Police called).

    (c) Youths break into the group home's adjacent garage – thought to have been about to set it on fire. (Police called)

    (d) Outside electricity box tampered with; youth seen in the vicinity.

(e) A female resident approached by youth in the street asking her questions about her place of residence.

(f) A gang of youths make fun of a resident in the street.

(g) Another female resident mugged by youth who took her purse. (Police called)

(h) General abusive behaviour by a gang of youths outside the home who pour contents of a bottle through an open window.

2. Network connected (where those involved are known to each other, Schutz's (1967; 1982) term 'consociates' is utilised):

(a) Two men seen trying to prise open a bedroom window – disturbed and ran off (one of them was definitely identified by a resident). (Police called)

(b) A resident alleges that for two months he has been followed from the bus stop back to the group home.

(c) An aggressive, abusive phone call to a resident from an outside consociate – several subsequent calls to the same person.

(d) A young male resident beaten up and hospitalised in a fight with an outside consociate. (Police involvement)

(e) Visits to a resident from a family member thought to have had an abusive relationship with them in the past.

(f) A consociate found banging on the bedroom window of a resident – who was, in fact, ill in hospital.

3. Sneak-thieving (where property or goods are at risk in the group home):

(a) Man came to the group home looking for his pet that had escaped. He returned a second time (nothing came of it – perhaps genuine or perhaps too many people about).

(b) A residents room broken into. (Police called)

(c) Television and video stolen.

4. Interaction with the local economy:

(a) A resident buys an over-the-counter drug which is consumed excessively and detrimentally to her condition.

(b) Several separate incidents of residents running up debts at local shops. (group home staff intervention)

(c) The selling of local authority property by a resident to a second-hand shop.

But is evidence such as this of any value? This has to be a question worth asking in the context of Care in the Community when vulnerable people's well-being might well depend on an informed answer. Even to the extent described here, there is in the report books no other real measure of social process and social relation between the community of the group home, the community of neighbourhood and the wider society than the ones outlined above. After interaction with health care professionals, clinicians, social workers and case managers all other associations and affiliations, interactions and involvements pale in comparison – apart from when they surface in an incident. There is no evidence, then, of any other systematic nexus or points of connection for extended relationships beyond this. The caring comes from health and social work professionals and female members of families at which point such qualitative relationships are exhausted. The trick then appears to be in this case to imagine what might 'go on' when the professional is no longer present. When considering how we might monitor the ongoing experience of 'the residents', the suggestion might arise as to why they should not have kept diaries. Ironically, residents are often not well enough to keep diaries while being well enough to be 'taken for a ride'. An example of this and the kind of thing from which we cannot afford to take our eye, came shortly after the conclusion of the period of study (and not included in the data). The brother of an infamous mass murderer and a drugs baron in his own right picked up one of the residents to go out for a ride in his BMW sports car. The two were old school pals, someone thought. The resident stayed over with the sports car owner and returned to the unit the next day. Shortly afterwards a residential social worker noticed that the client had a severe burn mark on his back. When asked what had happened the answer came back that '– had burned me with an iron because I knocked a cup of coffee over his new carpet' (like a sketch from Monty Python, he had to do it didn't he?). The drug dealer some months later phoned the unit to accuse his 'pal' of stealing his £9000 Rolex wristwatch. What punishment might be in store for their next outing together does not bear thinking about – or does it?

Discussion

Not only is this alter-world of a strange status ontologically for case study research, but also the tenets of sociology and the canons of research method would be rhymed-off at us to confirm why such endeavour is of no use social scientifically whatsoever. What, then, would we have done wrong (apart from exploring vectors of time and space that are apparently out of bounds to us)? It would be acceptable to work up a participant observation or life history study as a unique account of events; a one-off, from which we would not presume to generalise. It would also be fine to take quantifiable and statistically rigorous occurrences that we might generalise from to a wider population (for example, the number of times someone was assaulted). It would certainly be legitimate, too, to draw on hermeneutic techniques, or discourse analysis perhaps, which would problematise the very social construction of a text.

What would not appear to be of much value would be to try to reconstruct from reported events what has actually been going on and then attempt to relate that to a wider-ranging (theoretical) interpretation. That, itself, would undoubtedly constitute an unwarranted escalation to explanation based on, after all, pretty flimsy evidence. Conventional wisdom in social scientific research method advises that we would not be in a position to extrapolate and generalise from the findings of this case study – not even to 'connect-up' with theory. The case study would be viewed as at best an exploratory or pilot study producing a series of snapshots of a situation requiring further explication, with any findings, such as they are, being merely 'suggestive of' further lines of inquiry. There are, however, precedents for attempting to theorise data and evidence at this level of abstraction, ranging from Karl Marx (Marx and Engels 1975–1979) to Mass-Observation (1987) – who had no compunction in rehearsing theory that had not been generated out of their fieldwork in any particular way. It may be all well and good for the likes of Simmel (1964; Simmel and Levine 1971) or Schutz (1967; 1982) to speculate on the form of social relations without the slightest shred of evidence – on strictly empirical terms – but not so the journeyman (*sic*) researcher.

Ironically enough, then, the kind of data generated in this case study might be more trouble than it's worth. Why not just escalate the whole level of abstraction to haute theory and have done with it? No need, then, to get an obdurate real world to fit the theoretical 'facts'. The idea of generating theory from data as a process of discovery was famously promulgated by Glaser and Strauss (1968) as *Grounded Theory*. Though models and ideas can be imported from outside they must be related to the data. Not only is this a case for letting theory develop from data but Glaser and Strauss draw a distinction between *substantive* and *formal* theory, that is, two separate kinds or levels of theory. Substantive theory is an empirical area of sociological enquiry such as patient care (their example) while formal theory is a conceptual area of social thought, an example being the concept stigma. The substantive dimension should, in their view, emerge first, based largely on the comparison of 'facts' with like cases (we might use the number and type of invasive encounters). Concepts and ideas emerge from this process and established formal theories should not be applied prematurely. The evidence contained in the report books is not of sufficient status to warrant substantive comparisons with other data sets. In many senses, such evidence is the first tiny fragment of collateral damage resulting from an encounter 'over the ridge'. There might have been more or less of it depending on circumstance. Even if it were construed as being scattered correspondence from the front line we need to move theoretically into the 'war zone' at the earliest opportunity. To be squeamish about working up theory at a formal level would be like looking, to extend the analogy a final time, at the dead and wounded in a MASH (Mobile Army Surgical Hospital) unit and being unable to dream up 'armed conflict' without going through the process of comparison with other field hospitals elsewhere.

A case study of our type would tend to be viewed ideographically, *sui generis*, and would not, therefore, be a candidate for any nomothetic, generalizing measures. To not make connections with a wider population is one thing but to emphasis internal relations at the expense of acknowledgement of the influence of external relations is quite another. The Chicago school (see Plummer 1983), for instance, tended not to problematise the nature of the social relations of the wider society in order to contextualise their microlevel of analysis. In fact, we would need to come at the case study in question from quite the opposite direction. We would actually need to bring to the situation what we know, as much as we can know anything, about the world. What we need is to be able to establish certain variables early on: biography, social competences, reputation and previous record of the individuals in question, and what we know of images that circulate about mental illness as they relate to gender and 'race'. These things at very least. To this would be added what we can safely assume about the spatio-temporal context. This would include the history of the location, its political and economic dimensions, levels of unemployment and crime, and so on. Certain parameters of the wider society have to be taken for granted; for example, that Britain is an urban, industrial, capitalist, liberal-democratic society. Marx's critique of capitalism would be a major point of reference in this regard, though its finer points will not be rehearsed here. Incorporating this dimension would provide a further object lesson in having to take stock of what goes on when we are not around in order to make sense of the world (that is, capitalist accumulation). Once this level and its emergent properties are established as a direction of influence it is possible to map over it characteristic forms of social relations.

In the wider 'community' of negative identity – characterised by unemployment, poverty, lack of opportunity and the creation of alternative opportunity structures – residents do not participate in the world of production and they are in receipt of various kinds of benefits. This, itself, is not dictated directly by the state of the economy but by their history of ill health. Conversely, in the community there is a high level of unemployment and youth unemployment which may not have been the case historically in times of greater prosperity for the town and region. Thrown together in a 'common' exclusion from the world of work residents and community are living out recognisable social forms: they are failures on universalisable criteria of worth (Parsons and Shils 1952) or in the process of being failed through education; there is the adoption of different (illegitimate) codes for the creation of material life to that of the mainstream, market economy, and; a consequent attenuation of life across time where the structuring of employment and employment relations has receded. In modern, industrialised Britain the need to sell labour power in the creation of material life and shop-floor discipline dictated where people were, that is, in the mill or factory. There is some evidence (Sennett 1986) that not only do people now not know *what* others are (that is, their role) as they did in former times but neither do they know *where* they should be, which is particularly the case with youth not having work or not being in school or college. Settings of public life between the atomised mass (say, a football crowd) and the officers and roles of an organization (for example, a political meeting) have receded. People once came together as individuals to debate issues in public places where such individuals were face to face, cheek by jowl with a social, public world outside of a convened meeting or an organisation (though this was a predominantly male forum and initially a bourgeois perogative). Such levels of semi-spontaneous immediate interaction to deliberate on action in the world have virtually disappeared (Habermas 1989). What has to be taken into account is the context of a transformed public sphere. Although it is beyond the scope of this paper, it is worth noting that after the disappearance of the old working-class community (based on the social relations of employment in capitalist industrialism), residual public space, which is crossed only to arrive at the locus of the community of identity and personal actualisation, has been allowed to become characteristically *consociative* though in a 'cooler', 'emptier' sense than described by Schutz (1967; 1982).

We would need to plot the webs that are woven in the interaction order of the public world, including their points of 'anchor'. The intricacies of this construction would resolve themselves into the relief of characteristic forms of social relations. Coming into this case study work we would have to regard as veridical that forms of social relations are not arbitrary but are replete with the intentions and expectations of institutional settings – or the very lack of them. We have to conceive of an area whose properties are dependent on the locations that make it up; a 'field' of spaces of positions in a historically specific arrangement (see Bourdieu 1993). Though it may be argued that social action will always instantiate the 'field' it can suffice as an analytical construct independently of agency. In accounting for the social world we have to bring to that situation much, if not all, of what we know, and need to take into account the nature of the 'thing' we seek to analyse. One well-rehearsed maxim should be that the disaggregation and reduction of social process into its respective powers will seldom distil its combinative, emergent properties. In this regard, Sayer (1992, pp.241–251) has drawn attention to the distinction made by Harré between *extensive* and *intensive* research designs. The former works with units unconnected relationally but that fall into the 'right' taxonomic category for representativeness and generalisability. Such an approach does not consider the significance of context and spatial location and abstracts from interactional social forms which, *in situ*, weight the outcome in real social situations. In the latter, units may not be of the same order necessarily but are connected to each other relationally with consequent implications for structure and cause. Here, the contingent properties of the social context of relationality is explored as vital for explanation of how things work out in a particular case. Individuals who may have been excluded on taxonomic criteria may come seriously into play in a 'set-piece' conjuncture. Sayer remarks that in some instances 'the unusual, unrepresentative conjuncture may reveal more about general process and structures than the normal one. Rare conjunctures such as experimental communities, social or institutional crises, psychological abnormalities … etc. may lay bare structures and mechanisms which are normally hidden' (Sayer 1992, p.249). Although we should, indeed, guard against over-extended inferences from such an intensive case study as this, there may be virtue here after all.

Conclusion

This case study, then, did not generate data for comparative purposes as might an experiment or quasi-experiment seeking after a cause and nor did it comprise a survey of opinion where the accuracy of descriptive measures is at a premium. Neither was it, as it turns out, an ethnographic-type design such as a participant observation or life-history study where naturally occurring behaviour in a specific context is 'watched over' by the researcher. As a research project the case study tends to fall down on most of the criteria applied to both quantitative and qualitative method. In fact, the evidence was never meant to be revelatory at the level of explanation or description but, instead, provided confirmation that we might be in the right location for a certain kind of interpretation. One of the reasons this case study may not be wholly redundant is because it reports a rumour of the matrix of the spatial world in question and of the social relations that might be mapped over it. Perhaps what the report books enable us to do is to:

imagine social processes represented as tracing out paths in space-time. What happens to objects, whether people or things, depends on contacts and connections made within space-time; where are we in relation to others? Whom are we likely to come into contact with? (Sayer 1992, p.146).

The content and form of the physical and social environment constituting space-time makes a difference to what happens. Within a relative concept of space, constituted by objects having spatial extension, there is room for particular spatial configurations to take shape. Given different elements there will be different potential for movement. The integration of the elements of social forms in space-time is a critical dimension of emergent social relations. Indeed, a case could be made that the study confirmed the ontological status of the research location and its emergent context, with the theoretical edifice to which we might turn being related to that, *not* to the individual fragments of evidence itself in any way. It is ironic that if we were there as eyewitness to an incident that eventually ended up in the report books we would still need to *imagine* the world in which such things take place – might we have guessed it all along?

Note

1 This contribution is dedicated to the irreplaceable David Boulton who, as was his wont, saw the virtue in it.

References

Bourdieu, P. (1993) *Sociology in Question.* London: Sage.

Glaser, B. and Strauss, A. (1968) *The Discovery of Grounded Theory: Strategies for Qualitative Research.* London: Weidenfeld & Nicolson.

Habermas, J. (1989) *The Structural Transformation of the Public Sphere.* Cambridge: Polity Press.

Harré, R. (1979) *Social Being.* Oxford: Blackwell.

Marx, K. and Engels, K. (1975–1979) *Collected Works.* Vols 3–11. London: Lawrence & Wishart.

Mass-Observation (1987) *The Pub and The People.* London: Cresset.

May, T. (1993) *Social Research – Issues, Methods and Process.* Buckingham: Open University Press.

Parsons, T. and Shils, E. (1952) *Toward a General Theory of Action.* New York: Harvard University Press.

Plummer, K. (1983) *Documents of Life.* London: Unwin Hyman.

Sayer, A. (1992) *Method in Social Science.* (2nd edn). London: Routledge.

Schutz, A. (1967) *The Phenomenology of The Social World.* Northwestern University Press.

Schutz, A. (1982) *The Problem of Social Reality, Collected Papers 1.* The Hague: Martinus Nijhoff.

Sennett, R. (1986) *The Fall of Public Man.* London: Faber & Faber.

Simmel, G. (1964) *The Sociology of Georg Simmel.* Translated, edited and introduced by K.H. Wolff. New York: The Free Press.

Simmel, G. and Levine, D.N. (eds) (1971) *On Individuality and Social Forms.* Chicago: University of Chicago Press.

CHAPTER 9

Community Auditing

Appropriate Research Methods for Effective Youth and Community Work Intervention

Carol Packham

Introduction

This chapter seeks to make the case that some research methods are exploitative and deskilling of their subjects, and are therefore inappropriate to use as part of youth and community work practice. It suggests that a community auditing approach is an empowering process and can achieve desirable qualitative outcomes. It will make the case that many of the current research approaches used in community settings, although having specific value, do not meet youth and community work criteria, particularly those of participation, informal education and inclusion. It will chart briefly the development of participatory research methods, and will give examples of participative community audits. The characteristics and uses of community auditing methods, and the advantages and ethical considerations of the participatory process will be discussed.

Community auditing: appropriate research methods for effective youth and community work intervention

There is an increasing need for research in voluntary and statutory youth and community organisations that can give evidence of need or effectiveness of services. Youth and community workers are operating in an increasingly competitive climate, where we are required to justify the work being undertaken to funders (for example, for Single Regeneration Budget baselines), and policy makers, with statistical evidence and 'outcomes'. In addition, students and academics alike are researching our communities and agencies, needing to meet course and university funding requirements. It is therefore timely and necessary to develop and implement appropriate research methods which adhere to the principles and intervention strategies of youth and community work.

The youth and community work courses at Manchester Metropolitan University have taken account of these requirements while being sensitive to the needs of communities, and have developed a 'community auditing' approach to community-based research. Experienced youth and community workers are trained to undertake participative community audits with a youth or community group to enable the development of their knowledge of needs and resources in their community or evaluate their agencies. Through the audit process the participants develop skills, confidence and awareness of micro and macro issues affecting themselves and their communities.

The youth and community worker facilitates an audit process with members of the community group based on negotiation and consultation, sharing their knowledge and skills as part of the agency audit team. Most importantly the focus of the audit is identified by the agency and carried out with its full participation. As an example, a female youth and community worker was informed by a group of young women of their unhappiness with the opening hours of their local family planning clinic. They wondered if other young women felt the same, and wanted to find out the most appropriate times and location for a clinic. The worker helped the group, who became the audit team. They discussed and agreed on appropriate methods and devised a questionnaire for young women in their area. The worker helped them collect information about other family planning facilities in the area and arrange meetings with the relevant health workers. The young women collated their findings and used the results to persuade their councillors and the family planning clinic to alter the opening hours. The young people were best able to identify the needs, and the lack of resources in their area. Not only did the results of the audit bring an improvement in service, but also the process built the self-confidence of the participants, and developed their administrative and research skills and their knowledge of decision making and resources in their community.

What is community auditing?

Audit, a familiar method of financial accounting, is used increasingly to evaluate the effectiveness of service delivery where contracting of work requires providers to give evidence that they are meeting targets, and are using resources efficiently. This is particularly so in the English National Health Service, where clinical and medical audit has become a statutory requirement. The last 20 years have seen a 'proliferation of procedures for evaluating performance' (Strathern 1997, p.305). Power (1997), in charting what he terms the 'audit explosion', warns of the 'audit society' where 'institutionalised checking' has reduced trust, and increased control and regulation (p.213). Although Power is unable to define non-financial audit he, along with Kogan (1986) and Strathern (1997), identifies the main characteristic within many forms of auditing (for example, of academic institutions) of 'accountability'. The notion of accountability 'assumes institutional authority to call an individual or group to account for their actions... it is to be contrasted with responsibility which is the moral sense of duty to perform appropriately' (Kogan 1986, p.26). Power's analysis focuses on the contractual nature of audit, where the verifiability of accountability is crucial, 'making the invisible visible' (Strathern 1997, p.1). For Power, verifiability requires the use of systematically effective, empirical research methods, usually involving external, objective expertise, to authenticate and make reliable the outcomes of the audit:

> Audit has become a benchmark for securing the legitimacy of organisational action in which auditable standards of performance have been created not merely to provide for substantive internal improvements to the quality of service, but to make these improvements externally verifiable via acts of verification. (Power 1997, pp.10–11)

Although Power identifies three approaches to auditing, (self-examination, dialogical/participative, and the external professional), his analysis concentrates on the latter. Halstead (1996) has devised six models of educational accountability, ranging from the 'central control model' (contractual, where the employer is dominant) to the 'partnership model' (where the consumer is dominant). Here, all of those directly affected by a particular decision, or involved in a process (for example, an audit), have a share in decision making and are accountable to each other, not to an outside interest group. The auditing approach advocated here aligns with the partnership and moral accountability models, and with Power's dialogical approach. It is based on audit as having the potential for change through improvement (Strathern 1997), not control through checking.

The original meaning of audit (from the Latin 'audire', to hear) has largely been lost. Auditing has become merely a method of evaluation and accounting, rather than one of 'hearing' people's views, opinions, needs or what resources are available. For the outcomes of youth and community based auditing to be trusted it must include the involvement of the auditee. To enable this it requires the use of participative research methodologies as opposed to traditional research, in which both positivist and ethnographic methods involve researcher control and the 'extraction' of information from those involved (Martin 1994).

The courses at MMU have developed an audit method which embodies youth and community principles and is designed to enable people to 'be heard' throughout the process. This approach is appropriate to be utilised by youth and community workers whose aims are to foster conversation (Jeffs and Smith 1996) and critical dialogue (Freire 1972) as a medium for informal education and challenging oppression. A 'community audit' is therefore a method of evaluation or the obtaining of information useful to and by a community. It can use a variety of research methods, and be carried out by any number of people, the 'community' being any self identified group. Effectively it is a piece of developmental group work using informal education or community development principles.

These principles identify that the 'process' can be as important as the outcome of the audit, that the work is 'concerned with the involvement of people in issues affecting their lives' is carried out 'through collective action' with the aim of 'leading to empowerment of both groups and individuals'. The underpinning values of the work are those of 'confronting discriminatory attitudes and practices; and promoting equality of opportunity' and aiming to 'build skills and confidence of individuals, and capacity in organisations' (Smith 1993). The process should show a commitment to 'self-help' and have a central commitment to change and social justice (Humphries and Truman 1994, p.186).

Appropriate research methods in youth and community work would therefore aim to meet the criteria of:

- the full participation of the community
- a commitment to informal personal, social and political education
- the research process being facilitated and enabled by the youth and community worker as co-researcher.

The importance of participation as a key element is supported by Gough (1992), who places the ability to participate along with the need to avoid serious harm as being commonly desired by all individuals. However, participation has been used to describe varying degrees of involvement by the community, ranging from passive recipients of information to contributing to a consultative exercise and finally to 'self-mobilisation', where the community take independent initiatives (Pretty *et al.* 1995, p.61). The degree of participation sought by youth and community workers falls between Pretty's 'self-mobilisation' and 'interactive participation', where the community participates in joint analysis, 'seeking multiple perspectives and making use of systematic and structured learning processes' (p.61), the community having control over local decisions and so having a commitment to the research and its outcomes.

Applying youth and community work principles to auditing requires that participation does not mean solely the act of taking part in the research process, but in addition the research should be anti-oppressive and inclusive. The onus is on the audit team to enable the participation of community members, actively seeking representation and utilising appropriate research methods. As an example, an evaluative audit of 'specialist' services for a group of adults with learning disabilities was carried out through role-play and drama, the medium chosen by the community to express their experiences. Treleavan (1994) shows the value of participation when discussing collaborative enquiry with women as staff development. She states: 'participation can be empowering as participants engage directly in understanding and acting on issues of concern in their own lives' (p.141).

The educational outcomes of participatory research have been recognised as an important element of the developments in 'co-operative enquiry' (Reason 1994) which have been closely linked with experiential learning. The process of learning through experience is central to informal education, and 'the skills required for this research methodology are already held by youth workers' (De Venney-Tiernan *et al.* 1994, p.137). The youth and community worker enables the participants to view critically what is familiar to them, and purposefully engenders learning opportunities which foster the development of skills and knowledge. The focus on experiential learning encompasses valuing qualitative outcomes and acknowledges that quantitative and scientifically valid outcomes are not necessarily desired or achievable from the process of the communities' participation in this research method.

The role of the worker, then, is crucial in community auditing. They are not researchers who alone make strategic decisions about the focus and direction of the research (Denscombe 1998) but are trained developmental group workers and informal educators. Their role is to facilitate the participative process. Once the agency members have identified the audit focus the worker can help them make informed choices about the appropriateness of methods for collecting information, the value of secondary sources, ethical considerations, who to involve and how. As Haverlock states, 'to be effective change agents (workers) should act as collaborators and not as directors' (in Nicholls 1983, p.17). The rationale for this emphasis on participation is not only that it will develop the skills and knowledge of the participants as well as achieving useful outcomes, but also that participative research is potentially the most accurate method of identifying needs and resources. Importantly, the audit group throughout retains ownership of the information, method and outcomes, not the student/worker/researcher as is the case with many other forms of information gathering. It would be hypocritical for youth and community workers to use methods which flouted community development and informal education principles.

What distinguishes community auditing from other supposedly participatory methods is, first, in addition to participation in the research process the community has identified the focus and methodology of the audit, and should therefore have a sense of commitment to and ownership of the audit and its outcomes. Second, the workers' role is not to identify and control the direction or the focus of the research but to share their skills and knowledge and enable the audit team from within the community to carry out the audit. The comparable methods and outcomes of participatory and non-participatory research are shown in Table 9.1, within which the characteristics of a variety of participatory research methods can be located.

Table 9.1. Characteristics of research approaches	
Participative research/community auditing	**Non-participative research methods**
Agency or 'clients' identify issue to be audited	Researcher (funder/policy maker/ provider) decides area for audit/research
Internal audit team of 'users' or agency workers	Audit research team external to the agency – viewed as experts/professionals
Worker/student informs and enables audit process	Researcher-led process, although consultation may take place
Negotiation of methods; who to audit and how. Compilation of research tools, e.g. writing of questionnaire	Methodology and sample, researcher determined
Agency team carries out the audit research	Researcher carried out audit/research
Local knowledge of information, history and appropriate methods available and utilised	Researcher has limited access to local knowledge
Audit team collates information	Researcher collates information
Audit team prepares appropriate method of reporting back to agency, community and funder (e.g. by video, display, booklet, report, etc.)	Researcher reports to agency/funder/ policy maker/provider
Information obtained and skills acquired through the audit process are owned by the audit team (i.e. the agency and 'users' involved)	Statistical information, increased knowledge and skills benefit the researcher in the main
Evaluation of success of the audit and possibility of ongoing change and further auditing	Unless 'contracted' for further work, cycle of evaluation stops

Health and social welfare research methodologies: consultation or participation?

The growth in demand for customer satisfaction and cost effectiveness has resulted in the emergence of a multitude of auditing and participatory research methods. These developments seek to include consumers in evaluating services. These are mainly consultation exercises and do not meet the informal education/community development criteria or participatory research approach of full 'client' participation. Some research methods, although having historical roots in youth and community work, do not themselves contribute to the process of community development – in particular, community profiling and the social action approach.

Community profiling

Community profiling is a method that has traditionally been used by community workers to identify need and prioritise intervention. While useful in finding out secondary statistical information about a community, profiling is usually a non-participatory process involving subjective interpretation of the data obtained. Twelvetrees (1991), an advocate of the value of profiling as part of the process of 'contact making analysis and planning', suggests:

> to find out what it is like to be a resident in a particular locality it is often quite a good idea to behave like one for a day; to travel across town by bus or approach estate agents about accommodation. If you are working in a disadvantaged area try to find ways of getting a real feel of what it is like to be a person living there. (p.27)

He sees the worker as an information gatherer, and decision maker, and in the main the 'community' are the providers of information. Many youth and community work and applied community studies courses expect students to undertake community profiles, to learn about communities in relation to their needs, resource prioritisation and policy implementation. There may be some value in this approach as an initial perception, but it can be problematic in that it may lead to prioritising work on subjective and perhaps stereotypical perceptions. Additionally, communities become 'over-researched', the information obtained is very rarely 'owned' by them or of benefit to them either through the research process or outcomes. Community profiling approaches rely heavily on the controlling and interpretative role of the researcher and would therefore fall within Power's 'external expert' approach to auditing.

Social Action Approach

The social action approach comes closest to Power's dialogical and participative approach to auditing. It takes as a starting point the 'empowerment' of those involved in the research process. The approach draws heavily on the influences of community development, feminist and disabled people's perspectives, which necessitates an ethnographic approach emphasising collaboration, participation and mutual respect in all stages of the research process. Participants identify and define their needs and the researcher consults on the appropriate methods to be used, and where appropriate 'local' people are trained as 'peer researchers'. However, although advocating a non-hierarchical approach, participation at all stages is not an overriding requirement, and takes place where feasible. It is advocated as a means of enabling service user participation, to ensure the provision of appropriate, needs-led services. The educational benefits of the participatory process are not emphasised and the work is facilitated by a 'professional researcher' not a youth and community worker trained to enable research.

The growth of participative research methodologies

There have been several factors in the growth of participative research methods. First, the development of self- and agency awareness, and the notion that research should not be done solely on the needs (weaknesses) of a community or organisation. It can also be used to take stock of and evaluate the agency or community's own strengths and resources. This approach was developed as part of the British co-operative boom in the 1970s and 1980s, and encouraged a self-help approach to identifying the skills, knowledge and abilities available within communities or projects and enabling these to be aired and shared. For example, a 'social enterprise audit' (Spreckley 1984), is used to evaluate the success or failure of a social enterprise, such as a co-operative.

A second factor is the recognition that 'researcher-led' identification of need is often inaccurate and can lead to the imposition of inappropriate responses (for example, the determining of social policy). The topics and subjects chosen for examination are 'usually dictated by political interest or research or funder priorities', leaving some research 'undone' (Humphries and Truman 1994, p.28). This has been coupled with a growing recognition that the requirement of the self-identification of the needs or issues, that is, what is to be researched, is crucial if there is to be a move away from traditional 'needs assessment', often based on positivist, quantitative research data. As Croft and Beresford (1996) state:

> while needs assessment draws on people's view, in practice this seems only to inform and complement…services existing perceptions and policies. Clearly this is a step out of the department's own cocoon, but it certainly is not any kind of partnership or involvement. (p.180)

Third, there is a recognition that research which is aimed primarily at 'needs assessment' rather than examining the social construction of issues, is not challenging discrimination, rather it perpetuates the exclusion of particular groups and individuals. As Gough (1992) states, 'needs are defined by those with power, whether experts, men, whites, the able bodied, and are imposed on the powerless … a needs based strategy, far from being a path to liberation, is all too often a source of oppression' .

Additionally, researchers such as Humphries and Truman (1994) argue that who, as well as what, is to be researched is a crucial consideration. Early feminist research (see Roberts 1981), strove 'to "add women" to the previously male dominated view of the world' (Morris 1995, p.211). Truman (1994) argues that research which has sought to add marginalised groups' experience to dominant ideologies, enables these experiences to be viewed as alternative and 'sensitive' topics, or as being deviant. These areas are therefore made vulnerable to be 'picked off' and will still exist outside the dominant thinking. She suggests that what is required is a redefinition of the 'problem'. The social model of disability developed by the disabled people's movement demonstrate this redefinition of the 'problem'. In the medical model the individual's impairment is problematised, whereas in the social model there is a recognition that disabilities stem from society's failure to meet the requirements of disabled people.

This view is developed by Oliver (1992) who argues that traditional positivist and empiricist research paradigms are oppressive and alienating to many research subjects, often disempowering people and not leading to any improvement of their material conditions. He argues for 'emancipatory research', which includes people's self-definition, and where the 'researcher and researched become the changer and the changed' (p.107). Here, in order to challenge power relations, researchers must 'put their knowledge and skills at the disposal of the research subjects' (p.111).

Fourth, the actual methods of collecting information have been recognised as being discriminatory, resulting in demands for the 'revolutionising' of how research is done (Morris 1995, p.211). This means building in methods to create 'space ... for the absent subject' (p.217) to be heard and included. Research using hermeneutic principles, where the value of engaging and understanding social life is central, has used approaches such as storytelling (see Wilkins, Chapter 12, this volume) where, for example, groups of women, from their personal starting point (perhaps with a particular focus, such as a workplace), begin to see common themes emerging and can move towards ways of responding.

Last, writers have criticised the value of research that has not had the participation of the research subject. Heron's (1971) idea of 'co-operative experimental inquiry' is based on the assumption that 'persons are self determining' and that participation in inquiry can aid in a process of 'education and self development'. Reason (1994) develops this: 'those involved in the research are both co-researchers, who generate ideas about its focus, design and manage it, and draw conclusions from it; and also co-subjects, participating with awareness in the activity that is being researched' (p.41). Not only should the participants learn from their involvement in the research process, but they can also recognise that participation is crucial to ownership of, and commitment to, the research. Motivation is increased if participants have an understanding of the area of action and, as Haverlock (1969) has stated, self-initiated and self-applied innovation will have the strongest user commitment and the best chance of long-term survival.

The method of auditing that MMU youth and community workers are trained to use holds similarities to Heron's (1971) 'co-operative enquiry', incorporating Freire's (1972) notion of critical dialogue. Like 'Participatory Learning and Action' (Pretty et al. 1995) research methods (for example, Participatory Rural Appraisal), an underlying principle is the full participation of those who are normally regarded as the 'subjects' of research. The research is seen as a learning process that is facilitated by the worker with the aim of bringing about change. This may be individual, through capacity building and increased level of awareness, and on an organisational and community level. Participation is not only central to the educational principles of youth and community work, but it is also crucial if we are to avoid mis-identification of needs, community issues and resources. Heron (1985) describes a co-operative research cycle (as outlined by Wilkins in Chapter 1 of this volume), involving the participants in three types of 'knowing', propositional, practical and experiential. As an example, a group of young people excluded from school wanted to explore if their feelings of alienation and dissatisfaction with school were shared by other young people still attending school. They wished to challenge being labelled as deviant, and to find a way of having a voice. The youth and community worker enabled the group to identify how best to gather this information and present their findings (this initial stage of exploring of ideas being Heron's propositional knowledge stage). The group carried out informal videotaped interviews (feeling written questionnaires were excluding) in a number of locations where young people met, both in and out of school (Heron's practical knowledge stage). The results of their research were edited into a video by the young people and shown in schools and youth clubs to raise issues about school with staff, and to encourage pupils' participation through school councils (the 'deep' engagement in the research activity and the opening up to new experiences being Heron's stage of experiential knowing). The young people retained ownership throughout the process of their community audit, and were able to challenge their 'excluded' experience, and to use their findings to inform and empower themselves and other young people. Without such participation of the research 'subject', and resulting failure to engage in the cycle of co-operative enquiry, Heron (1988) argues that traditional methods are not only epistemologically unsound, but they also contribute to the impoverishment of the world.

Uses of participatory community auditing

Agencies who took part in participatory community audits facilitated by youth and community workers in training were asked to identify if the audit had been a useful tool, enabling participation and equipping the agency to continue the cycle of audit. From evaluation of 230 community audits involving audit teams from a range of statutory and voluntary projects, it was apparent that the method was invaluable to the agencies both in terms of educational process and usable outcomes. The feedback showed that the method could be used to achieve a variety of outcomes:

- *Identifying skills.* A group of young people attending a school exclusion project carried out a skills audit using a simple questionnaire to identify their existing skills and skills gaps in relation to 'the world of work'. The audit helped them identify strengths and weaknesses, and to network with other agencies. It also helped the agency target ways to develop the young people's skills for employability.

- *Evaluation of a service.* A group of Bangladeshi young people at a youth centre in Oldham carried out an audit to assess if local facilities were meeting the needs of young Bangladeshi people.

- *Identifying ways of improving a service.* An audit was carried out by 'New Deal' participants to inform a further education college 'of the views and needs of prospective New Deal clients' to enable the college to plan appropriately.

- *Confirming hunches.* Young people 'dropping in' to a city centre project audited the need and appropriateness of counselling services for young homeless people which 'confirmed a need we had previously suspected existed' (project co-ordinator).

- *Enabling people to be heard.* An audit carried out with immigrant men in Helsinki in relation to their training and education needs gave 'voices to the group and maybe for the first time has given the possibility for the group to tell their needs' (social services officer, Adult Education Centre).

- *Identifying needs.* Youth and community workers were employed to carry out an audit with 'excluded' young people in a 'Single Regeneration Area' in Manchester to help set a realistic qualitative baseline from which to target resources and measure change. Five hundred young people were involved in a range of agency and detached settings, using focus groups, audit teams, drama, art, video and residential methods.

- *Evaluating the impact of local and national policy.* A group of young people in an accommodation project in Bolton assessed the likely impact of housing benefit cuts.

- *Identifying resources.* A local amenities group audited community resources (people as well as services) in their area, to help improve local communication and access to facilities.

- *Directing funding and resourcing.* A group from a youth centre in Shropshire carried out an audit of young people's needs and interests to enable them to plan a range of activities on a set budget.

- *Meeting contractual obligations.* Providing information on the uptake and success of contracted services.

- *Establishing new initiatives.* A group of 'victims and bullies' in a secondary school carried out an audit of students on their experiences of bullying and possible responses. They used questionnaires and poems, prose and video to express their feelings. The results were given to the school in an 'anti-bullying' presentation and served to 'increase their self-esteem and confidence and give them "status" in front of their audience' (teacher), as well as informing the school's new anti-bullying initiative.

- *Determining policy.* University tutors have been involved in a large-scale audit with young people and workers from several school and project sites in an area of Manchester. The aim was to 'establish young people's views, needs and feelings about aspects of their lives as Moss Siders and their perceptions of their future and that of Moss Side itself' (Kenny and Cockburn 1997, p.4). The foci of the audit were negotiated with the young people, who were involved in the process throughout, and results of the audit were used to help determine future policy, particularly in relation to the delivery of services for young people.

Blocks to participatory community auditing

To prepare for community auditing it is important to think about possible blocks, and how to overcome or avoid them. The 'lead-in' time, particularly in relation to using youth and community principles is crucial for successful participatory research. Initial resistance could be the result of a lack of understanding of what the term means and what the process will involve. Part of the worker's role is to clarify the method of work and to identify the advantages to the agency and individual participants. The agency workers may feel it is easier and quicker to do the work themselves, and this may indeed be the case. From the outset it is important to be aware that, as with all developmental processes, this method of community auditing, if it is to be truly negotiated and participatory, will be slow and therefore 'expensive' in researcher effort (Humphries 1995, p.74). Participation of a voluntary nature should not be viewed as a low-cost option, the audit requiring resourcing both in relation to worker time, physical space and administration. For the work to be effective the agency has to be committed to support its resourcing and to the participatory nature of the work. All workers need to be informed and committed to the approach even if not involved directly, and ideally the ethos of the agency should support participation. Without these commitments the potential for change is reduced. The project on bullying described above had a number of benefits of the young people's involvement in the audit group work, where discussion, teamwork, research design and presentation skills were invaluable. The benefits for the school were that the youth worker 'occupied' a group of 'problematic' young people. Sadly, the methods of informal education and the findings of the work were viewed as marginal to the didactic teaching of the school and the priorities of the governing body.

Managers are often unwilling to relinquish power. It has to be recognised that there are likely to be many people who have entrenched attitudes that are opposed to participation, for professional, practical and political reasons. Attitudes of health and welfare personnel may be reinforced by the structures of large-scale and inflexible organisations. We have to work with 'issues of power, of oppression, of gender ... so we are confronted with ... the hostility or indifference of our organisational contexts' (Reason 1994, p.2). The audit team has to recognise institutional constraints and to be aware of their own perspectives and biases, 'and the limitations of our skills' (p.2), and to seek to make the audit as representative as possible.

People's experiences or knowledge of focused, researcher-led positivist models and methods of research may have engendered a sense of powerlessness and 'unskilling', in relation to professional experts. Other factors may be related to people's experiences of previous research or consultation, which may have been negative or unproductive. Community members may be hampered by an overemphasis on the technicalities of the 'method' of the research as opposed to the group process and potential benefits of participation. There may be a general apathy in the community or agency, or a fear of what is perceived as 'activism' and change. The voluntary nature of participation in many youth and community work settings may also result in a changing or reducing audit team, who may not have the ability or experience of a regular commitment to teamwork. In some agencies the nature of the 'user group' may make ongoing participation problematic, as in detached and street work, and work with drug users with erratic lifestyles. There may also be divisions within the agency or community which may work against a truly representative and participative audit, where for example the agency's users all come from one part of the community, geographically or in relation to interest/experience. The audit may also raise unexpected issues. The work with young women evaluating the family planning service cited earlier was represented in the local press as promoting under-age sex and led to intervention by the local MP – a truly educational experience!

To overcome these blocks the facilitator and audit group should be sensitive to their existence, and incorporate methods to deal with them. It is vital that the people involved in the work see that it is a positive process of innovation with the intention of improvement and possibly change, from which they will benefit. Recognising that many people feel comfortable with the existing situation and may be reluctant to change, participants may usefully carry out a 'SWOT' exercise (an exploration of their Strengths, Weaknesses, Opportunities and Threats). This can help identify the advantages and disadvantages of their own and agency involvement, and what may need to be overcome to enable the audit to succeed. For example, members of the community or agency are most likely to know who are the 'gatekeepers' of information and resources. They will know if there is a history of previous research which may influence the response to and therefore method of the audit, and they are the most likely people to have access to information about 'community assets'. It is also important to recognise that facilitating people through an educational process of 'empowerment' and articulation involving 'critical dialogue' is potentially threatening, both for the recipients and the participants. A critical examination of agencies, communities and services potentially can result in the exposing of hidden truths, and has to be seen as part of a positive process towards change and improvement. It should therefore be recognised that 'support structures for effective community action, (such as training, workers and resources) are crucial, particularly in those communities already alienated and disempowered by disadvantage and discrimination' (Lynn Brown, community audit worker, Salford 1996).

Ethical considerations in community auditing

Although community auditing has many advantages over other research approaches used in youth and community work, the participatory nature of the work has potential difficulties which the audit team should consider. Participation as a concept is problematic, particularly in relation to policy making: 'it is an idea whose development is restricted, whose role is ambiguous, and whose focus has been limited' (Croft and Beresford 1996, p.190). This, coupled with a non-empirical approach to research, has meant that the nature and value of the method has to be clearly stated and understood.

Consideration of research ethics is particularly important as the auditors will be collecting what is often sensitive, qualitative information. The guaranteeing of confidentiality and the ownership of information may be crucial to the progress and success of the audit, and may need to be clarified at the outset of the partnership. The benefits of the participative process should be made clear and unrealistic expectations of the results of the audit avoided. For example, if young people are asking other young people what facilities they would like in their area, they should be aware that all (if any) of their wishes will not be granted due to financial constraints, Government priorities and so on. The discussion of these issues is part of the educational process.

Keogh argues participation is not necessarily an empowering process; it can be tokenistic, and 'a manipulative tool to engage people in a pre-determined process, an expedient way to achieve results, or an attempt to support a democratic, empowering process' (Keogh 1998, p.187). The mercenary or 'extractive' approach to participatory research is demonstrated where participation ceases after the data collection phase. It may be that the audit group has lost interest, or has insufficient time or knowledge to complete a complex analysis or, as Naponen (1997) suggests, that workers do not 'believe participants are able to manipulate and analyse their own data' (p.37). For the research to be truly participatory rather than extractive the worker has to make the analysis stage 'accessible and useable' for the community.

Additionally, the 'bottom up' approach to needs auditing can be problematic if the audit group has not taken an anti-discriminatory approach and attempted to 'give a voice' to all who should be involved in, or considered by, the audit – the issue of representativeness. Often those who have the loudest voices are heard rather than a 'genuine distillation of the perspectives of the wider community' (Murtagh 1999, p.189). It is therefore important that the composition of the audit team, who is to be audited, and how, are considered, to avoid advantaging those 'already privileged in a group, or those groups with more resources' (Gough 1992, p.13).

Community audits of the scale undertaken by youth and community workers cannot usually be used to establish 'common criteria of welfare' (1992, p.13) on which policies can be based, or to claim representativeness and thus generalisation (Denscombe 1998). However, they can be used to complement or challenge other research findings, often adding a more qualitative dimension. The adding of such information to the triangulation process for comparison of findings can be contentious if outcomes make contradictions apparent. An example is where needs identified by the clients are found to be different from client needs perceived by the organisation, its workers or funders.

The benefits of the community audit approach are multi-faceted, with outcomes for the individuals involved, the agency/service and the wider community. The individual participants have the opportunity to be heard, to act upon felt needs, with the possibility of influencing policy and practice. They may also develop knowledge about their community, about networking, research methods, the provision of services and decision making. Through the actual carrying out of the audit they may have developed skills such as typing, researching secondary information and inter-personal abilities (for example, interviewing).

The value to the agency or service can be seen in relation to 'capacity building' within the agency and in relation to its community. It will benefit from the enhanced skills and knowledge of its members, and by using developmental groupwork methods the audit can develop cohesion and group identity within the agency. The outcomes of the work should form part of an ongoing process of evaluation, and can help prioritise needs and issues, the effective allocation of resources and applications for funding, thus influencing agency policy and delivery of services. The agency may be able to identify volunteers, activists and other resources within the community. The agency's profile will also be raised through increased awareness of its services resulting from the process of participation and consultation.

The implications for the wider community are that it should be better informed and resourced, and will have enhanced facilities and communication through improved networking and co-operation.

Conclusion

Youth and community workers in the UK are working in an increasingly finance- and outcomes-led environment. There are increasing demands for their work to be accountable. There is therefore a need, and often a requirement, to evaluate and audit their work. The importance of auditing for youth and community workers was shown by Erault (1995) who, when mapping the English Youth and Community Service, identified 'planning and evaluation in consultation with stakeholders' (p.28) as being one of the competencies required for youth and community workers. In addition, there is a need for community based research that recognises the 'context of deepening inequality, poverty and social exclusion' (Humphries and Truman 1994, p.xii) within which we work, and that uses anti-discriminatory principles. Participative research based on youth and community work principles allows communities an 'active involvement in challenging assumptions based on unequal social relations, through reflexive, explicitly committed participation in the process of social change' (Truman and Humphries 1994, p.14). These issues are central to the renewed emphasis on citizenship and democracy (Crick 1998) which seeks to encourage social and moral responsibility, community involvement and political literacy. Participatory research within a youth and community work framework can engender these qualities.

It is therefore important that managers, resource holders and providers of services are aware of the range of research methods available and the need to identify those which sit most comfortably with an approach as agents of informal education, community development and change. As with all challenging and developmental work we need to work with the issues and requirements of the participants, recognising that effective lead-in time, coupled with the commitment to participation, are crucial to the successful process and outcomes of the audit.

The method of community auditing advocated here meets the youth and community work criteria of participation, informal education and anti-discriminatory practice. It therefore has advantages over other research methods for facilitating youth and community development. The British Council of Churches (1985) report, *Faith in the City*, argued that the only way of overcoming powerlessness is to create new means by which people can be brought together to define their own local issues and begin to work with them. I suggest that community auditing is one such means.

References

British Council of Churches (1985) *Faith in the City: Report of the Archbishop of Canterbury's Commission on Urban Priority Areas*. London: Church House.

Crick, B. (1998) *Education for Citizenship and the Teaching of Democracy in Schools*. London: Qualifications and Curriculum Authority.

Croft, S. and Beresford, P. (1996) 'The politics of participation.' In D. Taylor (ed), *Critical Social Policy*. London: Sage.

De Venney-Tiernan, M., Goldband, A., Rackham, L. Reilly, N. (1994) 'Creating collaborative relationships in a co-operative inquiry group.' In P. Reason (ed) *Participation in Human Inquiry*. London: Sage.

Denscombe, M. (1998) *The Good Research Guide*. Buckingham: Open University Press.

Erault, M. (1995) Consultation Document in Mapping the Youth and Community Service: Preparatory Study to explore the scope for NVQ standards for Youth and Community Work. Unpublished paper for Her Majesty's Government.

Freire, P. (1972) *Pedagogy of the Oppressed*. Harmondsworth: Penguin.

Gough, I. (1992) 'What are human needs?' In J. Percy and I. Sanderson (eds) *Understanding Local Needs*. London: Institute of Public Policy Research.

Halstead, M. (1996) 'Accountability and values.' In D. Scott (ed) *Accountability and Control in Educational Settings*. London: Cassell.

Haverlock, R. (1969) *Planning for Innovation Through Utilization of Knowledge*. London: Centre for Research of Scientific Knowledge.

Heron, J. (1971) *Experience and Method: An Inquiry into the Concept of Experimental Research*. Human Potential Research Project, University of Surrey.

Heron, J. (1985) 'The role of co-operative inquiry.' In D. Boud, R. Keogh and R. Walker (eds) *Reflection: Turning Experience into Learning.* London: Kogan Page.

Heron, J. (1988) 'Impressions of the other reality: A co-operative inquiry into altered states of consciousness.' In P. Reason (ed) *Human Inquiry in Action.* London: Sage.

Humphries, B. (1995) *Understanding Research.* London: Whiting & Birch.

Humphries, B. and Truman, C. (eds) (1994) *Rethinking Social Research.* Aldershot: Avebury.

Jeffs, T. and Smith, M. (1996) *Informal Education: Conversation, Democracy and Learning.* Derby: Education Now Books.

Kenny, S. and Cockburn, T. (1997) *The Moss Side Youth Audit Final Report.* Manchester: Manchester Metropolitan University.

Keogh, N. (1998) 'Participatory development principles and practice.' *Community Development Journal 33,* 3, 187–196.

Kogan, M. (1986) *Educational Accountability: An Analytical Overview.* London: Heinemann.

Martin, M. (1994) 'Developing a feminist qualitative research framework: Evaluating the process.' In B. Humphries and C. Truman (eds) *Rethinking Social Research.* Aldershot: Avebury.

Morris, J. (1995) 'Personal and political: A feminist perspective on researching physical disability.' In P. Potts, F. Armstrong and M. Masterson (eds) *Equality and Diversity in Education 2*: National and International Contexts. London: The Open University/ Routledge.

Murtagh, B. (1999) 'Listening to communities: Locality research and planning.' *Urban Studies 36,* 7, 181–193.

Naponen, H. (1997) 'Participatory monitoring and evaluation.' *Community Development Journal 32,* 1, 30–48.

Nicholls, A. (1983) *Managing Educational Innovations.* London: Unwin Education.

Oliver, M. (1992) 'Changing the social relations of research production.' *Disability, Handicap and Society 7,* 2, 101–114.

Power, M. (1997) *The Audit Society: Rituals of Verification.* Oxford: Oxford University Press.

Pretty, J.N., Guijt, I., Scoones, I. and Thompson, J. (1995) *A Trainer's Guide for Participatory Learning and Action.* London: International Institute for Environment and Development.

Reason, P. (ed) (1994) *Participation in Human Inquiry.* London: Sage.

Roberts, H. (ed) (1981) *Doing Feminist Research.* London: Routledge & Kegan Paul.

Smith, J. (1993) Community Development Foundation Presentation, Leeds.

Spreckley, F. (1984) Community Co-operatives (a two-day workshop), Beechwood College, Leeds.

Strathern, M. (1997) "Improving ratings": Audit in the British university system.' *European Review 5,* 3, 305–321.

Treleavan, L. (1994) 'Making a space: A collaborative inquiry with women as staff development.' In P. Reason (ed) *Participation in Human Inquiry.* London: Sage.

Truman, C. (1994) 'Feminist challenges to traditional research: have they gone far enough?' In B. Humphries and C. Truman (eds) *Rethinking Social Research.* Aldershot: Avebury.

Truman, C. and Humphries, B. (1994) 'Rethinking social Research: Research in an unequal world.' In B. Humphries and C. Truman (eds). *Rethinking Social Research.* Aldershot: Avebury.

Twelvetrees, A. (1991) *Community Work.* London: Macmillan.

CHAPTER 10

Documentary and Text Analysis
Uncovering Meaning in a Worked Example
Steve Morgan

Introduction

The purpose of this chapter is to explore the potential of document analysis for research purposes and to introduce a particular theoretical method. It begins with a brief summary of the main methodological approaches before identifying discourse analysis as the focus of a worked example. This is a comparison of the text of two documents which construct the causes and meaning of delinquency from two very different viewpoints. It is hoped that the use of a worked example will help to demystify and render concrete, in an economic manner, the use of theoretical terms and constructs.

Examination of a range of contemporary texts of research methodology (Atkinson and Coffey 1997; Prior 1997; Silverman 1993) reveals that the words 'text' and 'document' are frequently undifferentiated and are usually 'taken as read' in that authors offer no explicit definition of these terms. Their meaning is presented as self-evident. Within linguistics and language research, the word 'text' has acquired a specific sense as 'any product whether written or spoken' (Fairclough 1992, p.4) but also extended, particularly where the method is discourse analysis, to 'cover other symbolic forms such as visual images and texts which are a combination of words and images' (p.4).

For the purpose of this chapter, it appears important to identify working definitions for both words. Text refers to the concrete products (distinct from oral utterances) of discursive practices in a broad sense: books, articles, transcripts, TV and movies, photographs and cartoons which, borrowing from Stanley's (1992) term, are representations of a knowing and artful kind. 'Document' refers to a more limited physical object. Documents use forms of printed language upon paper or other similar surfaces and electronic signs within computers to create storable records of lives and experiences, identities, social practices and imaginative creations.

Texts need not be documents but documents contain texts. Analysis is therefore of the document as text. Such documentation is pervasive in advanced contemporary societies and, as a central practice of bureaucracies, defines personal, social and occupational identity. It is a major vehicle for the creation of technologies and relations of power (Foucault 1972). Many occupational groups, particularly those involved in people work (social workers, the police, health professionals), are defined by their documentation (Atkinson and Coffey 1997).

Given this significance, it appears incomprehensible that so little emphasis has been given to the systematic study of texts and documents in research methodology in the social sciences. Where such analysis has been part of research it has tended to be a secondary adjunct or a supportive method in a triangulation of approaches whose primary focus is on talk-based and observational investigation.

This chapter starts from the premise that the theoretically informed critical analysis of texts and documents should be recognised as a central and valuable element in social research. This recognition does not deny that, as with all forms of research, the method has its inherent contradictions and problems. Approaches to analysis are based within different research paradigms so that there is no single coherent approach to analysis which is self-evidently 'true'. Document analysis is as much bound up in political and ideological disputes as is all social research. There are three major approaches to analysis.

Semiotic analysis of narrative and narrative structures (approaches to telling stories) using socio-linguistic methods are based on the work of de Saussure (1974) and Barthes (1967) and subsequent analysts (Hawkes 1977; Propp 1968). Their primary emphasis is on language systems and narrative structures, seeking to identify whether there are certain common organising ways of representing meaning.

Ethnographic analysis places its central emphasis on issues of authenticity, credibility and representativeness (Garfinkel 1967; Hammersley 1992; Hammersley and Atkinson 1983). Key questions concern the extent to which documents represent reality (the intention for those who produce documents) as well as their social organisation: the context and process of their production and use and the contribution this makes to an understanding of their meaning as social artefacts. Ethnographic approaches have tended to concentrate on the study of files produced by bureaucracies and on the problems of the production of official statistics as representations of social reality (Cicourel 1968; Gubrium and Buckholdt 1982; Prior 1987).

These two approaches to documentary analysis use a variety of methods summarised in a recent paper (Atkinson and Coffey 1997) by the word 'audit'. Techniques of agent categorisation, classification and counting are common. A well-known example is MCD (membership categorisation devices) (Sacks 1992). There is a tendency for the research techniques to 'cross over' between the socio-linguistic and ethnographic approaches.

The third approach is the analysis of texts and documents as representations of discourse and discursive practice. Foucault (1972), the initiator and most influential exponent of the method, argues that, unlike other forms of language analysis, his interest is not based on the identification of rules but on the question: 'how is it that one particular statement appeared rather than another?' (p.27) and what must be related, in a particular discursive practice, for such and such an enunciation to be made, for such and such a concept to be used, for such and such a strategy to be organised (p.74).

A subsequent crucial issue related to these questions, is that of the status and credibility of statements and the way in which these are related to other supporting or conflicting discourses. Foucault argues that such an analysis, in refusing to privilege discourses of the powerful, creates a space for the release of 'an insurrection of subjugated knowledge' (Foucault 1980, p.81).

The very existence of a document testifies to its coherence as a text 'simply because it is there' (Prior 1997, p.66). In his references to archaeology as a critical metaphor, Foucault (1980) suggests a function of analysis as excavation, working through deposits of meaning, identifying the linkages and relations between the elements of discourse, the social actors and social practices which create the discursive practices of which the document and text is a product.

Methodology

Discourse analysis is the chosen theoretical basis for this paper and, in terms of its practical method, draws primarily on the work of Fairclough (1989; 1992) and Smith (1990). An important characteristic of documents as texts is developed by Smith who analyses their 'active' nature, referring to their capacity 'to be seen as organising a course of concerted social action' (1990, p.21). She goes on to argue that:

> The investigation of texts as constituents of social relations offers access to the onto-logical ground of institutional processes which organise, govern and regulate the kind of society in which we live, for these are to a significant degree forms of social action mediated by texts. (pp.121–122).

Alongside this approach, some techniques drawn from linguistic analysis will also be used where these are helpful and appropriate. Two properties of documents: intertextuality and interdiscursivity will form the basis of the analysis.

Intertextuality refers to the property of documents to contain explicit and implicit references to or 'snatches of' pre-existing or anticipated documents which are yet to be produced. Fairclough (1992) argues that the capacity for interplay between the texts of such documents is not unlimited or arbitrary. It is dependent on relations of power and credibility between document producers, whether they are identified individuals or anonymous and corporate authors within bureaucratic agencies. Such an analysis stresses the interdependence of documents and texts and the difficulty of comprehending meaning in one example without relating it to the context of other documents within the discourse.

Interdiscursivity is closely linked to intertextuality and refers to the configuration of conventions which create the conditions for document production, distribution and consumption. Figure 10.1 illustrates the key elements for analysis.

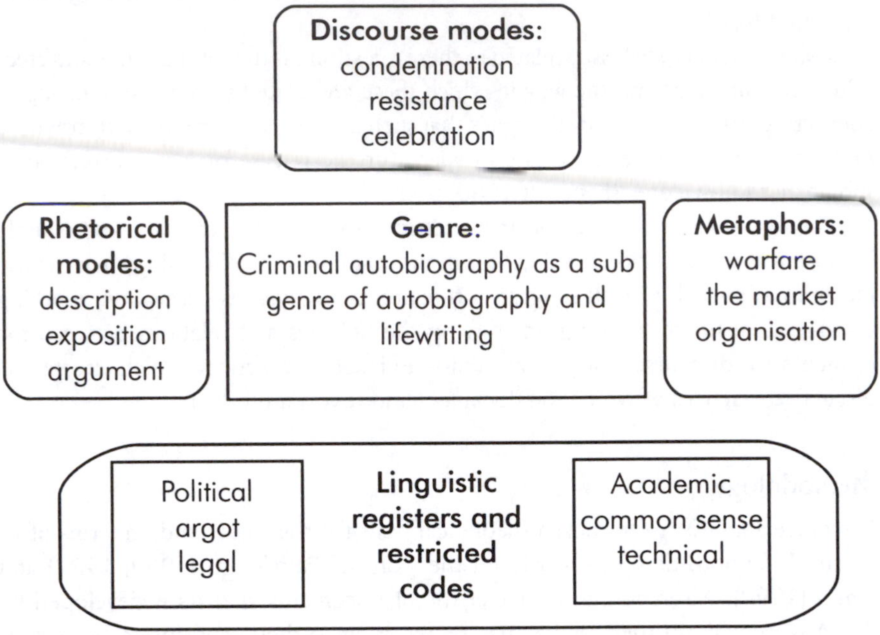

Discourse modes:
condemnation
resistance
celebration

Rhetorical modes:
description
exposition
argument

Genre:
Criminal autobiography as a sub genre of autobiography and lifewriting

Metaphors:
warfare
the market
organisation

Political
argot
legal

Linguistic registers and restricted codes

Academic
common sense
technical

Figure 10.1 Criminal autobiography: intertextual relations and the context of discursive relations.

At the centre is 'genre', a relatively stable set of conventions constituting the type of document with its specific textual conventions and format. A 'particular configuration of genres in particular relationships to each other' (Fairclough 1992, p.126) constitutes a system. For the purpose of this chapter the examples of genre are criminal autobiography and a populist monograph on juvenile delinquency, both of which are located within the system of discourses of criminal justice.

The texts of documents within this system represent three possible dominant modes of discourse on crime and criminality, namely condemnation, resistance and celebration. These are produced using rhetorical modes of description, exposition and argument which are emphasised by characteristic metaphors. In the case of contemporary criminal justice these tend to be dominated by metaphors based on warfare, the free market and the organisation as machine. The system also has its characteristic linguistic registers and restricted codes ranging from criminal argot through ideological common sense to complex legal and academic language.

The complexity of the discursive relations between social actors, social practices and discursive practices is illustrated in Figure 10.2 which is a development of a diagram in Fairclough (1992, p.73).

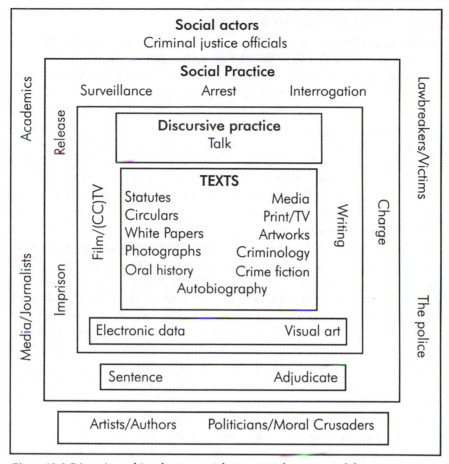

Figure 10.2 Discursive realtions between social actors, social practices and discursive practices

This reveals the intricacy and richness of possible relationships and the multiplicity of potential influences upon the production and consumption of texts and documents. In this case these are often fiercely contested and the question of hierarchies of credibility is frequently problematic.

A critical and characteristic aspect of this are the invariably rigid and oppositional relationships between groups of social actors and the nature of the ontological positions they adopt. The voices and accounts of offenders are regularly discounted and ignored by the official discourse (Burton and Carlen 1979) of criminal justice officials, politicians and the media. The dominant discursive mode is condemnation; the characteristic metaphors those of warfare: 'a militarised discourse of criminality, built around the metaphor of criminals being "at war" with society, and society having to "mobilise forces" to "fight them off" (Fairclough 1992, p.130). Discourses of resistance are subject to constant denigration while those of celebration tend to be confined to crime fictions.

Analysis of extracts from two documents

The first extract (Appendix 1) is from a criminal/prison autobiography (Probyn 1977) and describes a first appearance by the author before a juvenile court in East London during the Second World War and his understanding of its subsequent impact on him. The second (Appendix 2) is a passage from a populist monograph on juvenile delinquency (Jones 1945) written by a magistrates' clerk working in London during the period contemporaneous with the events described by Probyn. Both describe the process of the creation of a delinquent. The subtitle of Probyn's book is *The Making of a Criminal*. The intention of this chapter is to explore the intertextual relationship between the extracts to investigate the ways in which the discourses within them 'feed off' and confront each other, the official ideological discourse of Jones seeking to establish an authoritative meaning of delinquency which is resisted by Probyn's personal testimony.

To help the reader, the lines of the two extracts (Appendices 1 and 2) have been numbered to clarify the references used in the analysis. Identification of the discursive practice related to both documents, their production, distribution and consumption, reveals obvious common elements. Both are commercially published, printed books with associated characteristics of relative permanence, portability and authority. Each has its place in a genre within a system of discourse. As physical objects, they are sold in bookshops, kept in libraries, homes and colleges. They confer on the writer the authoritative status of author. They are aimed at a commercial market that is both preconceived and researched. They have been subjected to processes of editing and typographical design and presentation. All these elements are part of the interdiscursive context of their production.

Both are educational in the broadest sense. Probyn's text, as an autobiography, is presented as an authoritative, knowing insider account of a lawbreaker and prisoner, indemnified against its potential lack of credibility as the testimony of a criminal by an authoritative introduction by Stan Cohen, an eminent criminologist. Jones is published by Pelican Books, a series of populist texts in the traditions of adult self-education. The note on the author stresses, as a virtue, his self-made status from humble beginnings and the basis of his 'expertise' in 20 years work as a criminal justice official. In both cases the author and authorial status are constructed in a highly specific manner.

Extract 1

The quality of force in a text (Fairclough 1992) describes the way in which its social purpose is realised through language and structure. Here the delinquent as unknowing object is powerfully portrayed in the first paragraph by an assertive persuasive modality. This is combined with ambivalence created by the use of a series of dualities which construct the thematic meaning: guilt/innocence, knowledge/ignorance, power/vulnerability, childhood/adulthood, justice/discrimination. Strong nouns and adjectives – hard, cold, absolute, unrelenting, outrageous, disgusting (1–7) –, re-create the power of the remembered experience in an emotional sense.

The use of the active personal voice, the authorial 'I', gives the text a particular and characteristic tone. The author as child re-creates an account of a Foucaultian diagnostic process and creation of a criminal 'other' by the court bureaucracy which is internalised by the terrified child's sense of 'oppressive guilt' (4). The dramatic and theatrical nature of the proceedings also emphasises this. These are, however, the words of a highly literate adult who has studied some sociology, re-creating a specific experience from a vantage point of knowledge and reflection based on reinterpreted meaning. This process is fundamental to and highly characteristic of the ways in which autobiography 'writes' identity (Stanley 1992). By the end of the paragraph (11–16) a transition has been achieved from object to knowing subject which char-acterises the nature of the rest of the extract. Narrative gives way to exposition and argument. The oppression of social class and an explicit analysis of the meaning of the event described is constructed out of the narrative. The trial for theft of the 'tin of peas' becomes a critical, perhaps *the* critical event in which the author both receives and internalises the ascription of criminal status *and* constructs his political analysis of the way in which criminals are made.

The final two paragraphs also describe the process of autobiography as outlined above. The moment of time abruptly shifts from the court to the author-as-adult writing 30 years later after years in prison. It is the court which unwittingly *and* knowingly makes criminals (21–25). Ironically, the internalisation of the sense of being 'other' releases an awareness of an alternative explanation and identity through the recognition that this is the product of childish ignorance. The transfor-mation of awareness described echoes Hobsbawm's (1969) analysis of the bandit as a primitive political rebel and moves to a politics of knowledge and resistance. In Probyn's 'evil web' (45) there is also an implicit anticipation of Cohen's (1985) carceral net, a metaphor of the criminal justice system as a fishing net drawing indi-viduals into it, whose mesh becomes more tightly woven the deeper each is entangled.

The assertive modality is maintained by the strength of repeated 'I know' (19, 28), 'I have realised' (21), 'I rejected' (26). Despite the apparent lenience of the sentence (probation), the author's sense of outrage is based on recognition of dis-crimination and unfairness in the difference of treatment between the defendants. The emphasis on the contrast between the ignorance and confusion of the child and the awareness of the adult is maintained throughout the passage. The final paragraph summarises the message of the text, the author's intention of how it should be read. The first sentence artfully combines the mundane, the comic and the emblematic to create a powerfully ironic tone which is a key component of the extract. The legally and morally innocent child is sacrificed to the demands of quick and efficient court procedure by the setting aside of 'tiresome duty' (43–44). The final sentence summarises the incident and the author's reading of its significance, clearly and eco-nomically.

Extract 2

The force of the second extract is the product of a different grammatical construction. By adopting the indirect, passive voice, common to academic discourses, Jones creates authority by the removal of his own active voice. The use of 'there is' rather than 'I believe' or 'I consider' and the objectification of: 'the slum dweller' (7), 'father' (19), 'mother' (20), and so on, constructs a categorical authority which is maintained throughout the extract. The 'slum' (2) and 'slum life' (18) are not simply factually descriptive of social and human conditions but become an organising metaphor within the text of this document. The explicit tone of the discourse admits to no doubts and co-opts the agreement of the reader by omitting any references to an opposing argument.

Despite this, there exists throughout the text an implicit contradiction which the author struggles to resolve: the meaning of the impact of poverty and social and economic conditions, and the demands for a moral absolute. This produces a discourse of poverty and criminality linked to different environments which can be morally evaluated. As with Probyn, the rhetorical device of antithesis and balanced dualities is used throughout although the nature of these is construed differently. Working class/middle class, city/country, poverty/comfort, are expressed in references to: 'poorest types/better elements' (2, 3), 'slum dweller/farm labourer' (7, 26), 'slum child/middle class children' (32, 28). The juxtapositions are used to create a construction of a delinquent 'other', a precursor of the contemporary underclass (Murray 1990). The notion of slum dwellers as the dangerous classes is built upon throughout the extract by unfavourable comparisons with middle-class and rural life.

This is constructed through the creation of an insistent sense of inevitability and determinism: 'slum life is bound' (18), and the paragraph which follows it creates a pathological reading of slum life, which although qualified by some conditional modality ('may') changes in the final sentence to assertion. This is contrasted both with some quasi-idealised references to rural life: 'the farm labourer at least has his employment – and with it his cottage' (26) (with no recognition of its tied status), and later references to the economic security of middle-class children.

In contrast to the assertive tone conveyed through grammatical construction, ambiguity is expressed through use of vocabulary and the conflation of descriptive terms for children. In two sentences (12–14), 'friends', 'juvenile delinquents', 'playmates', 'school fellows' are all used interchangeably to describe the children of the slums, reflecting the moral ambiguity ascribed to the environment and the experience of such children. Similarly 'cadging', 'misdemeanour', 'normal instincts of boys', blur the distinctions between moral absolutes. This blurring derives from the first key theme of the extract, the argument that an important influence on delinquency is economic and social poverty and lack of legitimate opportunity within an urban environment. Particularly identified are the criminogenic influences of the street environment and the cramped life of the urban slum home. Jones categorically asserts that this environment creates children who 'from the circumstances of their existence become obsessed with such craving to acquire things that it has to be satisfied with stealing' (31–32). This deterministic certainty sharpens the dilemma posed within this particular discourse of delinquency.

The second important theme, reminiscent of theories of anomie, is that there has been a loss of traditional authority represented by the Church and of the social significance of shaming within a close-knit and known community. The anonymity of urban life is contrasted with the public knowledge and social opinion of the small rural village. What is constructed as the orthodox moral code of the latter is contrasted with the subcultural criminality of the slum where the 'poorest types of the population are all herded together' (1) and among whom are 'professional criminals' (4). The urban environment is by its very nature criminogenic. The countryside is portrayed as open free public space, the city street as a more ambiguous space, a narrow channel of public right of way through inviting but prohibited private property. This is an account by an urban author, ignorant of or disregarding the rigid class structures and jealously guarded property rights of the rural environment with its own relationships between poverty and crime. The tension between the social and economic analysis and the felt demand for moral certainty is not explicitly resolved but the author ultimately has to defer to the ideological imperative of morality.

Conclusion

Both documents contribute to the discourse of juvenile delinquency and its control. Both construct a delinquent 'other'. One is a personal, highly specific, lived account of a critical incident, the second a generalised discourse built on, but essentially ignorant of, other multiple potential accounts of anonymous children processed by the juvenile courts. Jones is a classic text of official discourse and an example of ideology. It can be read as a representation of a mundane and banal statement of general beliefs held about juvenile delinquency by a particular group of individuals in the criminal justice system: magistrates and the clerks who assist them. It makes strong claims to typicality and orthodoxy and to a special knowledge and expertise held by members of the group. It graphically illustrates the thesis that ideology is most effective and compelling when it operates as a discourse of common sense and when it is part of an ideological state apparatus (Althusser 1971; Gramsci 1971).

Autobiographical accounts, of which Probyn's is an example, have the capacity to challenge the generalising, normalising effects of ideological official discourse. Whereas Jones identifies a particular construction of slum life and its inherent lack of moral controls as the key producer of delinquency, Probyn identifies the way in which criminal justice officials and the court make delinquents through processes of diagnosis, explanation and classification to special status for forms of disposal. This diagnosis and explanation is in itself based on the ideological belief systems exemplified in Jones. In their separate ways each is based on a logic of inevitability and determinism. The important recognition achieved by Probyn is that society's rejection of the delinquent may create a space for him (for in both these extracts delinquency is unquestionably gendered as male) to develop a personal and political analysis of identity which can confront and challenge the official accounts.

In recognising and validating this potential for opposition, language and discourse analysis draw research methodology into the contradictions and problems cited in the introductory section. Critical to these are the issues of credibility and authority, discussed earlier, which are mirrored in the debates about credibility in research methods. Controversy concerning notions of research bias, representativeness and reliability are, for analysts of discourse, issues which cannot be separated from the right of excluded voices to be heard and to contribute to understanding of identity and experience. Positivist emphasis on scientific method and on the researched as problematic objects of study has restricted the range of material which is accepted as valid data. Discourse insists upon the possibility of redress to this traditional imbalance in credibility.

This chapter has used extracts from documents to identify and analyse two important properties of texts. Examination of interdiscursivity permits the reader to understand the conditions of production, distribution and consumption of a document, revealing the complexity of the context in which it may be read and understood. Intertextuality reads it, not just as a free-standing, unique product of discursive practice, but as an active contributor to a chorus of voices which respond to documents already existing as well as anticipating future possibilities. In undertaking such a project the researcher validates the written document as an important object of analysis in its own right.

References

Althusser, L. (1971) 'Ideology and state apparatuses.' In L. Althusser (ed) *Lenin and Philosophy and Other Essays*. London: New Left Books.

Atkinson, P. and Coffey, A. (1997) 'Analysing documentary realities.' In D. Silverman (ed) *Qualitative Research: Theory, Method and Practice*. London: Sage.

Barthes, R. (1967) *Elements of Semiology*. London: Cape.

Burton, F. and Carlen, P. (1979) *Official Discourse*. London: Routledge & Kegan Paul.

Cicourel, A. (1968) *The Social Organisation of Juvenile Justice*. New York: John Wiley.

Cohen, S. (1985) *Visions of Social Control*. London: Polity Press.

de Saussure, F. (1974) *Course in General Linguistics*. London: Fontana.

Fairclough, N. (1989) *Language and Power*. London and New York: Longman.

Fairclough, N. (1992) *Discourse and Social Change*. London: Polity Press.

Foucault, M. (1972) *The Archaeology of Knowledge*. London: Tavistock Publications.

Foucault, M. (1980) 'Prison Talk.' In C. Gordan (ed) *Power/Knowledge: Selected Interviews and Other Writings 1977–84*. London: Routledge.

Garfinkel, E. (1967) *Studies in Ethnomethodology*. Englewood Cliffs, NJ: Prentice-Hall.

Gramsci, A. (1971) *Selections from the Prison Notebooks*. edited and translated by Q. Hoare and G. Nowell Smith. London: Lawrence & Wishart.

Gubrium, J. and Buckholdt, D. (1982) *Describing Care: Image and Practice in Rehabilitation*. Cambridge, MA: Oelschlager, Gunn & Hain.

Hammersley, M. (1992) *What's Wrong With Ethnography? Methodological Explorations.* London: Routledge.

Hammersley, M. and Atkinson, P. (1983) *Ethnography: Principles in Practice.* London: Tavistock.

Hawkes, T. (1977) *Structuralism and Semiotics.* London: Methuen.

Hobsbawm, E.J. (1969) *Bandits.* London: Weidenfeld & Nicolson.

Jones, A.E. (1945) *Juvenile Delinquency and the Law.* Harmondsworth: Penguin Books.

Murray, C. (1990) *The Emerging British Underclass.* London: Institute of Economic Affairs Health and Welfare Unit.

Prior, L. (1987) 'Policing the dead": A sociology of the mortuary.' *Sociology 21*, 3, 355–376.

Prior, L. (1997) 'Following in Foucault's footsteps: Text and context in qualitative research.' In D. Silverman (ed) *Qualitative Research: Theory, Method and Practice.* London: Sage.

Probyn, W. (1977) *Angel Face: The Making of a Criminal.* London: Allen & Unwin.

Propp, V.I. (1968) *The Morphology of the Folktale.* 2nd rev. edn, edited by L.A. Wagner. Austin, TX, and London: University of Texas Press.

Sacks, H. (1992) *Lectures on Conversation.* Edited by G. Jefferson, 'Introduction' by E. Schegloff. Oxford: Basil Blackwell.

Silverman, D. (1993) *Interpreting Qualitative Data Methods for Analysing Talk, Text and Interaction.* London: Sage.

Stanley, L. (1992) *The Auto/biographical I: The Theory and Practice of Feminist Auto/biography.* Manchester: Manchester University Press.

Appendix 1

2 Hard, cold official eyes focused upon me as I came to a halt in front of the bench. There were tables to the left and right of me and seemingly hosts of people, all staring at me

4 with unnerving intensity. I felt an oppressive guilt, as though I had committed some outrageous and disgusting crime from which I could never be redeemed. The whole

6 attitude and atmosphere of that court seemed to me, from the very moment I entered it, to be one of absolute and unrelenting condemnation. The charge was read out and I was

8 asked if I had eaten the peas; because I was too terrified to speak, I nodded my head. Even had I known of the defence that was open to me by law, I could not have used it, I

10 was dumb with terror and I was a mere nine years old. Having overawed and cowed me into making this admission, advantage was then taken of my tender and naive innocence

12 and ignorance. My guilt was pronounced and I was sentenced to serve a period on probation, whilst Billy was let off altogether. Since neither Billy nor I had any previous

14 record, the disparity in our treatment could only be due to the fact that Billy came from a middle-class family whilst I came from a working-class family and that my humble origin

16 was considered to be a further aggravation of my offence.

18 I think now that this was one of the most significant points of time in my life. Looking back, I know, with the benefit of years of retrospective interpretation, that it was this act of

20 discrimination which I was later to relate to the prison scene and the political system as a whole. After careful reflection, I have realised how destructive this particular experience

22 was and how it was inevitable that it should influence my development and the sort of treatment I could expect from the system. The court, in its pompous incompetence,

24 inflicted upon me, at the age of nine, an enormous sense of guilt which I could not even
   begin to understand or cope with. Yet because, in a strange way that I could not
26 understand, I rejected the court's definition of myself as being irredeemably wicked and
   criminal, I also resented the oppressive sense of injustice that the gross disparity of our
28 treatment implied. I now know that my behaviour from that time on has been motivated by
   my rebellion, and that every subsequent punishment I have suffered has served only to
30 confirm, in my mind, my sense of alienation from a system from which I am both rejected
   and which I have rejected for its efforts to impose upon me an acceptance of social
32 inequality and social injustice. I was too young to know that, in a vague way, I was even
   becoming politically aware. Had I recognised this it is probable that my rebellion would
34 have taken a more effective and constructive form.

36 On the basis of my innocent admission that I had eaten a few peas, the court found me
   guilty of larceny. No consideration was given to the fact that, in my innocence, I could see
38 no wrong in taking that which had been abandoned as being unwanted and despite the
   fact that an essential requirement for the finding of guilt was that one should have had an
40 intention to steal, i.e. 'to permanently deprive the owner of his property'; it was not
   considered necessary by the court in this case. Being only 9 years old, I could obviously
42 know nothing of the requirements of law or of my legal rights, and the court took
   advantage of my innocence, ignorance and age to relieve themselves of the tiresome
44 duty of establishing whether or not there was a guilty intention. And so at the tender of
   nine I was convicted of a crime I did not commit, I was caught up in an evil web that was
46 destined to incarcerate me for thirty years of my life in various establishment institutions
   which have done everything possible to reinforce the patterns of criminality that they have
48 prescribed for me.

50 Walter Probyn (1977, pp.24–25)

Appendix 2

2 In the slum the poorest types of the population are all herded together with hardly any
   leavening of or intercourse with the better elements. There is invariably a fair sprinkling of
4 professional criminals and the standard of behaviour which will pass muster in such a
   community is bound to be on the low side. The Church exerts little moral influence, and
6 like other respected institutions, tends to be valued only for the opportunity of an
   occasional successful bit of cadging. If the slum dweller gets into trouble and has to go to
8 the juvenile court, he will not, therefore, be such an outcast as if he lived in a country
   village or a middle class suburb. There is no social opinion strong enough or sufficiently
10 unanimous to be a constant burden to him; and his disgrace will not be so widely known
   that it follows him everywhere as it would if he lived in the country. He can usually go a
12 few streets away and make new friends even if he cannot find other juvenile delinquents
   in his own street as playmates. His misdemeanour may not even reach the ears of his
14 school fellows – an impossibility in a village.

16 In addition to the weakened force of outside opinion in the poorer industrial districts there
   is also a big difference in the home atmosphere as compared with that of the rural
18 population or the middle classes. Slum life is bound to carry with it a lack of that sense of
   security which is so necessary for the happy and normal development of a child. Father
20 may be out of a job quite often; mother may have to go out to work; the child gets
   neglected; bits of the home may disappear into the pawnshop; rent may be owing and the

22 family may have to move; food may often be scarce and of poor quality. The youthful
mind becomes over-burdened with wants and prematurely conscious of the economic
24 struggle for existence.

26 The farm labourer has his employment – and with it his cottage – at least secure, no matter
what their other deficiencies; and he can procure for his family with the help of his own
28 garden a sufficiency of reasonably good food. Middle class children too can generally
grow up in economic security and taking the finance of life for granted. Neither of these
30 sections of the population is likely to produce children who, from the circumstances of
their existence, become obsessed with such a craving to acquire things that it has to be
32 satisfied by stealing. The slum child is, on the other hand, under a very strong temptation
to allay his nagging feeling of deficiencies by taking from society without leave what he
34 lacks.

36 Economic factors have another unfortunate effect on many children. They restrict poor
working class parents in providingg their offspring with indoor amusements and hobbies to
38 occupy their leisure; in addition, the home, with its sleeping, eating and sitting
accommodation concentrated often in the same room, is not a place to attract the child to
40 spend his time in; nor is he wanted to stay in when pressure on space is so great. The
village child may live in a cramped cottage, but when he is forced out he has plenty of
42 scope for his energies in the fields and hedgerows and woods and rivers. His advenurous
spirit can find plenty of outlets without the community being affected.

The natural playground of the town child, on the other hand, is the street; anything he
46 does there is bound to affect society, and any misbehaviour is bound to be at the expense
of somebody else' s property. So his chance of being haled before the juvenile court for
48 the ordinary mischief of youth is very much greater. He commits an offence even by
playing football or cricket; the normal instinct of boys to throw things may lead to a charge
50 of wilful damage or assault; if he wants to go exploring it will have to be in some
unoccupied (or occupied) private property, and he will find it difficult to resist taking there
52 any portable articles he discovers lying about unprotected.

54 A.E. Jones (1945, pp.26–28)

CHAPTER 11

Hidden from History
Research and Romantic Friendship
Janet Batsleer

Introduction

How can research in feminist studies, often conducted in other disciplines, in particular in the area of cultural history, assist investigative work in applied community studies? By drawing on the case of 'romantic friendship' as it has been investigated, debated and analysed by feminist historians, I would like to illustrate how new areas for research and investigation can emerge and how concept-ualisations developed by historians can influence the framing of contemporary research in applied community studies, just as contemporary preoccupations in-fluence the work of recovery which historians undertake. I will do this by offering a brief outline of the feminist scholarly work and then attempting to show the connection with my own documentation of the 'girlswork' movement in *Working with Girls and Young Women in Community Settings* (Batsleer 1996). In this book I documented the recent history of working with girls and young women in the context of youth and community work with young women in the United Kingdom. This work was usually referred to as 'the girlswork movement' and in my experience had been closely connected with the Women's Liberation Movement of the 1970s. At the time I was writing the book, feminist work was at a low ebb and feminist ideas were widely under attack, from many different points in the political spectrum. It seemed entirely possible that the girlswork movement would disappear without trace, together with many of the insights and understandings it had generated. As a student, and then as a youth worker, I had been very involved in this movement – organising young women's conferences, access to non-traditional activities for girls and young women, challenging the absence of women from senior positions in the local authorities and well-established voluntary organisations, encouraging young women's alternative publications, and so on – and did not wish to see it become utterly hidden from history. At the same time, as a lecturer in a polytechnic (now university), I had taken the opportunity to become familiar with another distant offshoot of the Women's Liberation Movement, feminist scholarship. It is the connectedness between these two apparently separate streams that proved so fruitful for my own practitioner research.

The notion of 'hiddenness' and 'recovery' has been particularly important to historians of subordinated groups. The past does not only belong to the victors and rulers, but also to the vanquished and overruled. Historical investigation of hidden or forgotten relationships and struggles can challenge the dominance of certain taken-for-granted common-sense assumptions in the present. One of the most powerful aspects of hegemonic cultural patterns is their seeming 'naturalness' or 'eternalness'. In his pioneering work of social history, *The Making of the English Working Class*, Edward Thompson (1963) wrote that one of his aims was 'to rescue the poor stockinger, the Luddite cropper, the "obsolete" handloom weaver, the "utopian" artisan and even the deluded follower of Joanna Southcott from the enormous condescension of posterity' (p.13). The same imperative informed Sheila Rowbotham's (1973) early feminist work *Hidden from History: 300 Years of Women's Oppression and the Fight Against It*. Peter Fryer's (1984) *Staying Power* reclaims the long history of a black presence in Britain. And Martin Bauml Duberman, Martha Vicinus and George Chauncey Jnr (1989) have also used the phrase 'Hidden from History' in their collection of essays *Hidden from History; Reclaiming the Gay and Lesbian Past*. Each of these volumes contains a challenge to orthodoxies and to the too-simple acceptance of Marx's dictum that 'the ruling ideas in every age are the ideas of the ruling class'. They show that no cultural practice or body of ideas is uncontested. Class cultures are made and remade. So are relationships between men and women. So are patterns of relationship between nations across the globe and between peoples within nations, in neo-colonial and postcolonial contexts. And even heterosexuality is not natural, universal and eternal in the forms it takes. Nor, as the case of romantic friendship shows, are heterosexual relationships necessarily the primary relationships through which women or men make sense of their lives.

Revealing romantic friendships

Are the communities whose lives I am interested in researching, communities with a history? Have they been 'hidden from history'? Is there any existing critical scholarship which might throw light on that history? These are important questions for all community-based research. In addition it is useful, following from feminist questioning, to ask how the separation of the domestic world from the public space of work and politics might have been lived in earlier generations and how it is changing. Have men been associated primarily with the public domain and women with the private? This analysis of the separate roles of men and women and of their relative access to power and ability to exercise their rights has been a foundation of the feminist case for separate work and was particularly strong in practice in the girlswork movement in the UK in the 1980s. Access to feminist scholarship generated new questions about this public/private split, and the experience of 'separate spheres'.

Lilian Faderman's (1985) book *Surpassing the Love of Men* took as a central motif the connection or otherwise between romantic love between women and lesbian love, in which romantic love is conceived as non-genital, and lesbian love as sexual. In this she acknowledged her debt to Carroll Smith Rosenberg's (1975) pioneering scholarship which demonstrated the impact of 'separate spheres' on the forms which significant personal relationships could take, and which highlighted the importance of love relationships between women. Faderman provided a wealth of evidence of loving relationships between women from the sixteenth century onwards. She sees these relationships as primarily non-sexual and argues that they were condoned by society rather than seen as disruptive of the social structure. On the other hand, trans-vestite women (that is, those who dressed and often attempted to pass as men) were usually persecuted and sometimes even executed. Why, Faderman asks, was a woman's choice of dress such a weighty factor in determining whether men would praise her love for another woman as being noble and beautiful or flog her for it? Issues of how to dress have always been central for women, and for feminists in a culture in which appearance is a powerful marker of status, 'race', class and femininity. Early campaigns in the girlswork movement – recorded, for example, in the collection of writings by young women, *Girls are Powerful* (Hemmings 1982) – included campaigns about wearing trousers at school and also, for some Asian girls and for some Rastafarian girls, the right to wear culturally acceptable dress. Feminists wearing dungarees in the 1970s were certainly marking their distance from powerful codes of femininity, and were creating a sense of mutual recognition. The fact that this meant feminists, of whatever sexual practice or desires, 'looked like lesbians' did not go unnoticed and led to, on the one hand, a sustained attack on feminists via an attack on their dress sense, and on the other hand, an opening up of possibilities for 'looking like a lesbian' among lesbian women who did not want to be identified with what was perceived as a narrow and limited sexual politics among lesbian feminist women. Haircuts and dress codes continue to play a significant part in the making of femininities.

The complexity of the relationship between lesbian identity and feminist identity or politics is being addressed by Faderman (1985) in this quote, as is the issue of the place of the sexual in the definition of the term 'lesbian':

> Certainly the degree of sexual expression among romantic friends must have varied, just as it does among women who are avowedly lesbian today. However, it is likely that most love relationships between women during previous eras, when females were encouraged to force any sexual drive they might have to remain latent, were less physical than they are in our times. But the lack of any overt sexual expression in these romantic friendships could not discount the seriousness or the intensity of the women's passions toward each other, or the fact that if by 'lesbian' we mean an all-consuming emotional relationship in which two women are devoted to each other above anyone else, these ubiquitous sixteenth, seventeenth, eighteenth and nineteenth century romantic friendships were 'lesbian'. (p.19)

But this conclusion presented me again with a major question. If these romantic friendships were in the quality and intensity of the emotions no different from lesbian love, why were they so readily condoned in earlier eras and persecuted in ours? Why were they considered 'normal then and abnormal now'? Faderman answers her own question about the shift from seeing love between women as normal to seeing such love as perverse, as related to the changes in the status of women and the development of 'medical knowledge' via sexology which cast love between women as a disease. She argues that as the status of women began to rival that of men, same-sex love between women became more threatening to the patriarchal order, and that the development of sexology was an effective counter to the threat posed by such female power. Sexology neutralised the power of lesbian love by pathologising and morbidifying it. Faderman's historical research challenged contemporary definitions of the sexual, of love relationships and the role of women. It also engaged with the debate, which was a powerful current in Anglo-American feminist politics from the mid 1970s to the mid 1980s, about the connection between the personal and the political and specifically about the connection between lesbian identification and feminism. Two pieces by Mica Nava (1992) reminded me of the hornet's nest which the debate about 'revolutionary feminism' stirred up in the then small world of feminist politics as well as of the appalling climate of moral censoriousness which some feminists associated with the girlswork movement managed to develop. Borrowing from the traditions of the revolutionary left, in particular from the tradition of polemic, pamphleteering and attack, the Leeds Revolutionary Feminist Group suggested that feminists who continued to have sexual relationships with men were taking energy from the movement and were therefore a kind of 'enemy within'. This led to the emergence – briefly – of a category 'political lesbian' and it is certainly the case that some of the key figures in the girlswork movement in the UK in the 1970s and 1980s identified – however momentarily – as political lesbians. Others, for whom the term referred primarily to their love relationships, remained lesbians, and also feminists. Others remained feminists and, more or less defiantly, heterosexual. It is in this context that many of the fears of separate work with girls and women that youth workers who established separate work with girls in this period have attested to, need to be understood. Homophobia often formed a border for the work – it was important for some workers to demonstrate that their work was not about challenging heterosexuality, and there was a good deal of emphasis laid on valuing traditional arts of femininity via make-up, body care, taking responsibility for contraception, and so on. Dungaree-wearing feminists running bricklaying courses and motorbike maintenance classes may have been happily heterosexual in their personal lives, but they were very often perceived as 'dangerous dykes'. It was all extremely confusing.

Adrienne Rich (1986) and Janice Raymond (1986) had developed discussions of the 'lesbian continuum' which Rich significantly argued could encompass many forms of primary intensity between women:

If we consider the possibility that all women – from the infant suckling at her mother's breast, to the grown woman experiencing orgasmic sensations while suckling her own child, perhaps recalling her mother's milk smell in her own, to two women, like Virginia Woolf's Chloe and Olivia, who share a laboratory, to the woman dying at ninety, touched and handled by women – exist on a lesbian continuum, we can see ourselves as moving in and out of this continuum, whether we ourselves identify as lesbian or not. (Rich 1986, p.54)

Rich then goes on to identify from across the globe, and across millennia, a number of examples of women's strong bonds with other women. In the following extract Rich is drawing deliberately on literary and historical evidence which crosses not only time and space but also the divides created by class and racism:

We can then connect aspects of woman identification as diverse as the impudent, intimate girl friendships of eight or nine year olds and the banding together of those women of the twelfth and fifteenth centuries known as the Beguines who 'shared houses, rented to one another, bequeathed houses to their room mates...in cheap areas of town', who 'practised Christian virtue on their own, dressing and living simply and not associating with men,' who earned their livings as spinsters, bakers, nurses or ran schools for young girls, and who managed – until the Church forced them to disperse – to live independent both of marriage and conventional restrictions. It allows us to connect these women with the more celebrated 'Lesbians' of the women's school around Sappho of the seventh century BC, with the secret sororities and economic networks reported among African women, and with the Chinese marriage resistance sisterhoods – communities of women who refused marriage or who, if married, often refused to consummate their marriages and soon left their husbands, the only women in China who were not footbound and who, Agnes Smedley tells us, welcomed the births of daughters and organised successful women's strikes in the silk mills. It allows us to connect and compare disparate individual instances of marriage resistance: for example, the strategies available to Emily Dickinson, a nineteenth century white woman genius, with the strategies available to Zora Neale Hurston, a twentieth century Black woman genius. (p.54)

It is in this discussion of a continuum of resistance to marriage that Rich finally locates lesbian sexuality: 'and we can connect these rebellions and the necessity for them with the physical passion of woman for woman which is central to lesbian existence: the erotic sensuality which has been precisely the most violently erased fact of female experience' (p.56). Here lesbian experience is seen as an aspect of a wider feminist political rebellion against the controls, subordinations and even erasures imposed on women in the name of male dominance and heterosexuality as an institution. In the context of this discussion it became possible for me to make sense of some of what was happening both around me and inside me in the practices of the girlswork movement, and in my attempts to document it. First, we had been working and living in the context of an erasure of that lesbian continuum from our sense of ourselves and of the past. So any connection with the term 'lesbian' seemed deviant and potentially threatening. Mica Nava's (1992) account in 'A Girls' Project and some responses to lesbianism', written in the same period, seems to me to be an important record both of the climate of the time in relation to homosexuality and the ways in which girlswork could change things. In 1980, Nava could write: 'In our culture lesbianism falls outside the boundary of what constitutes tolerable behaviour for women; it is taboo' (Nava 1992, p.40), and then could offer a documentation, through interviews with young women who were 'coming out' in the context of a girls' project, of how that taboo was being challenged. Rich connects the erasure of lesbian experience with male dominance, suggesting that female bonding is always a threat to male dominance. Perhaps the threat is however only really powerful when it also entails a threat to male-dominated forms of heterosexuality. Women's liberation-inspired girlswork was certainly countering male dominance and in doing so opening up the possibilities of consensual heterosexualities as well as lesbian existence. This feminist scholarship helped me turn my attention away from focusing entirely on issues of the threat to men, and helped refocus attention on the agency and creativity of young women (Batsleer 1996).

British literature

The largely US-based research was taken up in the British context too. Liz Stanley in particular has drawn on this research to explore the epistemological issues that link lesbian and feminist research. Stanley's work is important because she emphasises strongly the need for feminist researchers to pay attention to the specific accounts of the women whose lives they are researching, and to admit the complexity of the evidence, rather than attempt to draw up evidence for contemporary political battles within women's movements. It seems clear to me that both Faderman and Rich are highly involved in those contemporary battles. In her essay 'Feminism and friendship' Liz Stanley (1992) shows how Faderman's approach ignores the understandings of the protagonists of romantic relationships in favour of a researcher-imposed set of understandings and meanings. Stanley argues:

> It is crucial to treat biographical subjects as agents of their lives and not as puppets whose thoughts and actions were determined, whether by social structures or by ideological prescriptions of how men and women were supposed to be, or indeed by others within their social and political circles. It would be ironic indeed if a feminist approach to friendship, by wanting to recognise women's oppression in the past as well as the present, should treat these friendships as determined by patriarchy. (p.219)

Stanley provides convincing evidence of the eroticism of relationships which Lilian Faderman suggests were non-genital and she also shows how, contrary to Faderman's argument about the 'morbidifying' nature of sexology, the sexologist Havelock Ellis's wife Edith Lees most certainly did see herself as an invert and that 'mannishness' existed in particular women's behaviours and identifications in the absence of any demonstrable influence by sexologists. The patterns of women's friendship took and take many shapes and meanings, one of which was erotic genital sexual involvement. In her concluding remarks Stanley suggests that:

> through the lens of friendship all the varied relationships women of the past had with each other can be looked at and their meanings – for the protagonists and also for present day readers – pondered. Writers of biography have always had available to them such patterns of friendship in the lives of their subjects; however, the conventional form that biography has been written in has denied this information to readers, and its absence needs to be redressed in feminist auto/biography. (1992, p.235)

Phillipa Levine's (1990) study of patterns of friendship and kinship among nineteenth-century feminists supports this perspective. She cites a number of passionate declarations of love between women, such as this one from Bessie Rayner Parkes about Barbara Leigh Smith:

> Oh how dearly I do love and reverence Barbara; how I long for her to love me dearly. Her face seems to me a summing up of herself; how I long to look at it, to gaze long and to drink in her revelations. (Levine 1990, p.72)

She argues that such friendship was often the foundation for feminist political work and says that one of the most striking features of feminist friendship in the period is the absence of vituperative enmity. Particular cultural organisations developed to support these friendships, particularly Women's Clubs, which emerged in most major cities in Britain:

> Just as these new women's organisations offered new social opportunities for women breaking out of the mould by taking up careers of various sorts, so they also provided a new channel for the development of women's friendships. It was often female friendship that helped women resolve the problems of independence and rebellion which a feminist stand invariably invoked. (p.72)

This significant body of historical scholarship has implications for contemporary research. For example, research into political organising, including community-based organising, could reveal more adequately the meaning of particular patterns of friendship as a support for organising. It would be interesting to understand how changing patterns of households, increased mobility and new forms of communication have affected the development of the 'new social movements'. In analysing the girlswork movement as an aspect of the Women's Liberation Movement, it would surely be possible to explore how particular urban centres (often with strong student communities), have created sustainable spaces and sustainable communities for women, including lesbians, committed to new patterns of household and with a desire to create new forms of community and different forms of sociability. It is through these friendship networks that women have made a difference, inciting one another to take on new challenges in the public sphere and bringing about systematic change in relations between men and women and in the acknowledgement of lesbian and gay relationships. Family life has been widely analysed as the basis of community and also of the fragmentation of community, but rarely has this been considered as a network of female bonding and support, of mothers, daughters, sisters, aunts, grandmothers, nieces and cousins. Female friendship, including the possibility of lesbian relationships, could be recognised as a force to be reckoned with in the communities studied. Most community studies assume the norms of heterosexuality as a framework. The scholarly research on romantic friendships suggests that such assumptions should be questioned, and that a more open set of expectations is needed when female friendship and kinship networks are analysed. Interestingly, this relates also to the challenges posed by developing black feminist scholarship on the meaning of community and the significance of othermothering (Hill Collins 1991).

The impact of historical knowledge on research into girlswork

Practitioner research for me (Batsleer 1996) has been rooted in my own practice commitments, my own experience of working with girls and young women and my knowledge of a wide network of practice which never seemed to be fully visible, never fully acknowledged, even at the height of the girlswork movement in the 1970s and 1980s. So there is an immediate sense of connection between the hiddenness identified by social historians and the hiddenness of the particular practice I was concerned to document. Also, I have struggled with the political question of how and in what ways I might define myself as a feminist for 20 years or so. The term 'feminist' has encompassed a wide range of references, ranging from questions about intimate relationships to a set of political and cultural projects – of which the girlswork movement was certainly a part – and has also encompassed an enormous body of intellectual work, all of it containing a set of epistemological challenges in relation to the practice of research. Also I am an intellectual. Ideas matter in my life. They can have a profound effect. The discovery of this body of writing about romantic friendships and the debate surrounding the term 'lesbian' had an enormous impact on me, both in terms of my own evaluation of my relationships with other women and in terms of my understanding of girlswork as a practice of informal education. Angela McRobbie (1991) has described the passionate enquiry which constitutes feminist research as caught 'between talk, text and action' (p.61). The practitioner research on girlswork could be understood as caught between my talk within a feminist political and intellectual community, the texts of feminist historians and the action of organising spaces for and with young women. Seeing talk and conversation as the basis from which research emerges is not only a way of rationalising talking late into the night or non-stop over the kitchen table in academic terms. It is a way of acknowledging the power of friendship, and of the embedded experience of friendship, in feminism. Passions, excitements, animosities fuel the work, and fuel feminist inquiry, and also limit it. I wrote *Working with Girls and Young Women in Community Settings* (Batsleer 1996) because of conversations with women youth workers who said such a book was needed. We saw that 'girlswork' as we called it was again about to be lost, again hidden from history, and we recognised the existence of such written reports as a method of challenging that process of erasure.

Written texts, both the texts we create as scholars and the texts we read, formalise and extend this conversation. They deepen it and maybe narrow it. The texts are the aspects of the work that are validated as 'academic'. They are very important and it is through this written material that we have much access to the past and to the wider communities in which the work is located in the here and now. But the written record is only one moment in the process of practitioner research. The actions that followed from my writing of the book have included the continued involvement in the organisation of spaces for and with young women. Increasingly these have been spaces with young women whose experience has been one of exclusion from or marginality to the norms of femininity. Lesbian young women and bisexual young women are no longer erased under the general heading of 'girlswork'. Asian young women are no longer responded to separately on the basis of their supposed 'difference' or 'language/cultural issues'. Rather their critical perceptions of the norms of femininity provide some pointers to changes yet to come. The impact of all of this has been to generate new questions, both for research and teaching.

New questions

The scholarship about romantic friendships poses new questions about the place of women's friendships in political organising. Recognising women's friendships within the context of the development of national organisations such as the National Organisation for Work with Girls and Young Women which represented women youth workers throughout the 1970s and 1980s, allows testimony to the power of self-identified lesbian networks within feminist politics in that period. It may also point to some of the causes of the collapse of the same organisations, as the tensions surrounding openness to lesbian friendships were negotiated. At the beginning of the girlswork movement there was a great deal of hostility which lesbian women who were active in girlswork had to negotiate (Nava 1992) and this led to the perpetuation of a closeted existence for lesbian workers within a feminist organisation. The term 'women' was often read as a code for 'lesbian', resulting in a great deal of confusion and misunderstanding. Some of the difficulties experienced in women's organisations might also be related to the powerful emotional dynamics – negative as well as positive – involved in female friendships, compounded by the impact of homophobia. It seems likely that much feminist political energy in this period came from a network of female friendship which contained more than a commitment to a set of specific demands for equality but involved deep personal commitments too, involving love for as well as jealousy of and rivalry with other women. But by the mid 1980s a lesbian caucus was in existence in both the Community and Youth Workers Union and in the National Organisation for Work with Girls and Young Women, and in the early 1990s the National Organisation for Lesbian and Gay Youth and Community Workers had been established. The impact of the introduction of Section 28 of the Local Government Act (1988) was largely positive for the flagging energies of lesbian and feminist politics. And it meant that girlswork ceased to act as a 'closet' for lesbian workers, beginning to enable some critical separations to be made between lesbian demands and a wider feminist politics. In particular, the issue of alliances with gay men became strong again, and themes such as 'bisexuality' and 'queer' and the possibility of a coalition of sexual minorities re-emerged into sexual politics. The problem of 'hiddenness' and 'invisibility' remains but now can be attended to in all the particularity of the experience for a huge variety of different groups of women. The breaking down of the closet created by the category of 'woman', which happened for lesbian women in women's organisations in the UK in the late 1980s, happened alongside challenges from black women and South Asian women. Female friendship, including romantic friendships 'across the tracks', can now be validated as part of the house of difference rather than subsumed into one category.

Moreover, recognising romantic friendships in the past challenges assumptions about girlswork in the present. Why assume that girlswork is about countering male dominance primarily? Might it not also be about affirming many patterns of love (and other bonds) between women, including lesbian relationships and identifications? Are the 'best friends' of today the 'romantic friends' of yesterday? These questions very much changed my understanding of the place of girlswork in sexuality education. Initially I had seen girlswork primarily as a safe space away from boys, in which (among other things) a view of female autonomy and autonomous female (hetero)sexuality could develop. The writings of feminist historians about romantic friendship helped me to see that this was at the same time a female and potentially lesbian space, with all its complexity. This became particularly evident to me while I was documenting the work on sexuality. Analyses which emphasised the social construction of sexuality and of hetero-patriarchal homophobic space helped me understand both why the simple demand for separate space for work with girls had been so threatening as well as the importance of feminist work which could continue to enable young women to speak about their sexuality and name their desires in ways less controlled by the dictates of normative heterosexuality. One of the first young lesbian groups to meet openly as such in Manchester had published a report on their work, which explicitly addressed the theme of friendship, in the following poem by Shona:

Friends

You hold my hand
Smile and talk
We're friends aren't we
Would you walk off
Or hold me close

I want to hold you
Kiss you
You let go of my hand
Hug me
And turn to leave
I call your name
You turn
I smile
Maybe I'll tell you tomorrow

This poem seemed to me to be further testimony to the power of friendship, as documented in the work of feminist historians, and an important focus for sexuality education, in direct contrast to the appeals to 'the values of marriage and family life' embedded in Section 28 and the sex education guidelines for schools. Further, much of the research on feminist friendship and on 'romantic friendships' in the late nineteenth century identifies the place of feminist women in relation to the political elites of the day, particularly the network of liberal families. Practitioner research in youth and community work, by definition, is less concerned with the elites than with the subaltern class of professionals and with poor and subordinated communities. In this setting, questions of the place of friendship in building defensive solidarities emerge. What is the nature of mutuality in community work? Are women skilled, from necessity, at crossing class and racialised divides? The conversation between feminist cultural history and practitioner research in youth and community work needs to be a two-way conversation. What histories are there of 'romantic friendships' among poor women? Between women of very different class and/or national backgrounds? Some of the sources for historical research in this area might be in oral histories facilitated in community projects and even in classrooms. When teaching a course on sexuality education recently, I introduced some material relating to 'romantic friendship'. After the class one of the students came and spoke to me about her grandmother's diary, which had been read by the family after her death and had contained the account of her relationship with another woman who, as the student said to me, 'had always been there'. This 'romantic friendship' had outlasted two husbands. On what basis had it been 'hidden from history'? And how many more such diaries are there to be discovered, including those still being written today?

Conclusion

There is always a history and a story to be told about subordinated groups which is not the story of the dominant responses to them. Stigma and pathology have contributed to the hiddenness of romantic friendships and lesbian relationships, and this has prevented a recognition of their place in community organising. But as I believe the case studies taken from the girlswork movement show, these are now being challenged in talk, text and action, in the passionate scholarship of feminist academics and in community-based actions and research. The resources of cultural history and the work of feminist scholarship are important resources for practitioner research. And practitioner research offers one method to feminists based in universities to resist some of the stultifying effects of the university environment.

References

Batsleer, J. (1996) *Working with Girls and Young Women in Community Settings.* Aldershot: Arena.

Bauml Duberman, M. Vicinus, M. and Chauncey, G. Jnr., (1989) *Hidden from History: Reclaiming the Gay and Lesbian Past.* Harmondsworth: Penguin.

Faderman, L. (1985) *Surpassing the Love of Men: Romantic Friendship and Love between Women from the Renaissance to the Present.* London: The Women's Press.

Fryer, P. (1984) *Staying Power: the History of Black People in Britain.* London: Pluto.

Hemmings, S. (ed) (1982) *Girls are Powerful: Young Women's Writings from* Spare Rib. London: Sheba.

Hill Collins, P. (1991) *Black Feminist Thought: Knowledge, Consciousness and the Politics of Empowerment.* New York: Routledge.

Levine, P. (1990) 'Love, friendship and feminism in later nineteenth century England.' *Women's Studies International Forum, 13,* 63–78.

McRobbie, A. (1991) 'The politics of feminist research: Between talk, text and action.' In A. McRobbie (ed) *Feminism and Youth Culture: From* Jackie *to* Just Seventeen. Basingstoke: Macmillan.

Nava, M. (1992) 'A Girls' Project and some responses to lesbianism' and 'Youth Service provision, social order and the question of girls.' In *Changing Cultures: Feminism, Youth and Consumerism.* London: Sage.

Raymond, J. (1986) *A Passion for Friends: Towards a Philosophy of Female Affection.* London: The Women's Press.

Rich, A. (1986) 'Compulsory heterosexuality and lesbian existence.' In A. Rich (ed) *Blood, Bread and Poetry: Selected Prose 1979–1985.* London: Virago.

Rowbotham, S. (1973) *Hidden from History: 300 Years of Women's Oppression and the Fight Against It.* London: Pluto.

Smith Rosenberg, C. (1975) 'The female world of love and ritual: Relations between women in nineteenth century America.' *Signs: Journal of Women in Culture and Society 1,* 1, 1–29.

Stanley, L. (1992) *The Auto/biographical I: The Theory and Practice of Feminist Autobiography.* Manchester: Manchester University Press.

Thompson, E.P. (1963) *The Making of the English Working Class.* Harmondsworth: Penguin.

CHAPTER 12

Storytelling as Research
Paul Wilkins

Introduction

People make sense of their experience and communicate it to others by telling stories. Cragan and Sheilds (1995) take the view that 'regardless of context, all human communication exhibits the characteristics of narration or stories' (pp.91–92). This view is widely held in the social sciences and, as Rennie (1994, p.234) points out, in many disciplines in the humanities and social sciences storytelling is considered to be a fundamental way in which people make sense of our lives. Many authors (for example, Bettleheim 1976; von Franz 1982) write of how metaphor speaks widely and generally and of the importance of symbols and archetypes in the understanding of life and life events. Jones (1996, p.10) writes of the dramatherapy paradox that 'what is fictional is also real' and Goddard (1996, p.4) has pointed out the 'metaphorical nature of everyday talk'. So there are many reasons to believe that storytelling and metaphor are the ordinary language of ordinary people, a universal mode of communication understood in some way (however deeply or shallowly) by both teller and listener. Because they are a natural form of expression, it makes sense to use them in any investigation of human experience: as a means of inquiry, as a way of processing data and as a way of presenting findings. With the possible exception of the use of narrative analysis (see Manning and Cullum-Swan 1994; Riessman 1993) as a method of handling (for example) interview data, this is rarely done. Instead, research methodology and the presentation of findings privileges the language of an academic elite and still tends to favour a positivistic paradigm and to ignore the creative expression which is everyday dialogue. Perhaps there are good reasons for this – somehow the faculties of imagination, intuition, expression and creation are undervalued in a world apparently devoted to outcome research and the power of number. In *The Little Prince*, de Saint-Exupéry (1991) writes:

> Grown-ups love figures. When you tell them that you have made a new friend, they never ask you any questions about essential matters. They never say to you, 'What does his (*sic*) voice sound like? What games does he love best? Does he collect butterflies?' Instead, they demand: 'How old is he? How many brothers has he? How

144

much does he weigh? How much money does his father make?' Only from these figures do they think they have learned anything about him. (pp.15–16)

Perhaps in our struggle to fit in with 'the grown ups', social science researchers have used their methods and their language. Rather than hearing the stories in which reside a richness of detail, we have sought to measure, otherwise, like de Saint-Exupéry's Turkish astronomer (1991, p.15), we have risked not being listened to because we are not wearing the right clothes. Even with the move to qualitative research – (the 'fundamental goal' of which McLeod (1994) describes as 'to uncover and illuminate what things mean to people' (p.78)) – social scientists have tended to use what Reason and Rowan (1981) refer to as 'old paradigm' research. Although these methods are of value, they are not necessarily at their best when used in an effort to understand human experience. In human inquiry, the accounts informants produce of their experience more often than not are closer in form to a story (maybe as narrative, perhaps as poetry or some other form of artistic expression) than to an orthodox account of positivistic or other 'old paradigm' research. To move such accounts to a more conventional form involves the researcher in *doing* to rather than *working with* the people on whose experience the research draws. Keeping to the story form preserves personal meaning *and* is more likely to produce an account which is meaningful to the population from which it is born but is also accessible to others outside the academic elite.

Stories in qualitative research

The value of storytelling has been widely discussed in the literature of qualitative research. For example, McLeod (1994, pp.76–102) writes of qualitative approaches as 'listening to stories' and Clandinin and Connelly (1994) consider the contribution of narrative in its various forms. Some accounts deal more directly with the use of the story form.

Reason and Hawkins (1988) describe a way of using stories in research. They consider how 'stories and storytelling might be part of an emergent paradigm of inquiry'. Of this paradigm, they write:

It tends to be co-operative rather than unilateral; to be qualitative rather than quantitative; to be holistic rather than reductionist; to work in natural settings rather than artificial laboratories. When we start to see storytelling as an aspect of inquiry we discover an important new dimension: inquiry can work either to explain or to express; to analyse or to understand. (p.79)

They distinguish between 'two paths of inquiry', explanation and expression.

- *Explanation* is the mode of classifying, conceptualising, and building theories from experience. Here the inquirer 'stands back', analyses, discovers or invents concepts, and relates theses in a theoretical model. This is essentially an analytical approach: dividing holistic experience into manageable components. Orthodox science is an exercise in explanation, endeavouring to answer questions of *what* and *why*.

- *Expression* is the mode of allowing the meaning of experience to become manifest. It requires the inquirer to partake deeply of experience, rather than stand back in order to analyse. Meaning is part and parcel of all experience, although it may be so interwoven with that experience that it is hidden: it needs to be discovered, created, or made manifest, and communicated. (Reason and Hawkins 1998, pp. 79–80)

They argue that, for example, creative acts (storytelling, acting, painting, etc.) are all encounters with the meaning of experience and that the expression of experience is inquiry into meaning. This 'is an important aspect of research which has been almost ignored by orthodox science' (p.80). In their view, the storytelling model of inquiry they propose offers at least some steps towards a viable and valid research strategy.

Riches and Dawson (1996) present an account of a piece of research based on the 'making and taking' of stories. This was an inquiry into 'grief and marital tension following the death of a child'. In their section on 'making stories' (pp.360–362), they report that 'each parent had a distinctive story to tell' and express the view that 'the role of the audience may be crucial in parents' successful construction of stories'. In other words, in storytelling the role of the listener is as important as that of the teller – in some sense it is a process of the co-construction (or co-discovery) of meaning. In their section on 'taking stories' the authors expand on this, stating 'by explicitly adopting a collaborative paradigm, research knowledge can be conceived of as a "co-production" of the interviewer and interviewee'. (pp.362–363)

Riches and Dawson (1996, p.363) stress the importance of a collaborative relationship in this kind of inquiry and that their 'naiveté' or explicit 'willing suspension of disbelief' were essential elements of their authenticity. By appearing as fully human and fully present, and avoiding the mystique of the researcher, they presented themselves 'as an informed and sympathetic audience'. This is best expressed in their own words:

> On many occasions, parents illustrated their stories through photographs, school books and things children had made, won, drawn or done with their lives. We found talking about lost children whilst looking at these mementoes both moving and insightful. During these interviews we were not scientists researching social processes but ordinary people talking intimately about children who lived, mattered and needed remembering.

In the process of inquiry, 'stories' can be understood to be not only words but a variety of other forms of creative expression. I (Wilkins 1995) have shown how techniques from art therapy and psychodrama may be used to explore the client–therapist relationship and its possibilities. This amounts to an attempt to understand (but not necessarily to explain) the relationship between two people via the creative process. True, this understanding stems from the particular perspective of one person (the therapist) and as such reveals but part of the elephant. However, feedback from supervisees indicates that there *is* some link between what happens in creative group supervision and their relationships with clients. This suggests that the stories told in art and drama (and I guess music and movement) have some value as investigative tools. Others have used creative techniques as research processes. Hawkins (1988) writes of psychodrama as an instrument of research. He sees this as a way of bringing life back from the (fieldwork) stage of research into the reflection and writing.

A storytelling research process

The mistake of the blind men investigating an elephant was that each of them 'knew' what kind of creature it was from the little bit they felt. The one who seized the tail thought an elephant was like a snake, the one who had hold of a leg thought that an elephant was like a tree-trunk and so on. They all knew *something* about an elephant but none of them knew *everything* – or even came close. Now, suppose each man had told his story of the elephant to the others. Given a willingness to listen and to learn, each individual story would be moderated by that of the others and a meta-story could emerge. This may still have fallen short of the totality of 'elephant' but it would represent a more complete understanding.

In collaborative research, each person tells their own story, paints their own picture, and so on. An objective is to make collective sense of individual 'stories'. This may be done by a process of story building which is about responding empathically and acceptingly to the authentic experiences of the co-researchers and which has parallels with the cycles of co-operative inquiry (see Reason and Heron 1986). Story building occurs in stages, which are:

- the 'telling' of an individual, highly personal story as a largely intra-psychic process

- the mediation of that story through writing a journal, painting a picture, etc.

- the more public retelling of that story where it is modified by the input and influence of others

- the recasting of the personal stories in the light of the previous stages and pre-existing stories (which may include anecdotes or the literature) and the production of an encapsulating account. This account may take notice of or even be based on a variety of 'creative' output.

- the synthesis of a group story from the personal stories in such a way that all feel and believe 'that is our story – I see myself and my colleagues in it'. This may be done accumulatively (two get together to combine their stories, the result is then combined with the product of another couple and so on) or by an individual or subgroup who then refer back to their collaborators in the research.

It is possible to use one or more of the recognised techniques for handling interview data at this stage (see Denzin and Lincoln 1998). These include thematic analysis (see Boyatzis 1998), narrative analysis (see Riessman 1993) or discourse analysis (see Nunan 1993). Of these, narrative analysis is to be preferred because it takes the perspective of the teller. In my view, over-formalisation of this stage risks moving from the frame of reference of the participants to that of the researcher and, if the objective is to produce a co-owned account, it is better to stick with the reiterative process. However it is produced, this collective story takes account of disagreement as well as consensus and, if properly constructed, will be far from bland.

It is a mistake to consider these stages as entirely discrete. Because this creative approach to research is a story of interaction, the processes are enmeshed from the very start. It is also important to note that there can be a continual cycling through the first three stages. Sharing thoughts, ideas and experiences is likely to be a constant feature of such research; these stories are constantly impinged on and altered by the stories of others.

Although it has stages in which other forms of expression may be important and (see Rogers 1985), movement from one to another often seems to deepen the experience/understanding, I have used story building only to generate an account in words. I see no reason why the same process could not apply to any other medium. In my view, the door is wide open for dramatherapists, music therapists, art therapists and dance movement therapists to build on these ideas (or to develop something entirely their own) in such a way as to use the techniques of their own disciplines as research tools.

The validity of a story building approach lies in that it 'rests on a collaborative encounter with experience' (Reason and Heron 1986, p.465). Because it is concerned with people's perceptions, the knowledge they create through doing, not with 'objective' reality, story building has intrinsic validity. As McLeod (1994, p.97) has pointed out, in qualitative research the concept of reliability cannot be applied in the same way as in quantitative studies. He suggests that 'trustworthiness' may take its place. Heron (1996) writes:

> There can be personal, idiosyncratic truth, as well as shared, intersubjective truth; and both are always formed within the context of a particular language and culture. This makes truth a variable, unfolding, artefact of creative minds in ever-shifting social contexts, participating in, and shaping, given being ... and a proposition, in my view, is not true because it works, rather it works because it is true. (pp.168–169)

If, in the story-building process, attention is paid to group dynamics and action is taken to ensure that 'consensus collusion' (Reason and Heron 1986, p.466) is reduced (for example by the devil's advocate function), then it will accurately reflect the authentic experience of the participants. This authenticity corresponds to Heron's 'truth' and contributes to the trustworthiness of the research.

The product of story building may be presented in the form of an orthodox report (as in Wilkins et al. 1999) but if accessibility is an objective, there are other possibilities. Reason and Hawkins (1988, pp.90–93) describe a similar process to story building. They experimented with storytelling as inquiry and, in a workshop, found that the main approach they developed was to respond to a story with stories. They write:

> Typically, one person would tell a story from their own lives which carried some meaning about male and female; the rest of the group would listen, and then privately compose some kind of response – another story, a poem, or a retelling of the original story. (p.90)

They found that these responses were of four types:

1. *replies* – which are the listener's reaction to the original story 'an expressive way of giving shape to the feelings and ideas arising while listening to the story'

2. *echoes* – which are the listener's own story on the same theme

3. *re-creations* – in which listeners 'take the story and shape it into another form, finding their own way of telling the tale. This could be a poem, a fairy tale, or some other kind of story; it may stay at the same "level" as the original or move toward the archetypal level'

4. *reflections* – which are the listener's story about the story they have heard – 'essentially the reflection involves standing further back ...pondering the story'. (p.90)

Storytelling and the presentation of research findings

In his novel set in the international conference circuit of literary criticism, Lodge (1984) acknowledges the widely held but seldom voiced view that, as engaging and invigorating as peers and colleagues may be in person, the papers they present may be less than gripping:

> Let's have a drink, let's have dinner, let's have breakfast together. It's this kind of informal contact, of course, that's the real *raison d'être* of a conference, not the programme of papers and lectures which has ostensibly brought the participants together, but which most of them find intolerably tedious. (pp.233–234)

If story, form, colour, movement, enaction, sign and symbol were used not only in the investigative part of research but also in its reporting phase, wouldn't this go some way to overcoming the tedium named by Lodge? If metaphor is the everyday language of ordinary people, isn't it more egalitarian and inclusive to convey the findings of research in an expressive form? There is precedent for fiction as research. For example, John Henzell, speaking at the European Consortium for Arts Therapies Education (ECArTE) conference in 1997, pointed out that Proust's seminal novel *A la Recherche du Temps Perdu* is not only the product of research but can be seen as giving a guide to a research methodology.

Moustakas (1990) refers to the final phase of heuristic research as the process of creative synthesis. He writes:

> The creative synthesis can only be achieved through tacit and intuitive powers. Once the researcher has mastered knowledge of the material that illuminates and explicates the question, the researcher is challenged to put the components and core themes into a creative synthesis. This usually takes the form of a narrative depiction utilising verbatim material and examples but it may be expressed as a poem, story, drawing, painting, or by some other creative form. (pp.31–32)

Such a creative synthesis may comprise the whole a research report or be but a part of it. For example, Sims (1998), as part of her study of the experience of adult only - children, reflected upon her own experience. She presented the results of this heuristic process as occasional entries in a fictionalised diary covering her life from childhood into early adulthood. Zafar (1998), whose account of racism is in effect the product of an heuristic study, produced a creative synthesis which interweaves poetry, prose, extracts from the literature and artwork. The power of this approach to the presentation of research findings is demonstrated in this poem taken from her paper:

> My skin – My skin is the trouble isn't it?
> It has too much pigmentation in it – whose fault is that?
> The sun's or mine?
> Sun why have you made me this colour?
> Why when you made me this colour did you not spare a
> thought for my pain?
> Sun, how can you stand to shine – How dare you,
> moon rise – How dare you,
> stars multiply – How dare the rivers run – Or the trees
> grow – Or the flowers bloom –
> How dare the world spin – How – When I am hated simply
> for the colour I am?
> World full of colour – Riotous, blossoming,
> living colour – World, you are colour – then why,
> why, is my colour reviled?

Perhaps this conveys more of the pain, confusion and rage of a 'person of colour' living in a predominantly white society than any factual account could.

In collaborative approaches, and especially in story building, a final stage would be to 'fictionalise' the collective story – to turn it into a myth, a fairy story even a cartoon strip (or perhaps a form suitable for performance or as 'visual art'). For example, in Wilkins *et al.* (1999) there is a brief reference to a difficult stage in group process, and in a paper I gave at the ECArTE conference in 1997 there appears a fictionalised account of this same stage:

We met, we ten in the glade that was to become central to our lives. The ritual circle was formed and our leader took his place at its head. We wondered mightily how a circle could have a head and yet it was thus. We smiled, made polite conversation and stressed our intent to be warm, open and helpful. Were we not met to support each other in our struggles for knowledge? But from the very start, little maggots of doubt and fear began to wriggle in our hearts.

We stumbled on, unsure, confused. Some of us began to freeze, others became unbearably loquacious. Some of us took up poison darts and other weapons of offence, others buckled on more armour, retreated further behind great shields of steel which bore no sign, no livery. Throughout all this our leader (who had entered many similar glades, participated many times in this ritual of learning) appeared calm. He responded to our pain and fear, told of his own and yet somehow he seemed to rise above our troubles. By turns, this irritated us and comforted us. Sometimes we sniped, probing for chinks in his armour, sometimes we looked beseechingly, willing him to save us from the unknown.

The third time we entered the glade, we became aware of another presence. In the very middle, between us all, separating us, was a dark and formless monster. As it writhed and grew, we became silent, not daring to look at each other lest we caught the monster's eye and it devoured us. And the monster fed and grew. It seemed invincible – we felt our energies being sapped. This went on – and on – and on. We were swamped by everlasting night but we dared not name what we could see nor even acknowledge its fearful presence to one another.

Then it happened. One of us, perhaps braver or more desperate than the rest, suddenly pointed at the monster in the middle crying 'I see you'. The monster quivered and seemed to shrink a little. Our companion took the hand of the person on her right and repeated her words. A warm, golden glow, at first feeble and flickering, embraced their linked hands. The monster shrank still further.

We ten saw that naming the monster was an invocation of the light, and joining together, we worked to banish it from our presence. In doing this, we declared common purpose and our work began. It was not a smooth path we trod together. The long, brooding silence of one of us turned into a vicious anger, sweeping over us as a festering wound burst. Because although we were many, we were one, we caught him as he threw himself. We bathed his wound, heard his grief. Some of us comforted, some named their guilt for their part in his sorrow or the sorrow of others, some told of their resentment that, by keeping himself apart, our wounded comrade had lessened the power of us all. For all its painfulness, it was a warming and cleansing rite.

And so it went. We walked the circle of our encounter carrying out the rituals of togetherness, becoming closer but also stronger in our separateness. As we walked, we encountered obstacles, snares, enchantments but these began to affect us less. It was as if as we circled, we climbed ever upward tracing a helix towards the sky. Our leader became our companion, another of the company. Like us, he had faults, human failings. We knew not how, but this made him stronger in our eyes. Then we looked at ourselves. The more we named and shared our vulnerabilities the stronger we became! How could this be? Somehow we had become more than the sum of our parts.

At last, our time together drew to a close and we knew that we must leave our now warm and sunny glade. We celebrated, danced our joys, wept our sorrows, touched each others hearts. We knew that we were for ever changed by our time together. There had been no miracles. (Well only the every day kind – the sort where you scramble up a great and terrifying precipice, roped together, using ice axes and crampons, always in mortal danger, Exhausted, aflood with tears of triumph and joy, bruised but happy you look back to find that the mighty cliff has become a gently rolling hillock.) We were neither blissful nor perfect, many more times we would be required to take arms against a sea of troubles – but we would be stronger. Each of us now carried part of all within themselves. So precious a gift is greater than gold or diamonds.

The above is the highly abbreviated, fictionalised story of a facilitator and ten students who met together once a week for two terms as a creative therapy group. It is drawn from the accounts of group process each of us produced, using our collective imagery and ideas. It is certainly very different from an account of group process as a number of defined stages. Does it say more, less or something different?

Conclusion

The creative and artistic products of research may stand alone. Far from being merely avenues of 'expression' (which is one way in which poetry, pictures, stories produced in the research process might be viewed) they are a communication. Perhaps this communication speaks most powerfully on an experiential level rather than on a cognitive level. It is none the worse for that: 'What I hear I forget, what I see I remember, what I experience I understand'. However, there is no reason why creative output should not be accompanied by a more traditional commentary.

References

Bettleheim, B. (1976) *The Uses of Enchantment*. London: Thames & Hudson.

Boyatzis, R.E. (1998) *Transforming Qualitative Information: Thematic Analysis and Code Development*. London: Sage.

Clandinin, D.J. and Connelly, F.M. (1994) 'Personal experience methods.' In N.K. Denzin and Y. S. Lincoln (eds) *Handbook of Qualitative Research*. Thousand Oaks, CA: Sage.

Cragan, J.F. and Sheilds, D.C. (1995) *Symbolic Theories in Applied Communication Research: Bormann, Burke & Fisher*. Cresskill, NJ: Hampton Press.

de Saint-Exupéry, A. (1991) *The Little Prince*. London: Mammoth.

Denzin, N.K. and Lincoln, Y.S. (1998) *Collecting and Interpreting Qualitative Materials*. Thousand Oaks, CA: Sage.

Goddard, A. (1996) 'Tall stories: The metaphorical nature of everyday talk.' *English in Education 30*, 2, 4–12.

Hawkins, P. (1988) 'A phenomenological psychodrama workshop.' In P. Reason (ed) *Human Inquiry in Action: Developments in New Paradigm Research.* London: Sage.

Heron, J. (1996) *Co-operative Inquiry: Research into the Human Condition.* London: Sage.

Jones, P. (1996) *Drama as Therapy: Theatre as Living.* London: Routledge.

Lodge, D. (1984) *Small World: An Academic Romance.* London: Secker & Warburg.

Manning, P.K. and Cullum-Swan, B. (1994) 'Narrative, content, and semiotic analysis.' In N.K. Denzin and Y.S. Lincoln (eds) *Handbook of Qualitative Research.* Thousand Oaks, CA: Sage.

McLeod, J. (1994) *Doing Counselling Research.* London: Sage.

Moustakas, C. (1990) *Heuristic Research: Design, Methodology, and Applications.* Newbury Park, CA: Sage.

Nunan, D. (1993) *Introducing Discourse Analysis.* London: Penguin.

Reason, P. and Hawkins, P. (1988) 'Storytelling as inquiry.' In P. Reason (ed) *Human Inquiry in Action: Developments in New Paradigm Research.* London: Sage.

Reason, P. and Heron, J. (1986) 'Research with people: The paradigm of co-operative experiential inquiry.' *Person-Centered Review 1*, 456–476.

Reason, P. and Rowan, J. (eds) (1981) *Human Inquiry: A Sourcebook of New Paradigm Research.* Chichester: Wiley.

Rennie, D.L. (1994) 'Storytelling in psychotherapy: the client's subjective experience.' *Psychotherapy 31*, 234–243.

Riches, G. and Dawson, P. (1996) 'Making stories and taking stories: Methodological reflections on researching grief and marital tension following the death of a child.' *British Journal of Guidance and Counselling 24*, 3, 357–365.

Riessman, C.K. (1993) *Narrative Analysis.* Newbury Park, CA: Sage.

Rogers, N. (1985) *The Creative Connection: a Person-centred Approach to Expressive Therapy.* Santa Rosa, CA: Person-Centred Expressive Therapy Institute.

Sims, N. (1998) 'The Experience of Adult Only-Children'. Unpublished BA dissertation, Manchester Metropolitan University.

von Franz, M.L. (1982) *An Introduction to the Interpretation of Fairy Tales.* Irving: Spring Publications.

Wilkins, P. (1995) 'A creative therapies model for the group supervision of counsellors.' *British Journal of Guidance and Counselling 23*, 2, 245–257.

Wilkins, P., Ambrose, S., Bishop, A., Hall, R., Maugham, P., Pitcher, C., Richards, E., Shortland, J., Turnbull, A., Wilding, S. and Wright, N. (1999) 'Collaborative inquiry as a teaching and learning strategy in a university setting: Processes within an experiential group – the group's story.' *Psychology Teaching Review 8*, 1, 4–18.

Zafar, M.M.A. (1998) 'Beyond boundaries.' Paper given at the 7th Person Centered Forum, Johannesburg, July.

CHAPTER 13

Demystifying the Doctorate: Why Do a PhD?

Ed Mynott

Introduction

This chapter has been provoked by the author's experience of studying for and attaining a PhD, and by conversations with other postgraduate students who have either completed their studies or have abandoned the attempt. It does not pretend to constitute a survey of a representative sample or a specific section of doctoral students. Nor is it intended to provide a detailed guide to the most common difficulties faced by doctoral students as they go through the process of research and writing up. There are several handbooks available which attempt to do this and every postgraduate student would gain from reading at least one of them as part of clarifying in their own minds what they are setting out to do (Cryer 1996; Phillips and Pugh 1994; Rudestam and Newton 1992; Salmon 1992).

Instead, this essay is designed to encourage students who are thinking about or have begun a PhD to ask themselves why they want a PhD. This may seem like a simple question but it is fundamental, and just as important to address as the subject matter of your research, where you intend to study and who is going to fund you. Therefore, consciously posing the question as early as possible can be invaluable for any intending PhD student. Doing this allows us to distinguish between the PhD as a product, a qualification which potentially allows the student to do things they could not otherwise do, and the PhD as a process, the researching and writing of a doctoral thesis which may allow the student space to do things they might not otherwise be able to.

The first thing to realise is that a completed PhD is essentially a passport to the status of academic. It is worth noting two things here. First, the PhD is not necessarily a passport to an academic post, only to the status of academic; and second that the majority of PhD students opt to leave academia. According to a survey carried out by the research councils, of those PhD students who graduated in 1995, 8 per cent had permanent academic jobs, 25 per cent were employed on short fixed-term contracts in universities, 47 per cent were employed 'in a variety of companies and industries' and 20 per cent were unemployed (Elliot Major 1999, p.xxxiii).

As part of posing the question of why you might want to study for a PhD, let us examine three things:

1. the nature of the academic environment to which the PhD offers access

2. the conflicting notions of how a PhD should prepare one for the academic environment or status

3. how different types of student motivation are likely to impact on the experience of studying for a PhD.

The academic environment

Universities cannot be understood in isolation from the wider capitalist society of which they are part. The division between mental and manual labour (which is characteristic of class-divided societies) has found various expressions as capitalism has developed. One of these is the existence of a set of quasi-autonomous institutions of higher education, some of which have their roots before the industrial revolution, some of which were founded in the classic period of nineteenth-century capitalism and some of which arose out of the post Second World War expansion of higher education across the Western world.

Universities have traditionally had a deep-rooted attachment to the ideal of university autonomy and, in practice, there has been scope for a degree of autonomy among academics with regard to their intellectual work (Neave 1988). However, these institutions are fundamentally shaped by the State and capital in a number of ways, from their funding and administration to the nature of the teaching and research which goes on within them. As Barnett argues, 'higher education is inescapably bound into its host society' and 'cannot pretend to a position of social and cognitive purity' (Barnett 1988, pp.88,90; see also Shaw 1975, pp.43–55).

At the same time, the fact that universities are separate institutions accentuates the division between 'society' and intellectual life. Intellectual life is conceived as the practice of professional thinkers, unencumbered by any ties to social forces external to the universities. This view is a powerful one, not least among academics themselves. One of its consequences is a conception of intellectual activity as a process which is compromised by too close a contact with social forces external to the academic world.

In one sense this can be a healthy response from academics who do not want to simply be an instrument of, or an apologist for, wealthy and powerful forces – be they governments, large corporations or rich patrons. They recoil from being, in the phrase used by Martin Nicolaus to describe successful sociologists, the 'financial creatures, functionally the house servants, of the civil, military and economic sovereignty' (Nicolaus 1972, p.51).

Yet this can often be accompanied by a suspicion of partisanship of any sort, a belief that the project of combining critical thought with open partisanship – even of the exploited and oppressed – is impossible or undesirable.

Another consequence of conceiving serious intellectual activity as the sole pre-rogative of professional thinkers is the creation of a hierarchy in which academic work is privileged over any other intellectual work. At its worst, this leads to academic writing becoming the exclusive focus of legitimate critical inquiry. A self-referential environment is created, whose concerns, controversies and modes of expression appear to have little relevance to any kind of activity outside the academy.

These consequences are compounded by the way that a particular division of labour has arisen within academia. The division of labour which characterises capitalist production has its counterpart in the division of intellectual activity into separate academic disciplines. This encourages a narrowing of focus which can lead to extreme specialisation and, at worst, obscurantism.

I have concentrated on these aspects of academia not in an attempt to caricature it, nor to suggest that it is impossible to carry out valuable research and intellectual work within it, but to outline the tendencies which operate and the pressures they give rise to. Familiarity with the academic environment and seniority offer valuable resources in negotiating these pressures; and negotiation is enormously aided by that increas-ingly elusive thing, a permanent contract. (In 1996–97, according to Higher Education Statistics Agency data analysed by the Association of University Teachers, 41% of all academic staff in UK higher education institutions were on fixed-term contracts.) However, familiarity and seniority are precisely what the PhD student usually lacks. Only the undergraduate student ranks lower in the academic hierarchy and the relative lack of power and standing of the PhD student, their status as an apprentice who has to be inducted into the club, can create problems which are not sufficiently recognised.

The PhD as a passport

If academia is conceived as a State, the PhD is like a passport which allows you into that State. It gives you, *in theory*, equal access as a citizen of the academic community:

> As the highest degree that can be awarded, it proclaims that the recipient is worthy of being listened to *as an equal* by the appropriate faculty ... When the examiners award the degree and recognise you as a full professional, what they are primarily concerned with is that you should 'join the club' and continue your contribution to developing your discipline through research and scholarship throughout your career. (Phillips and Pugh 1994, pp.18–21)

However, when we enquire what a student must do to gain their passport, there is some disagreement in the handbooks. According to Phillips and Pugh (1994), the outcome of a PhD project should be 'an original contribution to knowledge'. They are clear that:

the work for the degree is essentially a *research training* process and the term 'original contribution' has perforce to be interpreted quite narrowly ... apply this theory in a different setting, evaluate the effects of raising the temperature, solve this puzzling oddity or review this little-known historical event.

They contrast this with a 'major contribution', for example what Kuhn called 'paradigm shifts' – 'major changes in the science's explanatory schemes, which happen only rarely when the inadequacies of the previous framework have become more and more limiting'. Their advice is that 'You can leave the paradigm shifts for *after* your PhD' (Phillips and Pugh 1994, pp.34–35)

Other writers take a less narrow view of what is necessary to obtain a PhD, declaring that a student should make 'an original and major contribution to scholarship' (Delamont, Atkinson and Parry 1997, p.5). This difference in wording is not simply a verbal quibble, it signals a divergence between two models of what a PhD should be. Beard and Hartley (1984) noted that '[There] are certain styles of approach which we may caricature as the "science" and "arts" approaches respectively. At one end the PhD is a "training"; at the other it is an "opportunity for independent thinking" ' (p.262).

Decisions taken by the research councils in the 1980s shifted the emphasis in what a PhD consisted of toward 'training in research rather than discovering and reporting original research'(Beard and Hartley 1984, p.265). The historically high drop-out rate of doctoral students led the research councils (especially the Economic and Social Research Council) to abandon their formerly more relaxed view in favour of a more rigorous regime. Under the new system the student had to complete their PhD within four years of registration. If the rate of successful completions at a university fell below a certain level, that university was temporarily banned from holding research council studentships. Naturally, universities responded by taking greater control of the PhD process. For the student the results were mixed. On the positive side, more attention was paid by the university to making the process efficient. However, 'a possible negative effect is that you may be forced to take a narrower view of your research than you might like in order to complete within the stated time' (Phillips and Pugh 1994, p.29).

Some academics have been scathing about the effect of the research councils' policy. Conrad Russell described it as 'absolutely the paradigm case of the pursuit of "efficiency" threatening academic standards and interfering with academic judgement'. Forcing students to make up their minds on whether conclusions are true before having the research evidence on which to make that decision 'produces research which will not meet the test of the pursuit of knowledge for its own sake'. Perhaps most serious was Russell's claim that 'the present policy, by tempting people to tailor their findings to fit a time limit, is an invitation to scholarly dishonesty' (Russell 1993, pp.70–71).

Certainly, the conception of the PhD as a research training tends to narrow doctoral study to the acquisition of research techniques and specialised methods, making the subject of study secondary, if not irrelevant. But this development does not represent a sharp break with the older model of what a PhD should consist of. Rather, it accentuates those elements of the academic method – specialisation, an emphasis on technique, reference to a restricted field – which already loomed large in doctoral study. It may have been promoted by changes in the material relationship between funding bodies and the universities, but it was a development made easier by the ambiguity which has long existed over what constitutes an 'original' contribution to knowledge.

Given the characteristics of academia outlined above, the need for a PhD to make an original contribution has always held a danger of an even more drastic narrowing of focus and specialisation than that promoted by the existence of compartmentalised academic disciplines. At the same time, it is during the period of doctoral study that many students are encouraged to see as problematic any attempt to combine rigorous thought with writing for a popular (that is, non-academic) audience.

In the discipline of history, for instance, a 1994 survey of its members by the Organisation of American Historians found 74 per cent agreeing with the statement that 'the academic reward system encourages historians to write for academic audiences and discourages historians from reaching out to multiple audiences' (McPherson 1996, p.237). One group of postgraduate history students have described how such signals are sent out in the course of their studies:

> [O]ur professional culture still contains an undercurrent of disdain for works written by amateurs or for public audiences ... popular works may be credited as 'good narratives' but ultimately derided as lacking 'sufficient rigour'. We absorb it through hallway conversations and professional newsletters ... We rehearse it by learning to write ... in a style that favors subtle distinction and academic jargon at the expense of accessibility. (McPherson 1996, p.237)

It would be a brave academic who claimed that similar processes did not exist in their own discipline.

These, then, are some of the characteristics of doctoral study, whether practised as research training or seen as an opportunity to make an original contribution to knowledge. Which of them, if any, are perceived as problematic by the student is likely to greatly depend on the balance of the student's motivations.

Student motivation

One guide to PhD supervision states that 'We know relatively little about what motivates students to do a higher degree'(Delamont et al. 1997, p.186). Students about whom evidence was available tended to have mixed motives:

> Most had chosen to carry on and do a PhD in their undergraduate specialism because of their enthusiasm for the subject ... Other motivations mentioned were, in descending order, that the person did not feel ready to enter the labour market and/or wished to stay a student, that the challenge of the PhD was appealing, that

the respondent wanted a job in research or higher education which required a doctorate and that none of the alternatives appealed except a doctorate. (Delamont *et al.* 1997, p.186)

It is probably true that each student has a complex mixture of motivations which they may not necessarily have thought carefully about. There are certainly students who end up in postgraduate study simply because it seemed to be the next stage on an educational conveyor belt which has taken them from success at school to being a university undergraduate. There is also evidence that some students' initial psychological motivation is a desire to prove (whether to their peers, family or whoever) that they are capable of achieving the highest level of educational qualification (Salmon 1992, p.60). This is hardly surprising in an educational system dominated at every level by competition.

What is not in doubt is that without a strong self-motivation, the student will find it impossible to complete their PhD. Even if a student has not examined their own motivation before beginning a PhD, the process of doctoral study will force them to do so. Phillips and Pugh (1994) emphasise how important it is that the student really wants a PhD. Without that strong desire they will not have, or be able to acquire, the single-mindedness, determination and willingness to discover what is required which will be necessary to get them through the feelings of isolation and of pointlessness which recur throughout the period of doctoral study and which are described in every account of the experience of PhD students (Delamont *et al.* 1997, p.96); and this is in addition to the material pressures of money, time and family commitments which most students face.

When they deal with the question of motivation, Phillips and Pugh (1994) emphasise the need for both intrinsic and extrinsic satisfactions:

> You cannot expect with an activity as demanding as doing a PhD that the intrinsic satisfaction (such as the interest of doing the research, the enjoyment of discussing your subject with other like-minded researchers) will be sufficient on its own to carry you through. You must always have a clear eye on the extrinsic satisfactions (your commitment to the whole exercise of doing a PhD, its necessary place in your career progression, and so on); you must *want* to do it.'(Phillips and Pugh 1994, p.33)

Delamont *et al.* also agree that a high degree of motivation is required. They argue that 'to complete a PhD a person needs to be passionate about the discipline and want to advance knowledge within it' (Delamont *et al.* 1997, p.180).

In both of these accounts, the type of motivation identified is that of wanting to pursue an academic career. Given that a PhD is designed, primarily, to be a passport to academia, this is hardly surprising; and it is worthwhile for every PhD student to remind themselves of this elementary fact. However, it begs the question: what if forging an academic career does not rate very highly in a student's mix of motivations? There are certain forms of motivation which are likely to create more tensions within the process of doctoral study than others. In particular, wanting to do a PhD as part of tackling a practical issue which has arisen outside of academia is likely, in social science certainly, to create particular pressures given the characteristics of academia of separating theory from practice and privileging academic discourse above all others. This raises a further question. Is it possible to reconcile these tensions or should a student motivated in large part by these practical concerns give up doctoral study as an unsuitable vehicle for the kind of intellectual work they want to do?

The question of motivation is important because it has such a large bearing on the research questions a student wants to ask, and thus on the heart of their PhD. One author who examines this issue is Phillida Salmon. She outlines the experiences of ten students, most of whom were mature students from professional occupations whose research interests grew out of their work or life experience. Salmon (1992) emphasises the authorial character of PhD work in contrast with the predominant emphasis on training:

> A PhD is essentially a personal rather than impersonal undertaking. Like any creative endeavour, it involves its own prolonged and complicated course of development and demands of its students qualities of intellectual boldness and imagination. This perspective is, it seems, totally at variance with the 'training' view of such research. (Salmon 1992, p.10)

She believes that when the PhD is treated as a training, students' 'confused and tentative ideas' become 'prematurely crystallised'. The heavy emphasis on research methods is accompanied by a minimal attention to research questions. Research questions are defined along established lines at an early stage:

> When would-be research students are invited to present proposals to an academic selection panel, the usual expectation is that they will have derived their research questions from existing published work within the area... Such formulations... follow up 'the' questions – that is, the standard questions that previous researchers would agree to be important. How different 'the' questions would look if they were offered by the social groupings who are to act as the research subjects! In the perspectives of people outside the narrow academic community, what can be assumed, what matters, what urgently needs asking may be a world away from what is taken for granted by those who publish research findings about these people. (Salmon 1992, pp.12–13)

Salmon's contention that *all* research questions have an 'inescapably personal and personal-social character' cannot be properly debated here, nor her contention that 'Traditional scientific activity has no place for what is personal. Personal involvement is seen as suspect, as undermining the detachment and neutrality essential for science' (Salmon 1992, pp.12,13). What is certain is that for some students, their research questions are prompted by their personal experience, or practice of one kind or another, and originate from concerns outside of academic discourse. This can give rise to tensions which are not really recognised in the handbooks advising how to get or how to supervise a PhD. The point is often made that doctoral study differs from an undergraduate course in the sense that the student has to formulate their own research problems and that they are no longer guided by a formal syllabus. However, there is, so to speak, an informal syllabus. This is the body of literature with its history of controversies and research questions which is embodied in journals and publications.

Naturally, engaging with such work is necessary and may well lead the student to re-examine and refine their initial research questions. It might lead them to modify or even reject their initial methodology or theoretical standpoint. Yet the informal syllabus also acts to exert a constant pressure on the student to adapt their initial concerns and research questions to those questions and those theoretical standpoints which are legitimate according to the informal syllabus. This adaptation may be felt by the student to do damage to their essentially practical concerns, the motivation for doing the PhD in the first place. If they attempt to retain their original practice-motivated questions, this may be viewed by the academic world as a failure to leave behind the 'crude' or 'simplistic' forms of thought associated with practice and to ascend to the realm of rigorous thought exemplified by academia.

This conflict has been described by Salmon and some of her students. Salmon (1992) describes one intending PhD student's initial experience of the academic environment:

> It seemed that her own real-life understanding of race, class and gender inequality was being dismissed out of hand in favour of some other kind of knowledge which she did not have and which was the possession of people from another world than her own. (pp.31-2)

The student experienced a conflict between the role of professional teacher and the role of academic 'a role she deeply mistrusts, yet as a doctoral student must take on' (Salmon 1992, pp.56). She felt that the position of the professional was in opposition to that of the academic. While the professional, through their creative practice, was active, the academic was theoretical, speculative and retrospective. Yet in the academic world she felt that the professional was viewed as a 'nobody' in comparison with the elevated position of the academic.

Similarly, another student experienced 'uncomfortable disjunctions between the role of a PhD student and his role as a professional worker in the field of race relations' (Salmon 1992, p.58). He described his difficulty in writing for an academic audience as opposed to the 'policy makers, professionals, community groups' (Salmon 1992, p.58) who were the usual audience for the publications from his professional research projects:

> The problem, peculiar to my situation, is that of my two roles: policy development and academic work. I have to unlearn certain aspects of each aspect of my life, to satisfy both. I cannot use academic terminology and theory per se in policy/community development work, and vice versa. (Salmon 1992, p.58)

In these cases, the conflict described is that between academic theory and professional practice. However, the conflict between theory and practice can take other forms. For the student who has been motivated by an external practice of political activity there can be just as great tensions in attempting to hold on to research questions which derive from and seek to continue to interact with political practice. This can be further heightened if the student holds to a theoretical standpoint the legitimacy of which is widely questioned within academia. The student may feel a constant pressure to draw back from expressing themselves in the way they would prefer, especially when they face a firm and widespread conviction within academia that their standpoint is not sufficiently rigorous and cannot be defended intellectually. As Shaw has written, in the context of a discussion about Marxist economists:

> The critic is under immense pressure to compromise intellectually, not to admit the total opposition of assumptions, concepts and methods which must exist between any 'radical' economics and the mainstream. Marx must be transformed into a precursor of Keynes and so forth. And when a marxist economics is brought into existence and its autonomy recognised, the pressure still exists, in the more subtle form of a demand to match the technical abstraction and formal rationalisation of the bourgeois schools. Marxian political economy is resurrected, only to be instantly detached by such means from the broader context of a marxist theory and practice. The 'marxist economist' is still an *economist*, a peculiar kind of academic theorist accepting a basic divorce, first of himself from his subject matter, secondly of his subject matter from that which is regarded as the province of sociology, political theory, etc. (Shaw 1975, p.102; see also Rees 1998)

For the postgraduate student motivated to do intellectual work for reasons originating from and still connected with political activity, similar kinds of pressures exist.

Conclusion

Is it the case, then, that such pressures are so overwhelming or universal that the student whose motivation springs primarily from some source external to academia should withdraw from PhD study? Much will depend on the student's supervisor who is the key person in mediating their relationship with the wider academic world. Some models of supervision are overwhelmingly geared to training the student to take their place in an academic discipline: 'Guiding a new scholar into your specialism is intrinsically rewarding and the best way to ensure that your own work echoes down to the next generation and beyond.' (Delmont *et al.* 1997, p.164) This approach has the merit of making the supervisor keenly aware of their role in introducing the student to the wider world of journals, publications and conferences – but the student may find some of its assumptions deeply uncomfortable:

> The major international conference is rather like 'The Season' of a former era. You can 'bring out' your graduate students, your research assistants and other junior colleagues. Successful presentations can have a significant impact on research

students' reputations, and can also have a very positive effect on that department and the research group. (Delamont *et al.* 1997, p.164)

An approach to supervision which gives the student the opportunity to retain their focus on research questions motivated by practice, and which gives space to different methodologies and theoretical standpoints, is likely to be the most fruitful for students who experience an antagonism between professional or political practice and academic theory. Another way to try to negotiate the tensions produced by this antagonism is to consciously distinguish between two key aspects of the doctoral process – the intellectual aspect and the career aspect.

It *is* possible for a PhD student to follow their own research questions and engage with other academic work in so far as it touches on their primary concerns. They can fulfil the intellectual part of the process and thus achieve a PhD. However, there may be a cost.

Doing a PhD is not an intellectual process abstracted from any social context, it is a process which takes place within a specific institutional context, that of the academy. As such, there is a career component to the PhD process. Networking, attending conferences, delivering seminar papers, publishing. Decisions which the student takes in these areas will have an enormous bearing on their life after the PhD. To negotiate the career aspect of the process it *is* necessary to engage with the research questions, the theoretical and methodological issues, the intellectual fashions and even the personal rivalries which preoccupy an academic discipline at the time. If you separate the intellectual process from the career process, because you want to concentrate on the former without having to pay attention to the pressures of the latter (be they pressures of time or feeling that some of the questions which dominate in your discipline are too disconnected from practical concerns outside of academia), you may achieve a PhD but will not have fully 'joined the club' through networking, public speaking, and most importantly, publishing. This has a crucial bearing on what kind of work, if any, will be available to you within academia after your PhD is completed.

If your primary concern is to get a job outside academia, the strategy of separating the intellectual process from the career process will not have such severe consequences. The PhD will have intrinsic value and may have value as a commodity which enhances the price of your labour power and gives you wider choices about occupations. If you have not really considered whether you want to continue within academia after your PhD, it is worth thinking about it and what effect your decision may have on how you approach doctoral study.

Finally, I hope this chapter serves as an encouragement to students to evaluate their own mixture of motives as early as possible. Asking yourself *why* you want a PhD will help to evaluate whether studying for a doctorate is the most appropriate forum for you to pursue your intellectual work and the best way to achieve what is really important to you.

Acknowledgement

Let me put on record here the great debt which I owe to my own supervisor, Dr D.H.J. Morgan. Without his patient help and invaluable advice I am certain I could not have completed my own PhD.

References

Barnett, R. (1988), 'Limits to academic freedom: Imposed upon self-imposed?' In M. Tight (ed) *Academic Freedom and Academic Responsibility.* Milton Keynes: Society for Research into Higher Education and Open University Press.

Beard, R. and Hartley, J. (1984) *Teaching and Learning in Higher Education.* 4th edn. London: Harper & Row.

Cryer, P. (1996) *The Research Student's Guide to Success.* Buckingham: Open University Press.

Delamont, S., Atkinson, P. and Parry, O. (1997) *Supervising the PhD: A Guide to Success.* Buckingham: Society for Research into Higher Education and Open University Press.

Elliot Major, L. (1999) 'Altered image.' *Guardian Higher,* 16 March.

McPherson, J.M. (1996) *Drawn with the Sword: Reflections on the American Civil War.* Oxford: Oxford University Press.

Neave, G. (1988) 'On being economical with university autonomy: Being an account of the retrospective joys of a written constitution.' In M. Tight (ed) *Academic Freedom and Academic Responsibility.* Milton Keynes: Society for Research into Higher Education and Open University Press.

Nicolaus, M. (1972) 'The professional organisation of sociology: A view from below.' In R. Blackburn (ed) *Ideology in Social Science.* London: Fontana.

Phillips, E.M., and Pugh, D.S. (1994) *How to Get a PhD: A Handbook for Students and Their Supervisors.* 2nd edn. Buckingham: Open University Press.

Rees, J. (1998) 'Revolutionary Marxism and academic Marxism.' In J. Rees (ed) *Essays on Historical Materialism.* London: Bookmarks.

Rudestam, K.E. and Newton, R.R. (1992) *Surviving Your Dissertation: A Comprehensive Guide to Content and Process.* London: Sage.

Russell, C. (1993) *Academic Freedom.* London: Routledge.

Salmon, P. (1992) *Achieving a PhD: Ten Students' Experience.* Stoke on Trent: Trentham Books.

Shaw, M. (1975) *Marxism and Social Science: The Roots of Social Knowledge.* London: Pluto Press.

The Contributors

Note

David Boulton and **Steve Morgan** died suddenly and prematurely before this book was published. They were respected colleagues whose research enriched both their workplace and the wider research community. Their colleagues miss them greatly.

David's partner Yvonne Connolly, has written, 'David was very proud of being part of the team making the coming together of this book possible. He loved his work and had a special gift of making learning fun. He believed very strongly that anybody who could put the work in could reach the stars. He possessed a unique ability of listening and making potential difficulties seem less difficult. He cared deeply for his colleagues and his students, both at Manchester Metropolitan University and at the Open University, and the loss of David is felt by many. David had a passion for life and never tired of learning and teaching. This encompassed all aspects of social interaction and if his work has contributed in any way, he would be pleased. I hope that the memory of his white mop of hair, his twinkly eyes and friendly smile will continue to be an inspiration to all.'

Steve's partner Ann, his son Peter and his daughter Katherine, have written, 'Since Steve joined the probation service in 1970 he consistently kept what he knew to be his priorities at the forefront of his professional life. In terms of probation, that was a passionate belief that people can change and build a better life for themselves, and the way he could facilitate that. As a lecturer in social work, despite the frustrations of bureaucracy, he again never lost sight of the fact that his priority was his students and how they could learn to work with people who needed help. Towards the end of his career Steve returned to the concerns and voices of offenders, to how in expressing their experiences, hopes and fears, they could move on; and, in listening to those voices, how they in turn might help others, and might help people like himself to work towards making a difference in how their voices are heard.'

Janet Batsleer works as a senior lecturer in the Department of Applied Community Studies at Manchester Metropolitan University. She is author of *Working with Girls and Young Women in Community Settings* (Arena 1996), an example of practitioner research written partly to prevent important work from being wiped from the historical record. More recently she has edited, jointly with Beth Humphries, a collection of critical practitioner research-based essays entitled *Welfare, Exclusion and Political Agency* (Routledge 2000).

David Boulton started his career as a primary school teacher and moved into further and higher education as a lecturer in sociology. He was a principal lecturer at Manchester Metropolitan University, teaching research methods, from 1983 until his death in December 1999. He also carried out work for the Open University. He had a number of publications in the field of research, and carried out evaluation studies in a wide range of topics which include aspects of policing, lesbians' and gay men's experiences of crime, equal opportunities and career development in Greater Manchester Police Authority, and early treatment of drug misusers in custody.

Tom Cockburn is currently a lecturer in the Department of Applied Community Studies at Manchester Metropolitan University, a post he has held for five years. In 1996 he was awarded a PhD from the University of Manchester. His research interests are with research methods, past and present representations of children and young people, and social theory.

Philip Hodgkiss has degrees from the University of Cambridge and the London School of Economics. His research interests concern the conceptualisation of consciousness and its mapping over community and culture. He is currently senior lecturer in applied social thought in the Faculty of Community Studies, Law and Education at the Manchester Metropolitan University.

Beth Humphries has worked, taught and researched in social work and related fields for many years, moving from Northern Ireland to Scotland and then to England. She has been a principal lecturer at Manchester Metropolitan University since 1990. Her publications include *Rethinking Social Research* (edited with Carole Truman) and *Research and Inequality* (edited with Carole Truman and Donna M. Mertens). Her interests and commitment are in seeking ways in which professional practice and research can be used to combat injustice.

Adele Jones is senior lecturer in child care, and researcher at Manchester Metropolitan University. She is currently working on research projects examining issues related to black young carers, young black people and homelessness, and an international study of innovative family support projects. Previous research and development work has focused on residential care, child protection and work with black disabled young people. Her most recent research was an examination of immigration issues for children and young people. Adele has published on child protection and black feminism in social work research.

Marion Martin is a lecturer and researcher in community health and adult education at the University of Manchester, and has published on participatory and qualitative research in adult learning and professional education. She has worked in the UK, South India and East Africa. Marion is Director of the MEd in Gender Education and Development, and the MEd in Primary Health Care. She is joint editor with Korrie de Koning of *Participatory Research in Health: Issues and Experiences* published by Zed Books.

Steve Morgan worked as a senior lecturer in social work and applied community studies at Manchester Metropolitan University. He worked for ten years as a probation officer and his research background was in penology and criminal justice policy. His work on prisoner autobiography had its roots in concern for the recognition of offenders as credible voices in debates about crime and offending.

Ed Mynott is currently a researcher in the Department of Applied Community Studies at Manchester Metropolitan University, studying the ways in which local authorities interpret provisions for welfare within immigration legislation. He has also worked as an interviewer on the Office for National Statistics's Labour Force Survey. His doctoral research was a study of the 'social purity' movement in Victorian Manchester and was completed in 1995. He has published as a result of this and in the area of immigration controls and welfare.

Carol Packham is the course leader for the BA in Youth and Community Work at Manchester Metropolitan University, where she has developed community audit training and practice. She has recently managed a Social Regeneration Budget (5) Youth Audit. She has a commitment to participatory working and the changing role of youth and community workers, particularly with 'excluded' young people. She is chair of her local community forum and is joint organiser of an annual youth and community arts festival.

Mary Searle-Chatterjee spent two years as a Commonwealth scholar studying philosophy at Banares Hindu University before studying anthropology in Manchester. After being awarded a PhD in sociology in Banares, she lectured there for four years. She is the author of *Reversible Sex Roles: The Special Case of Banares Sweepers* (Pergamon 1981) as well as of 15 papers, and is co-author with U. Sharma, of *Contextualising Caste* (Blackwell 1994).

Paul Wilkins' background is in ecology, though in the 1980s life events led him to retrain as a counsellor and psychotherapist. After some years working in social services he joined the Manchester Metropolitan University to teach counselling. Most of his work is now on a course in Human Communication. His main interests are the application of his person-centred philosophy and 'storytelling' to learning and research.

Subject Index

Author Index